THE HAYMARKET CONSPIRACY

THE WORKING CLASS
IN AMERICAN HISTORY

Editorial Advisors
James R. Barrett
Alice Kessler-Harris
Nelson Lichtenstein
David Montgomery

THE HAYMARKET CONSPIRACY

Transatlantic Anarchist Networks

TIMOTHY MESSER-KRUSE

UNIVERSITY OF ILLINOIS PRESS

Urbana, Chicago, and Springfield

Library of Congress Cataloging-in-Publication Data
Messer-Kruse, Timothy.
The Haymarket conspiracy : transatlantic anarchist networks /
Timothy Messer-Kruse.
p.   cm. — (The working class in American history)
Includes bibliographical references and index.
ISBN 978-0-252-03705-4 (hard cover : acid-free paper) —
ISBN 978-0-252-07860-6 (pbk. : acid-free paper) —
ISBN 978-0-252-09414-9 (e-book)
1. Anarchists—Illinois—Chicago—History—19th century.
2. Haymarket Square Riot, Chicago, Ill., 1886.
3. Conspiracies—Illinois—Chicago—History—19th century.
I. Title.
HX846.C4M47   2012
977.3'11041—dc23   2011052785

CONTENTS

ACKNOWLEDGMENTS

There are many people who graciously lent to me their time, knowledge, and skill to help me advance my research. Russell Lewis, Julie Katz, and Debbie Linn of the Chicago Historical Society; Vincent Giroud, Morgan Swan, and Timothy Young of the Beinecke Rare Book and Manuscript Library at Yale University; Jeffrey Dunn and Pannee Burckel at the Instrumentation Center at the University of Toledo; and James O. Eckert Jr. of the Department of Geology and Geophysics at Yale University all helped me get this project off the ground. Joanne Hartough, Director of the Interlibrary Loan Department of Carlson Library found many essential items for me over the years. Barbara Floyd, Director of the Canaday Center for Archival Collections at the University of Toledo, has been an indefatigable and reliable colleague.

Special thanks to Dorothy Brown, Clerk of the Circuit Court of Cook County, and Phil Costello, Archivist, Circuit Court of Cook County, for their gracious assistance and for making their well-maintained collection of nineteenth-century legal records available to me.

I deeply appreciate Leon Fink's open-minded interest in new approaches to the field of labor history. Emily LaBarbera-Twarog helped in preparation of an earlier article for publication in *LABOR: Studies in Working-Class History of the Americas*.

Over the years I have benefited from the many conversations I have had with my colleague Peter Linebaugh, whose informed skepticism and deep knowledge of history has forced me to probe ever deeper into this material. Mark Lause's collegiality and encyclopedic knowledge of nineteenth-century radical movements distinguish him as a truly great scholar, but I appreciate him also as a fine friend. Gregory Miller has politely listened as I tried out all my more far-flung theories on him. I've benefited from the criticisms and comments of David Montgomery, Tom Goyens, Melvyn Dubofsky, Rebecca Edwards, Beverly Gage, and Allen Ruff, though I probably didn't take them as they were intended.

A very special thanks is reserved for Hank Browne, who, during my research trips, not only let me have the run of his Chicago apartment (which was just across the street from a police precinct station that stood at the time of the Haymarket bombing) but also was a constantly constructive critic of my work. I've also benefited from countless Sunday dinner conversations with Alan and Geri Messer, who are not afraid to punch holes in ideas that deserve a good poke now and then.

Stephanie Rader's day-to-day efficiency in running the Department of Ethnic Studies at Bowling Green State University allowed me to steal more time than I should have for this project. A number of graduate assistants slogged books back and forth from the library, copied articles, and assisted in countless small ways, including Rachel Constance, Michael Brooks, and Jerald MacMurray.

This project would not have been possible without the keen understanding of the nuances of the German language and the efficient translation skills of Jason Doerre and Claudia Schneider. Geoffrey Howes graciously offered his expertise on antiquated German constructions and consulted on the difficult and mysterious "fugitive letter to Ebersold." Noreen T. Hanlon expertly translated some important documents from French. Michael Bryant guided me through the nuances of meaning in the reporting on the McCormick strike in the *Illinois Staats-Zeitung*. Much of the research into previously untapped German-language sources was supported by the Office of Sponsored Programs and Research and the College of Arts and Sciences of Bowling Green State University. The staff of the Jerome Library at BGSU, especially Mary Keil of the Interlibrary Loan Department, were able to track down many obscure titles for me. Thanks to Cynthia Price, Donald Nieman, and Roger Thibault of BGSU for their consistent support. Thanks also to Griffin Messer-Kruse for his help in converting a stack of century-old industrial time sheets into usable data.

Many librarians and archivists assisted in tracking down rare and ephemeral materials. Thanks to William J. Shephard of the Catholic University of America; Bill Gorman of the New York State Archives; Joanie Gearin of the National Archives Northeast Region; Frederick J. Augustyn Jr. of the Manuscript Division, Library of Congress; John Reinhardt of the Illinois State Archives; Ella Molenaar of the International Institute of Social History, Amsterdam; Julie Herrada of the Labadie Collection, University of Michigan Library; and Jackie Graziano of the Westchester County Records and Archives Center. I very much appreciate Laurie C. Matheson's confidence in me and my work and Jill R. Hughes for her able copyediting

Finally, thanks to Griffin, Emmett, and Connor, who cheer me on. In the end, I would never have gotten to where I could write my books without the love and understanding of Diana Messer-Kruse.

THE HAYMARKET CONSPIRACY

INTRODUCTION

A few minutes after ten o'clock on Tuesday, May 4, 1886, in the midst of a national general strike for the eight-hour workday, nearly two hundred police officers poured out from the Desplaines Street station and marched the hundred yards to where Chicago's anarchists were holding a protest meeting. Captain William Ward stopped a few feet from where Samuel Fielden was just concluding his speech and loudly ordered the crowd to disperse. At that moment, someone partially sheltered by a stack of fish crates left on a nearby curb threw a round leaden bomb, slightly bigger than a softball, into the police ranks. The resulting explosion threw dozens of policemen to the ground, leading to the deaths of five cops. Gunfire erupted as police fired indiscriminately into the crowd and some protesters answered in kind. Two more policemen and at least three civilians were shot and killed.

The meeting had been called the day before in protest of the alleged police killing of six workers during a riot at the McCormick Reaper Works, one of the largest industrial establishments in the city. (In fact, two men had died as a result of wounds sustained in this incident.) Broadsides demanding "revenge" and calling on workers to arm themselves were hurriedly printed, and code words signaling the muster of radical armed groups were published in the *Arbeiter-Zeitung*, a German-language daily newspaper that had become the flagship of revolutionary anarchism in Chicago. A secret meeting of revolutionary militiamen was held in a basement room beneath a saloon known as Greif's Hall, and various plans for attacking police stations, cutting firemen's hoses, and aiding striking workers with force of arms were made.

What became known as the Haymarket Riot did not take place in the Haymarket, a widening of Randolph Street on Chicago's near west side, but commenced around the corner from Randolph on a narrow side street pierced with even narrower alleyways when anarchist editor and leader August Spies scrambled onto a freight wagon and addressed a modest crowd. Spies's presence aroused the suspicions of police hunkered in their station only one block away, as he had been speaking from the top of a boxcar the day before when a large portion of his audience suddenly attacked workers leaving the McCormick factory at the end of their shift.

It took only a few minutes for police to sweep Desplaines Street clear of all protesters, save those writhing on the ground, but it took them weeks to piece together a case that could make someone legally responsible for the tragedy. Orders were given to arrest all the men who had spoken from that wagon, and the following morning the police raided the offices of the *Arbeiter-Zeitung* and arrested all twenty-three editors, writers, printers, typesetters, and "devil boys" they found there. Jimmying open Spies's desk, they discovered receipts from an explosives company and two sticks of dynamite. More dynamite was found in a closet, and fuses and blasting caps were found in a trunk. Adolph Fischer, Spies's editorial assistant, was apprehended leaving the building armed with a revolver, a "dirk" knife, and a blasting cap. Over the next four weeks, dozens of buildings and homes were searched, and many anarchists and their associates were detained or arrested. Police rarely bothered to obtain proper warrants in these days before 1912, when the Supreme Court ruled that evidence illegally obtained must be excluded from trial. Only two anarchists resisted arrest: Reinhold "Big" Krueger, who shot Officer Michael Mueller in the chest as he was being apprehended and received a fatal bullet to the head in the return, and Louis Lingg, the bomb maker, who drew a gun and grappled with Officer Herman Schuettler until another cop subdued him. All the principal anarchist leaders in the city were eventually locked up, though two remained at large—Albert Parsons, one of the only native-born Americans among the anarchist leadership, and Rudolph Schnaubelt, whom police deduced had actually thrown the bomb.

When the conspiracy trial opened on June 21, 1886, Albert Parsons, the most wanted man in America, calmly walked into the courtroom. Parsons had come at the urging of anarchist lawyers, but this was a terrible miscalculation, for had he waited just one more day to surrender himself, legally he would have had the right to a separate trial. As it was, this was just the first of many legal misjudgments on the part of the anarchists' inexperienced and politically motivated lawyers that greatly aided the prosecution.

For their part, the prosecution took full advantage of the public's nativism and anti-leftist bias. Prosecutors festooned the courtroom with anarchist and socialist flags and banners seized from workers' meeting halls. Incendiary passages from anarchist books and newspapers were read into the record. As the trial progressed, an arsenal of weapons was heaped on tables in front of the jury, including loaded bombs. Such lurid displays were hardly necessary, though, as during the six-week trial prosecutor Julius Grinnell brought in witnesses and metallurgical evidence establishing Lingg as the bomb maker as well as witnesses who identified Schnaubelt as the bomber and Spies and Fischer as his accomplices. An old toy-maker, George Engel, was fingered as the man who had proposed bombing police stations at the secret meeting. Two other anarchists, Michael Schwab and Oscar Neebe, were implicated by witnesses as having knowledge of some sort of violent action at the Haymarket meeting, though they were never directly connected to the bombing. Parsons was shown to have attempted to purchase fifty pistols and was one of the speakers at the meeting, but beyond that little implicated him in the alleged plot.

Defense lawyers and witnesses described how the police charged into a peaceful meeting, guns drawn, and fired wildly in panic after the bomb exploded. The defense attempted to undermine the testimony of informants by getting them to admit they had been paid by the police, but the sums they admitted to were below what everyone in Chicago knew to be a decent bribe. In what might have been the greatest legal blunder of the age, the defense placed defendant August Spies on the stand, and he arrogantly admitted that the dynamite found in his desk was indeed his and that he kept a few bombs around his office for the purpose of frightening reporters and to "experiment" with.

The jury took little time to arrive at a guilty verdict, condemning all the men to death except for Oscar Neebe. The Illinois Supreme Court reaffirmed the verdict and dismissed defense claims that the jury had been illegally packed. When the U.S. Supreme Court refused to hear the case, pressure was turned on Illinois governor Richard Oglesby to commute the sentences of those who showed remorse for their actions. By this time a clemency movement had taken shape, based largely on several highly selective accounts of the trial that were published by friends of the condemned. Oglesby commuted the sentences of Schwab and Fielden, who wrote letters of confession, to life in prison. While the others held steadfast in their refusal to sign such letters, Louis Lingg was caught with four small dynamite bombs in his cell. Speculation was that they were to be used by four of the condemned men to cheat the hangman. Anarchist lawyers attempted to distance the other defendants from Lingg by petitioning the court to declare him legally insane. A few days later it was discovered that Lingg had managed to either squirrel away one last charge or have an accomplice smuggle another one into the jail; he had reclined on his cot and lit an explosive like a cigar, leading to his death a few hours later.

On November 11, 1887, Albert Parsons, August Spies, George Engel, and Adolph Fischer were hanged in the Cook County jail. A line of thousands of mourners followed their coffins to Waldheim Cemetery, where in 1893 a graceful monument to their martyrdom was erected. Four years earlier a larger and less elegant edifice was erected in Chicago's Haymarket Square to commemorate the heroism of the dead policemen. The same year that the anarchists' memorial was dedicated, Governor Peter Altgeld signed pardons for the remaining three imprisoned anarchists languishing in Joliet Prison.

The Haymarket bombing and trial marked a pivotal moment in the history of American social movements. It sparked the nation's first "red scare," whose fury disrupted even moderately leftist movements for a generation. It drove the nation's labor unions onto a more conservative path than they had been heading before the bombing. It also began a tradition within the American left of memorializing the Haymarket defendants as martyrs to the cause of the eight-hour workday, free speech, and the cause of labor generally.

Once the anarchist movement was safely broken up and suppressed, mainstream trade union leaders embraced the memory of the martyrs as a means of highlighting the hollowness of American liberties when it comes to industrial democracy. In the 1930s the Communist Party of the United States, seeking to overcome its own sectarianism, claimed the Haymarket martyrs as their own revolutionary predecessors. A generation later a New Left grew in opposition to cultural conformity and a Cold War consensus and rediscovered the indigenous roots of American radicalism, including the Haymarket anarchists, whom they now portrayed as organic intellectuals, adopting their radical tactics not from Europe but from their own hard experiences in the politically corrupt and economically exploitative cities of the Gilded Age.

Their poster child became anarchist Albert Parsons, a Texan, a former Confederate, great-grandson of a Bunker Hill Revolutionary War hero, namesake of a family whose lineage stretched back to the *Mayflower*. Parsons was as American as any hero they could hope to find. As if made to order for a movement arising out of southern campaigns against segregation and racism, Albert Parsons fell in love with a Texas woman of a richly mixed ethnic heritage that included African and Indian ancestors, thus making their marriage dangerous and their movement north to Chicago necessary. With Parsons placed at the top of their pantheon of useful martyrs, the New Left established a new historical interpretation of 1880s anarchism that soon became orthodoxy among both scholars and activists and distanced Chicago's anarchists from the anarchist movement campaigning in Europe. Chicago's anarchists were seen to be so different from the European anarchist movement that historians had difficulty distinguishing them from ordinary Marxists. Chicago's anarchists were depicted as die-hard union activists, as civil libertarians disillusioned with the realities of electoral politics but not its ideals, as "bomb talkers" filled with revolutionary fervor but actually pacifists at heart.

The new picture of Chicago's anarchists that emerged out of this reinterpretation was one that not only presumed their innocence in the Haymarket bombing but also flattened out their differences from other branches of the socialist movement. One result of this is that scholars have been largely unable to address the key questions that follow from the anarchists' advocacy of "direct action" and "social revolution." Did they, in fact, believe in organizing secret cells that could be called upon to take up arms and strike when the revolutionary moment arrived, or was such talk just another example of their bluffing to attract attention and make their movement seem larger and more threatening than it really was? If they did arm themselves and advocate the use of violence to throw off the yoke of capitalism, did they intend to use these guns and knives only in self-defense, or did they also contemplate taking the initiative and firing the first shot? Was their support of incremental trade union reforms like the eight-hour workday a sincere effort to lighten the daily burdens of ordinary workers, or did they push for strikes out of the hope that they might propel workers down the road to insurrection?[1]

Such questions must be answered in order to make sense of the bombing near Haymarket Square. What was anarchism in 1886? What ideas was it based on? What exactly did anarchists want, and how did they propose to get it? Such questions seem an obvious and crucial starting point for assessing the meaning of various anarchist leaders' actions in Chicago, yet contemporary scholars are maddeningly vague in answering them—so vague, in fact, that they seem to be avoiding the question; they seem to not want to lift up that particular rock, fearing what lurks beneath. Few scholars who have attempted to pin down the beliefs of Chicago's so-called anarchists actually define what the core elements of anarchism were at that particular moment, and those few who do then deny that Chicago's radicals held those beliefs.

Judging from the record of discussion, reporting, and debate of the 1880s, contemporaries of the Chicago anarchists had no such difficulty in defining what made the anarchists distinctive or in describing their core beliefs. In 1883 when American anarchists met in Pittsburgh to hammer out a manifesto, the other side of the socialist schism was represented in Baltimore, where a handful of delegates upheld the slow and laborious task of class organization and education against the stirring call for immediate insurrection. At the conclusion of their convention, the Socialist Labor Party clarified their differences with the anarchists: "We do not share the folly of the men who consider dynamite bombs as the best means of agitation. We know full well that a revolution must take place in the heads and in the industrial life of men before the working class can achieve lasting success."[2] Several years before the Haymarket explosion, economist Richard T. Ely succinctly explained the differences between ordinary socialists and anarchists (which he referred to as "Internationalists" in recognition of the previous year's London Congress of the International Working People's Association, where the anarchist movement was officially founded in 1881): "The Internationalists desire to begin the revolution, and do not shrink from an active initiative in deeds of violence. The Socialistic Labor Party believes in peaceful agitation and lawful means in behalf of their principles until their enemies force the struggle upon them."[3] Ely's British colleague John Rae, who published his taxonomic survey of socialism in 1881, likewise began by dividing socialism into two general categories: "the Centralist, which is usually known as Communism, Socialism, or Collectivism," and the "Anarchist, which—though also Communist, Socialist, or Collectivist—is generally known as . . . Nihilism." Rae elaborated that "nihilism may be said to be just an extremer phase of socialism. It indulges in more violent methods and in a more omnivorous spirit of destruction."[4]

The issue of *Frank Leslie's Popular Monthly* that was on sale as the Haymarket bomb exploded featured a cover story titled "Socialistic Movements in England and the United States." The anonymous author divided socialism into four great branches: Marxist, Christian, Aesthetic, and Anarchic. The latter was described as being distinguished by its threats and acts of "incendiary violence" and its rejection of "peaceable argument . . . for a reform of existing laws and social institutions."[5] George Engel, one of the men hanged for his part in the bombing, devoted part of his statement to the court before being sentenced to explain how anarchism differs from socialism: "Anarchism and Socialism are as much alike, in my opinion, as one egg is like another. They differ only in their tactics. The Anarchists have abandoned the way of liberating humanity which socialists would take to accomplish this. I say: Believe no more in the ballot, and use all other means at your command." Unlike modern historians, Engel saw clearly that what distinguished his brand of radicalism from others was not his principles or vision of the future, but his belief that violence was not only necessary but also the most effective tool with which to construct a new society.[6]

Thus, in spite of their widely accepted moniker, which suggests a philosophical basis of distinction, contemporaries of the anarchists understood them as being part of a movement that was less distinguished by their ideals, their social critique, or their vision of the future than by their commitment to violence. As detailed below, it was not until the late 1870s that advocacy of violence coalesced into a distinct movement within socialist ranks. As this tendency formed, it was variously described as "anarchist," "nihilist," and "social-revolutionary" to distinguish it from the glacial structural advances that were prerequisite to revolution as theorized by Marx and from the legalistic and electoral paths to socialism envisioned by Ferdinand Lassalle, Wilhelm Liebknecht, and other socialist politicians. More importantly, anarchism had not yet clearly separated itself from socialism, a development that would come in the 1890s with the republication of the philosophical writings of Pierre-Joseph Proudhon and Mikhail Bakunin, a flood of new and more systematic writings from Peter Kropotkin, and the subtle contributions of Leo Tolstoy. As a result, much of the confusion and imprecision surrounding the anarchists of the 1880s is simply due to the fact that they were labeled in a manner that failed to distinguish them from the different theoretical schools that they preceded and followed. For the purposes of this study, then, the terms *anarchism* and *anarchist* will be used only to describe those ideas, groups, or individual radicals who are distinguished by their complete rejection of ameliorative legal reforms and the voting systems that bring them about, by their advocacy of violence both collective and individual, and by their belief in the imminence of mass insurrection.[7]

In presuming the Haymarket anarchists' innocence, historians have had only to explain the tragic chain of events that led to the anarchists' martyrdom. Their jailhouse denials and post-bombing explanations were not only accepted uncritically but also became the lens through which the character of the anarchist movement was interpreted. When that lens is taken away, when the anarchist movement is chronicled according to what its members said and did over the course of years, rather than according to what they and their defenders claimed they had done when facing the noose, the whole story changes. From this new vantage point, one neglected question appears as the fundamental issue: did anarchist leaders plot a campaign of violent attacks to coincide with the general strike for the eight-hour workday that first weekend of May 1886?

Upon the answer to this question turns the whole history of the anarchist movement in America. If there was no organized conspiracy to attack the police in May 1886, then the relevant historical questions are those that are already fully answered by the many historians who have told the tale of the "Haymarket Tragedy" and the unjust execution of leaders of Chicago's labor movement. But if there was such a conspiracy, then the meaning of this radical moment is uncertain. If there was a conspiracy to make violent attacks, what did they hope to achieve? What beliefs, experiences, and presumptions about society could lead radicals to consider such drastic actions?

Though it goes against all of my historical instincts, I have endeavored to answer the fundamental question first—is there reliable and convincing evidence that the Haymarket bombing was the culmination of a coordinated plan to attack the police?—rather than recount the history of the anarchist movement in Chicago in the usual chronological progression. I must first address the question "Was there a Haymarket conspiracy?" because its answer defines and determines what is meaningful and important about the formation and growth of the anarchist movement that led to that dramatic juncture. The evidence uncovered by the police in their investigation and subsequently aired at trial provides a new means to understand what it was that the bomber and his or her accomplices hoped to accomplish, to get inside their heads and view the world through their eyes. Understanding the revolutionary anarchist movement on the participants' own terms rather than in the romantic ways their martyrs have been eulogized changes the meaning of their trial, their movement, and their memory.

CHAPTER ONE

THE CONSPIRACY

According to more than a dozen "squealers," the Haymarket meeting was originally conceived as the centerpiece of a larger plan to attack police stations throughout the city. It was the culmination of an idea that was conceived well before the strike for the eight-hour workday that commenced on May 1, 1886, and that was ultimately agreed to at a clandestine meeting of the "armed men" of the movement after rioting broke out at the McCormick Reaper Works on May 3.

That night the most militant men in the anarchist movement gathered after most other evening meetings had concluded at Greif's Hall, a saloon on Lake Street. Some of the men who gathered there had seen a coded message in that day's edition of the *Arbeiter-Zeitung*, the daily German-language newspaper of the anarchist movement. Others were at a meeting of the carpenters union being held just a block down the street above Zepf's Hall when a man burst in and shouted for all the armed men to go to a meeting at Greif's.[1]

Greif's Hall was a large saloon, not one of the poorer beer-bucket joints, and its owner, Thomas Greif, was chairman of the West Side Saloon Association.[2] Greif's had long been the most popular meeting place for radicals in Chicago. It was where the Socialist Labor Party held its main section meetings and nominated socialist candidates in the 1870s. The anarchists' publishing company, Socialistic Publishing Company, was organized there. Chicago's first city central labor union was founded there as was the city's branch of the National Liberal League, an organization that united "freethinkers . . . socialists, skeptics, and labor agitators" in their desire to keep the government free of religion. Unions of bricklayers, switchmen, carpenters, masons, plasterers, and even the union of saloon owners held their meetings in one of the two upstairs halls before adjourning to Greif's bar on the ground floor.[3]

Around 10:00 PM someone sent word that the armed men were to meet in the basement. A single set of stairs led down to a rough-hewn door sandwiched between the saloon's bathroom and the ice room where Thomas Greif cooled his kegs. Through the door was a low-ceilinged room that stretched the length of the building, furnished with six or seven rows of plank benches facing a small table that served as the rostrum. Despite the large size of the room, it was lit by only a single kerosene lamp slung from a beam. Before the meeting began, guards were posted: one at the door and one on the sidewalk to make sure no detectives bent their ears toward the squat cellar window.

Gottfried Waller, who later turned state's evidence and told his story before a packed courtroom, chaired the meeting, but most of the talking was done by middle-aged toy-maker George Engel and a typographer, Adolph Fischer. These two were among the most fervent and militant men in the anarchist movement. Fischer distributed copies of a circular, hot off the press, whose headline read, "Revenge!" that described the riot at the McCormick factory earlier that day and falsely stated that six workers had been shot and killed by the police. The thirty or more men in the room were angry, their passion easily stirred, and Engel proposed that they implement the plan he had devised.

Engel had unveiled this plan the previous morning, Sunday, May 2. While the devout entered their churches and the doubters filled the beer halls, leaders of the Second Company of the Lehr und Wehr Verein (the Educational and Military Association) and armed members of the Northwest Side group met secretly at Bohemian Hall on Emma Street. The little group included Big Krueger, who would be killed in a few days in a shootout with police; Gottfried Waller and Bernardt Schrade, both of whom would later turn state's evidence; and murder defendants George Engel and Adolph Fischer among others.[4] They discussed the coming resumption of the workweek and made plans for what to do if and when workers came into conflict with the police. Schrade, a commander of the Lehr und Wehr militia, revealed some of these plans when he was put on the witness stand. "It was said," Schrade reported, "that if they were to get into a conflict with the police that they were to mutually enlist themselves, assist themselves to make an attack." In particular, plans were established that in the event of such fighting, "the members of the Northwestern Group should go there [to Wicker Park] in case that it should get so far as that the police would make an attack." Among the contingencies considered by the meeting in order to aid the "revolutionary movement" was the possibility that firemen might be enlisted to clear the streets of protesters with their hoses. In one of the more dramatic moments in Schrade's testimony, prosecutor George Ingham asked:

Q. Was anything said as to what should be done with the firemen in such a case?

A. Well, it was said the best thing [was] to annihilate them, or to cut through their hose, and so forth, that they could not do anything.[5]

Gottfried Waller elaborated further and described a number of plans that were laid out, including one proposed by George Engel that "as soon as it came to a conflict between the police and the Northwestern Groups, that bombs should be thrown into the Police stations and the rifle men of the Lehr and Wehr Verein should post themselves in line in a certain distance and whoever would come out should be shot down." Others thought it better for the fighters to mingle in with "the people" and "fight right in the midst of them." But this idea was rejected by those who pointed out that no one would know who it was that stood next to them, and that person might just as likely be a detective as a comrade. In other words, the group had to decide between two fundamentally different military tactics: the armed fighters could either rush to the aid of the strikers and eight-hour rioters, throwing up barricades and fighting with them shoulder to shoulder like the communards did in Paris in 1871, or, as Engel proposed, they could operate independently of the masses and simply make it more difficult for the state to crush their uprising by attacking the police directly. In the end, according to Waller, Engel's plan was adopted by the Northwest Side group.[6]

By choosing the second of these tactics, the Northwest Side group maintained the initiative and control of their actions—riots were by their nature unpredictable and uncontrollable—but so much of the military advantage gained thereby depended upon the ability of the units to coordinate their actions and upon the dependability of the fighters, who were to take the first step and provoke a battle rather than responding defensively within a riotous crowd. The inescapable implications of this choice explain much of what did and did not actually happen the night the Haymarket bomb was thrown.

The following day, Monday, May 3, the confrontation between strikers and police that Engel and his fellow revolutionaries had hoped for burst out. An outdoor meeting across the prairie from the large McCormick Reaper Works addressed by August Spies turned into an assault upon workers filing out of the factory at day's end. A pair of uniformed policemen at the gates held the rock-throwing mob at bay for a few crucial minutes until wagonloads of reinforcements galloped through the crowd. Nightsticks and rocks quickly escalated to an exchange of gunfire in which several workers were wounded, at least one fatally.[7]

Later that same day a coded signal, "*Y.—Komme Montag Abend*" (Y.— Come Monday night), calling for a rare general meeting of the armed cells, appeared in the *Arbeiter-Zeitung*. (Gottfried Waller, the anarchist who chaired that meeting, testified that he had seen that coded signal used only once before.[8]) Since the *Arbeiter-Zeitung* was composed in the afternoon and put to bed by 5:00 PM for printing the next morning and distribution in the afternoon, this special call for a meeting of all the armed groups must have been written after the meeting at Bohemian Hall, where Engel first laid out his plan, but printed before the rioters had even begun to gather at the McCormick factory.[9]

Obeying the coded call to assemble, several dozen earnest men crammed into the basement of Greif's saloon. Engel was aware that he was addressing a general assembly of the armed groups of the city, not just his own notoriously militant Northwest side group. The plan Engel laid out for this larger group was a more general strategy for the whole city that included planning for a central precipitating event that would provoke a police confrontation and hopefully spark a wider workers' uprising, and agreeing upon rendezvous points for all armed groups across the city. In textbook military fashion, Engel's plan aimed to take advantage of the station system of policing that scattered the city's defenders across far-flung districts. Outlying stations were to be attacked once the riot in the center of the city had begun. Engel must have calculated that police were uniquely vulnerable to attack when they were summoned from their stations and piled into their patrol wagons. In that frenzied, distracted moment, the police were to be either shot or bombed as they rushed out into the open. Because the ultimate goal was not to kill them all but to keep the police divided and weak in the face of a workers' uprising, Engel stressed that under no circumstances were the patrols to be allowed to depart; fighters were instructed to shoot the draft horses rather than allow the police in distant stations to reinforce those in the heart of the city. By cutting telegraph wires and ambushing stations with the coordination of an agreed-upon signal, the police would be thrown into a state of panic and confusion, unable to combine their forces to confront the masses of striking and rioting workers taking over the city.

Waller remembered Engel's plan from the witness box this way:

> He told us that the Northwest Side Group had resolved as to that, that if on account of the workingmen—the strikers—something would happen to the police that we should gather at certain corners or meeting places. Then the word

"Ruhe"—translated as "Quiet" or "rest,"—if that was ordered to be published; if that was to appear it was to be the time for us to meet . . . the Northwest Side Group and the Lehr and Wehr Verein of the Northwest side should assemble in Wicker Park armed. Then a committee was appointed to watch the movement in the city. They should observe the movement and if something happened they should report, and if a riot should occur we should first storm the police station and should cut the telegraph wires . . . after we had stormed the police station we should shoot down everything that should come out, and by that we thought to gain accessions from the workingmen, and then if that police station was stormed we should do the same in regard to the second, and whatever would come in our way we should strike down.[10]

It was an audacious plan that required a high level of coordination among separated units. One code word, the German word *Ruhe,* or "peace," was to be printed in the next day's edition of the *Arbeiter-Zeitung* as a signal to all the armed men in different corners of the city if all the preparations had been completed, and they were to then muster at their various rendezvous sites. Once assembled and ready, they were to wait until they either got word that a riot had broken out in the city or could see the sky brightened by the "red fires" the rioters would set as a signal for them to storm the police stations.[11]

The missing piece of the plan was a demonstration that would lure police into a confrontation, draw large numbers of angry workers into the fray, and signal the armed groups to attack. But where could such a rally be held? Chairman Waller suggested that the demonstration be held in Market Square, a broad open area on the east bank of the Chicago River, running between Washington and Randolph Streets and bounded by Market Street on the east (today Wacker Drive). This was one of the two customary locations for mass demonstrations. Whenever a large crowd was expected, radicals held their events either on the lakefront or at Market Square. It was where workers first confronted the police during the great railway strikes of 1877. Denis Kearney, the popular and notorious anti-Chinese labor activist, spoke there on his visit to Chicago. In 1884 the newly formed anarchist International Working People's Association (IWPA) held one of its first protest meetings in Market Square, denouncing the hanging of Isaac Jacobson, a tramp who pled guilty to putting a bullet through the eye of his employer because his pay envelope was short one dollar. The IWPA's signature event, an annual protest against a Thanksgiving holiday, occurred there. When the anarchists organized to protest the dedication of the new Board of Trade building in 1885, they made their speeches and launched their demonstration from Market Square.[12]

It was completely customary for someone to suggest that a large open-air protest meeting be held in Market Square, but ultra-militant Adolph Fischer, who with his partner Engel published the monthly anarchist sheet the *Anarchist*, spoke out against it. Waller remembered this incident from the witness stand: "I had proposed Market Square and then Fischer said this was a mouse trap." Cabinet maker Peter Huber did not recall that it was Fischer who called Market Square a "mouse trap," but he did remember someone objecting to the meeting being held there and the reason why: "Some one else remarked, 'No, that is not a good place; it is a mouse trap.' If they held the meeting there and the police interfered, and the crowd resisted them, the police would drive them all into the river. Some said, 'That's so,' and then the meeting was fixed for the Haymarket, as Engel had suggested." Another man in attendance, Victor Clermont, who worked in a billiard table factory, also told Captain Michael J. Schaack of the "mouse trap" expression: "First Market Square was proposed, but some one objected by saying it was a mouse trap in case of trouble, and the Haymarket was agreed upon."[13]

Market Square, though a large area, was a box with only one open side. On the west was a branch of the Chicago River. The square was bounded on the south by a tall factory that extended clear to the waterline. Washington Street ended at the river, and the mouth of the Washington Street tunnel opened a block farther east. To the north another commercial building walled off the square. While much larger than the Haymarket Square, Market Square truly was a mousetrap, for police had only to draw their lines up along Market Street to close off all avenues of escape to those inside the square. In contrast, all the streets intersecting Haymarket Square were thoroughfares and cross-streets. This part of the city was well supplied with alleyways and bisecting lanes. Whether it was Fischer or someone else who observed the tactical advantages of Haymarket and the dangers of Market Street for anyone anticipating a skirmish, their assessment of the terrain was astute.

Only a couple of informants left a more detailed account of what plans were made for the Haymarket rally besides choosing its location. John Thielen, another carpenter and a friend of defendant Louis Lingg, told Captain Schaack of a sketchy plan for the Haymarket meeting: "The plan was to call out a meeting first and have no speakers there. The police would then come and drive us away. They then should fire on the police. There were a lot of armed people at the meeting, I know. But the police did not interfere, so they got speakers at the meeting. Finally the police came out, and the mob did what they had agreed to do."[14]

Likewise, Johannes Gruenberg, an older carpenter, remembered Engel's speech similarly: "We are . . . going to do this right, because all the boys look to us as the leaders, and we are going to call a meeting for to-morrow night at the Haymarket. Since all the people are excited, we will have a large crowd, and we will have things so shaped that the police will interfere. Then will be the chance to give it to them?"[15] Victor Clermont recalled the feeling at the meeting: "We expected that there would be present at the Haymarket meeting from 30,000 to 40,000 people and that then there would be a good chance for us to commence our revolution and attack the police and the government."[16]

Taking Thielen, Gruenberg, and Clermont at their words, their statements confirm that less detailed planning went into the Haymarket meeting than into the coordination of the various armed squads to be positioned on the outskirts of the city. At most, it was vaguely envisioned that armed militants would resist police interference with arms, but no one who sat on the hard wooden benches in the basement of Greif's Hall and later told authorities about it claimed that any specific plan was made to throw a bomb during that protest. It seems, instead, that the conspiracy's leaders had two different but related goals: (1) provoke a riot in the center of the city, and (2) coordinate an attack on its periphery. Given the ease with which confrontations had broken out over the previous day, it is understandable if these organizers did not think precipitating a riot needed much advance planning. If these accounts are correct, anarchist leaders like Engel and Fischer thought it sufficient to simply bring the volatile ingredients of violence together. Take some armed and angry men, plenty of bombs, a narrow street, a nearby police station, and mix to cook up a riot.

But though the Monday-night conspirators failed to develop a detailed plan of battle with police, they did take steps to be prepared for whatever actions might be called for. According to two of the militants crammed under the saloon, Louis Lingg offered to prepare dynamite bombs. According to Gustav Lehman, "the unanimous understanding among us all was that all who desired bombs must go to Lingg and get them."[17]

The ill-fated Haymarket rally was an event suspiciously unlike any the anarchists or socialists of the Chicago area had ever held. For prosecutors, the many departures from the usual anarchist routines that were apparent in the unfolding of this meeting were evidence of its unique purpose: to launch a coordinated attack upon the police. While none of the meeting's anomalies by themselves prove the existence of an insurrectionary plot, they do raise suspicions about just what the anarchists were planning for that night.

Sometime during the morning of the Haymarket rally, broadsides began to circulate calling "Workingmen" to a "Great Mass Meeting" that evening. These leaflets were unlike any others ever distributed in the city. They were anonymous, their origin and affiliations indicated only as a call issued by a mysterious "Executive Committee." In the past radicals had always been eager to claim credit and sponsorship of their events; both socialists and anarchists always included either the formal names of their organizations (the Socialist Labor Party or the International Working People's Association) or at least a line declaring their gathering to be a "socialist" picnic, parade, commemoration, ball, or mass meeting. Nothing in this flier revealed its organizers' ideological affiliations.

The broadside called workingmen to "Haymarket, Randolph St., Bet. Desplaines and Halsted," which was a most unusual location for radicals to hold a meeting. Anarchists had never held an outdoor rally in that place before. Only a couple of times over the previous seven years had any labor groups gathered there. In 1879 the Trades and Labor Assembly met there before parading off to a picnic at Ogden's Grove. Later that summer a parade of socialist militia companies came close but chose not to assemble in Haymarket Square; instead they drew up their ranks one block north on Lake Street. Just a week before the Haymarket bombing, the Central Labor Union assembled a parade promoting the eight-hour workday there before marching to the lakefront. Only missionaries from the YMCA were known to regularly ascend a soapbox there.[18]

Two editions of the broadside were printed, identical but for the line "Workingmen Arm Yourselves and Appear in Full Force!" that one version did not include. Apparently this was not empty rhetoric. Gottfried Waller, an anarchist leader turned state's witness, heeded this suggestion and later confessed that he came to the meeting with a revolver in his pocket.[19]

In spite of what the handbill advertising the protest meeting said, the Haymarket meeting did not actually occur in the Haymarket. Haymarket Square was a two-block-long stretch of West Randolph Street, between Desplaines Street on the east and Halsted Street on the west, where the already broad avenue widened to more than double its usual width. Its nickname was obsolete, no hay having been carted to the area for decades, but in 1866 it was formally designated one of three market districts "for the sale of poultry, vegetables, and meats by the carcass or quarter." From dawn to dusk, except on Sundays, this two-block run of Randolph was cramped with farmers' and peddlers' carts crowding dangerously close upon the dual lines of streetcar tracks that ran down its middle.[20]

Rather, the meeting actually took place a half block north of Randolph Street on the much narrower Desplaines Street. This block of Desplaines was distinctive. It was anchored on its north, on the corner of Lake Street, by Zepf's Hall, one of the radicals' favorite meeting places. A half block to the south was the city's newest and most modern police station. The Desplaines Street police station opened on May 3, 1882, with a sumptuous dinner and a formal ball. It was the home of the Third Precinct, a district commanded by Captain John Bonfield, a cop who may have been the officer most hated and reviled by the anarchists in all the city. It was also one of the few stations in the city that had been built with a pistol range in its basement, a feature that lent the officers of the Third Precinct the reputation of being good marksmen in an era when the clumsy handling of firearms by Chicago police was a common subject of jokes.[21]

Of all the streets intersecting Randolph in this part of the city, it was this block of Desplaines that was most crisscrossed by alleyways. Three narrow alleys intersected the block: one on the east that doglegged back to Randolph known as Crane's Alley, one slightly farther north on the same side of the street that ran through to both Jefferson and Lake Streets, and one on the west that was glorified with the name Eagle Street, though it was barely wide enough for two wagons to squeeze past each other.

Most uncharacteristically for the radicals' public meetings, which seem to have nearly always begun punctually at their advertised time, the rally at the Haymarket got started so late that many people who showed up left discouraged before it began. According to the announcement, the meeting was to begin at 7:30 PM, not an unusual time for such an event, but somehow the timing slipped and the event did not commence until an hour later. Mayor Carter Harrison, who arrived on the scene sometime between the appointed hour and five minutes to eight, thought that because of the delay about two-thirds of the people milling about Randolph Street looking for a meeting left before it began.[22]

Another unusual feature of the Haymarket meeting was that there seems to have been no provision made for the "Good Speakers" promised by its announcement ("Good Speakers will be present to denounce the latest atrocious act of the police, the shooting of our fellow-workmen yesterday afternoon"). The two featured speakers of the evening, Albert Parsons and Samuel Fielden, were asked to come and speak well after 7:30 PM. Both Parsons and Fielden were then at a different meeting, at the offices of the *Arbeiter-Zeitung* on Fifth Avenue, and were called to the Haymarket by Balthasar Rau, who showed up to fetch them between a quarter past eight and eight thirty.[23] August Spies, who called the meeting to order and was its first speaker, did not immediately begin his speech but asked the crowd if anyone had seen Parsons and then left to find him before returning a few minutes later and speaking. Clearly, either this was the most poorly organized meeting in the history of the Chicago IWPA, or it was a meeting in which arranging "Good Speakers" or keeping a large crowd was, for some reason, not of much importance. According to a number of informants and anarchist witnesses, these unusual features were not accidents, coincidences, or the result of poor preparation, but were all part of a plan to lure police into a trap.

The other leg of Engel's plan, the more coordinated military attacks on police stations, was to be triggered by a coded message published in the anarchist newspaper. It had been agreed in Greif's basement that if the word *Ruhe* appeared in the "Briefkasten" (letter box) column of the newspaper, all the armed units were to muster at their prearranged locations. As the informer Waller put it on the witness stand: "It was to be the signal to bring the members together at the various meetings in case of a revolution, but it was not to be in the papers until the revolution should actually take place."[24]

An even more interesting account of the meaning of the secret signal comes from William Seliger, the man who helped Louis Lingg fashion bombs on the day of the bombing. Seliger said he arrived back at the narrow frame house he shared with Lingg, who picked up a newspaper and said, "Here it is." When asked what Lingg meant, Seliger answered, "He said there had been a meeting on the West Side and he was going to go at once to it;—there was to have been a meeting on the West Side, there was to be that night." The back-and-forth examination continued:

Q. What else did Lingg say about the word "Ruhe"?
A. That everything was to go upside down—topsy turvy—that there was to be trouble.
Q. Give everything that Lingg said as fully as you can about what the word "Ruhe" meant.
A. He said to me that a meeting had been held at 54 West Lake Street and it was determined upon that the word "Ruhe" should appear in the papers as a signal for the armed men to appear at that meeting.
Q. Repeat what Lingg said to you about the meaning of the word "Ruhe."
A. Well, he said that a meeting had been held at which it was determined that the word "Ruhe" should go into the paper for all the armed men to appear at 54 West Lake Street, that there should be trouble.[25]

According to August Spies, the order for the insertion of the word *Ruhe* arrived at his office around 11:00 AM on the day of the bombing. He passed it along to the typesetters and thought little about it until later in the day, after the paper had been printed, and his ad manager, Balthasar Rau, asked about it. Spies describes what happened next:

He asked me if I knew what that meant. I told him no, I did not. He said the armed sections held a meeting last night, and they have resolved to put in that word, that it means as much as the armed sections should keep themselves in readiness, prepare themselves, that in case the police should precipitate a riot, that they should come to the assistance of the attacked. I asked him where he heard it. He said it was a rumor, and I sent up for Fischer who had invited me to speak at that meeting in the evening, and Fischer came down and I asked him in regard to that. He said Oh, it was just a harmless signal. I asked him if it had any reference to the meeting on the Haymarket. He said none whatever. He said that it was merely a signal for the boys, for those who were armed to keep their powder dry, in case they might be called upon in the next days; to fight. I told Rau it was a very silly thing, that such nonsense should be stopped, and he said he knew some persons who had something to say in the armed organizations and I told him to go and tell them that the word was put in by mistake, and he did.[26]

On the surface, Spies's explanation of how he came to insert the word *Ruhe* into his editorial page is convincing. There is no particular reason to believe that Spies was in cahoots with Engel and Fischer. After all, no witness or informer claimed he sat with them in Greif's basement. Spies seems almost naïve in his openness in describing what Rau told him of what was agreed upon at that meeting—the signal, the expected riot, the armed units making ready. None of this was necessary for Spies to answer the question posed to him.

But in his eagerness to defend himself by claiming he did not agree to this plan and took an action to stop it, he may have given himself away. For if Spies knew nothing about the secret meeting in Greif's cellar, if what Rau told him about it was from a "rumor," how did Spies know to ask Fischer about it, one of the men who was at that meeting? At that moment the *Arbeiter-Zeitung* office was filled with dozens of men who were equally connected to the anarchist movement. Why did Spies call Fischer down to explain the secret sign? Either Spies recognized that this signal was associated with the planned Haymarket meeting, or Spies knew that Fischer was privy to such information, or both.

Spies's version of events reveals an interesting dynamic between Fischer and himself. For when Spies asked Fischer about the meaning of the word *Ruhe*, Fischer reassured him that it was "harmless" and had no reference to the Haymarket meeting. Spies, however, clearly did not believe what Fischer told him and instead was convinced that the signal was related to the Haymarket meeting and told Rau to tell the armed groups to stand down.

Of course, it may very well be that Spies was only vaguely aware of the military wing's plan and that once he learned more about it, he took steps to call off the fool's errand. But if this were the case, why did Spies, rather than Fischer, dispatch Rau to tell the anarchist fighters that the signal had been published in error? Apparently Spies tried to tailor his testimony to accomplish two ends but did not quite realize that the two contradicted each other. Though he tried, he could not simultaneously deny that the code word *Ruhe* was a prearranged signal to stir the armed groups into readiness at the time of the Haymarket meeting and also claim that he had done his best to call off the attack.

Others also observed some sort of tension between Spies and Fischer. Balthasar Rau told his own story to Captain Schaack and supported Spies's claim of having attempted to rescind the coded signal. However, in Rau's telling, the signal was explicitly linked to both the Haymarket meeting and the throwing of bombs:

> When I saw that word in the *Arbeiter-Zeitung*, I was working in the office of that paper. I remarked to August Spies that that would make trouble in the city, and his answer was that Fischer did it, meaning that Fischer was responsible for it. Spies, after I had told him what trouble it would make, got excited and called Schnaubelt. Spies asked him, "How is this?" referring to the word "Ruhe." Schnaubelt replied, "Well they want to throw dynamite bombs." He also said that if the police interfered, then there would be trouble at the Haymarket. He further said that the people stationed on the outskirts of the city, east, west, south, and north, should be informed as to when the riot commenced and when their time had arrived for storming the city. When Fischer was asked about this word "Ruhe" he was close mouthed. He would not say anything to us. I heard Spies say in his office, "If that word 'Ruhe' is in the paper, there will be trouble, and I don't want that. That will break up our organization." Spies said: "I will print hand-bills to stop the meeting at the Haymarket May 4." He said he would attend to that himself. I said that we had better put up signs on the corners to notify the people that there would be no meeting at the Haymarket that night. Spies said that if there was a meeting, then there would be trouble. Schnaubelt was to go to the North Side that afternoon, May 4, and tell the people that there would be no meeting at the Haymarket that night.[27]

In Rau's account, Spies knew more about the code word *Ruhe* than he admitted in his own testimony. From the witness box Spies claimed the word had been just one of a bundle of anonymous submissions for the newspaper's letter box from a "number of labor organizations." Rau, however, indicated that Spies was aware that the code came from Fischer, though he did not know the full extent of its meaning. When Rau told him about the military plan, Spies first asked Schnaubelt for confirmation and then quizzed Fischer about it. Fischer refused to tell what he knew about the militants' plan. Of course, it is understandable that Spies might have chosen not to mention his conversation with Schnaubelt on the witness stand, as Schnaubelt had been identified by the prosecution as the man who threw the bomb. In this account the tension between Fischer and Spies is ratcheted up a notch, and it is Schnaubelt who is dispatched to spread the word that the meeting had been cancelled instead of Rau. Beyond these differences, however, Rau's version and Spies's account trace the arc of the same plot: Spies was not fully cognizant of the meaning of the coded signal, but he did know who was involved, and he believed the signal was tied to the Haymarket meeting and would mobilize the armed men.

Perhaps if Tuesday, May 4, had been a quieter day, peaceful like the ironic secret signal word *Ruhe*, the militant anarchists may not have made all their preparations for revolution. But that day the workers of Chicago seemed to grow even more rebellious, giving hope to those who believed the final conflict between labor and capital was near.

On the day of the bombing, riots broke out in far-flung corners of the city as they had the day before, from the lumberyards in the southwest to the factories of Goose Island in the north. McCormick's factory was tense but calm as fifty uniformed police officers kept watch in front of its iron gates. Armour's glue factory on the south side of Chicago was the first target, beset by hundreds of men, many with pick handles and other improvised clubs. Two patrol wagons were dispatched, and though no shots were fired, it was reported that the police resorted to a "vigorous clubbing" to induce some of the protesters to move on, and four were hauled to jail.

The epicenter of trouble on the southwest side of the city seems to have been the corner of Eighteenth Street and Centre Avenue. At noon a crowd numbering about five hundred gathered there and marched off to a nearby paint factory where scabs were working under the protection of armed guards. Shots were fired and the factory shut down. Regrouping back at this troublesome corner, three undercover detectives made a move to arrest a man brandishing a revolver and provoked another skirmish involving billy clubs and punches, bricks, shots fired over the heads of the crowd, three patrol wagons screaming to the scene, and seven more arrests.

Many in this neighborhood had by now realized that whenever a group of strikers gathered or marched and the mood turned ugly, a policeman or an undercover cop would call for reinforcements at one of two places: a wooden patrol box on the corner, part of a telegraphic alarm system that made Chicago among the most modern of large city police departments, or the telephone at Samuel Rosenfeld's Drug Store, which was across the street in the same building as Weiskopf and Porgie's Hall, coincidentally the place where Bohemian socialists and anarchists held their meetings. Once darkness fell, the wooden patrol box was dismantled by a mob that then moved on to Rosenfeld's and ransacked it, too, smashing it so thoroughly—every window, every glass jar, bottle, beaker and flask—that Rosenfeld was put out of business. Ammunition for the riot was provided by a nearby building site where bricks and boards were stacked. The breaking and looting spilled next door and gutted Samuel Weiskopf's saloon in turn on the rumor that Weiskopf had provided a suit of clothes to disguise a policeman so that he could make an escape from a pursuing crowd.[28]

Increasingly urgent rumors and reports, the two being hard to distinguish, pointing toward some sort of coordinated anarchist attack arrived at police headquarters. Informants reported that the anarchists were arming and preparing to march on the Chicago, Milwaukee, and St. Paul Railroad freight houses and burn them down. Concern among the police brass grew dire enough for a squad of police officers to be dispatched to seize a stand of muskets belonging to the Grant Zouaves, a parade militia whose drill hall was sometimes used by socialist groups. Fearing that arms might fall into the wrong hands, police seized the Zouaves' forty guns and hauled them to the First Regiment armory for safekeeping.[29]

One reporter noticed an unusual number of men gathered around the corner of Lake and Desplaines Streets that afternoon, the same block where the bomb would later fly. "They were mostly socialists, and they stood in close-packed groups listening to orators expounding the doctrines of Herr [Johann] Most. They made no demonstration of any sort, and it was difficult to see what they were doing there."[30]

Colonel E. B. Knox, commander of the First Regiment of the Illinois State Guards, hearing reports that a large number of strikers were preparing to attack the railroad freight houses, gave the order for the mustering of the guard. By two o'clock in the afternoon, two hundred men had assembled at the armory, and twice that many were expected to be in uniform before dinnertime.[31]

Once that day's edition of the *Arbeiter-Zeitung* with its *Ruhe* signal was distributed, some revolutionaries armed themselves and went to their assigned places according to Engel's plan. John Thielen, who helped Lingg hurriedly finish making his bombs that afternoon, told Captain Schaack that he spent part of the evening of May 4 waiting outside the Larrabee Street police station with another militant of the Northwest Side group, "old man Lehman." Following Engel's instructions, Thielen and Lehman waited for a signal to attack. Thielen claimed that nineteen other men lay in ambush at the Chicago station to their south.[32]

William Seliger, Lingg's housemate, testified in court that after dropping off a satchel of bombs at Neff's Hall, he and Lingg walked toward the Larrabee Street police station with Thielen and Gustav Lehman. Seliger had two pipe bombs in his pocket, and he assumed all the other men had bombs with them as well. While the others went ahead, Lingg and Seliger scouted out the Western Avenue police station, stopping for a glass of beer on the way, and then returned to the Larrabee station. They arrived just as the police were whipping their patrol wagons down North Street. Lingg prepared to throw his bomb and frantically demanded that Seliger give him a light. Suddenly reluctant to be party to murder, Seliger thought fast and pretended to have to duck into an alcove to get his match lit. By the time Seliger had sparked his fire, the wagon had clattered past.[33]

When Ernst Hubner saw the word *Ruhe* in the *Arbeiter-Zeitung* on the evening of May 4, he stuffed four bombs into his pockets and rushed to the Schiller monument in Lincoln Park, the spot his armed company, the North Side group, had arranged as their muster spot. According to what he told Captain Schaack, Hubner found only a few others who had responded to the call. The small group waited until they grew tired, and Hubner, apparently disgusted with either the cowardice of his comrades or the poor organization of his unit, walked over to the North Avenue pier and threw his bombs into the lake.[34]

The revolutionaries waiting in ambush outside the Chicago Avenue police station watched as events began to play out just as Engel predicted. Some sort of alarm was raised by the riot downtown, and suddenly scores of policemen scrambled out of the building into patrol wagons and sped off toward the Haymarket. But the men lost their nerve at the sight and simply went home or back to Neff's saloon, where some of them had earlier picked up bombs from Lingg's satchel, and blamed one another for their cowardice.[35]

By midnight it was clear that the bold and bloody plans laid under Greif's Hall had failed. One courageous militant had done his duty—he had resisted the police as they marched to disperse the workers on Desplaines Avenue— but aside from the brief exchange of gunfire that followed the explosion, his act did not inspire workers to rise up and fight. Police showed more grit and discipline than expected, and the armed anarchist groups whose attacks on the outlying police stations were key to Engel's plan proved themselves to be either less committed to their principles than they boasted or simply cowards.

While the testimony of informants and the actions of some of the arrested anarchists revealed the details of the anarchist conspiracy, one discordant fact that seemed to suggest the opposite remained. If there had been such a broad conspiracy, if so many bombs had been fashioned and handed out, and if the police had followed the script and marched as planned into the trap set for them, why had there been only one bomb lobbed that night? This discrepancy was discussed and explained a few years later by Max

Nettlau, a pioneering chronicler and historian of the nineteenth-century anarchist movement. Nettlau wrote that in the summer of 1888 he had a conversation with Victor Dave, one of the most internationally renowned "physical force" anarchists of the 1880s and a close associate of Johann Most. Dave confided to Nettlau that London socialist William Morris had shared with him a letter he had received from Chicago anarchist William Holmes. (Holmes had been a frequent contributor to Morris's magazine, the *Commonweal*.) In this letter Holmes admitted that the accused Chicago anarchists had developed a plan to respond violently to police attempts to break up their meetings. However, he explained, one of the men who had agreed to meet the police with bombs left the city on the morning of May 4 to spend the day in the countryside, enjoying life and nature before the battle to come. In the meantime, the earlier plans were changed, but word did not reach this man before it was too late. When the police marched up and ordered the crowd to disperse, this individual threw his bomb, fully expecting others to do the same.[36]

Unfortunately, no independent confirmation of the Dave/Holmes story can be found. Nettlau gave it additional credence when he related that another anarchist told him the same story, though he admitted that this man may have heard it from Dave as well. Still, the story is revealing in that on one level it attempts to exculpate the anarchists on trial from responsibility for the bombing, which here becomes an act they tried to stop. But the manner in which it distances the accused from the moral responsibility of the murders that night confirms their legal guilt. According to the law that was operative at the time of the Haymarket trial, the most relevant act was not the throwing of the bomb but the meeting at which this attack was planned. Once having set the conspiracy in motion, it did not matter that some members may have attempted to alter the plan. The arcing path of the bomb above the heads of the police on Desplaines Street was launched with a gavel's rap on an old wooden table in the cellar of Greif's Hall. Without the cellar conspiracy, the law could reach only the man who threw the bomb; with it, however, every man present in that cellar was as legally culpable as the bomber himself.

Revolutionary expectations proved quite portable. The initial expectation that the insurrection would begin with a massive strike wave on May 1 slipped when that Saturday passed peacefully without any large demonstrations. After the McCormick riot, anarchists looked eagerly to the Haymarket demonstration to spark an uprising. Even a week later, William Holmes still held out hope that the bomb had started the revolutionary rumbling and that the social volcano was about to blow: "All the world has by this time heard of last Tuesday night's affair. Who knows? Perhaps it is the opening of the Social Revolution!" Then the verdict in the trial was thought to be a red-letter date. Later Louis Lingg expected that the occasion of his hanging might push the working class into rebellion, writing in one of his last letters, "It is very likely that the carrying out [of] our sentence, which will be nothing more or less than our murder, will result in the overthrow of tyrants."[37]

In the years following the bombing an increasing number of people grew skeptical of the idea that any of Chicago's anarchists ever seriously plotted revolution. Those who loudly maintained that the radicals who had been executed, jailed, or driven to suicide were innocent men drew many to their cause on the grounds that no sane man could have ever believed that a plan like Engel's could succeed. Even if the men under Greif's Hall had sealed their dark agreement, what could they have hoped to achieve? Revenge was an understandable motive; the audacity of the anarchists' own plans is harder to believe.

Generations of historians have followed suit and dismissed all the evidence of a wider conspiracy. But given the many witnesses and turncoats and the often striking agreement of their accounts, those interested in understanding rather than just apologizing for the Chicago radicals must go further. They must follow the tantalizing glimpses through the low basement window into the inner sanctums of radical life that have been left to history and try to understand the ideas, experiences, and aspirations that could lead a group of principled men to take such drastic actions as Engel seemingly proposed in the spring of 1886. What thinking made Engel's plan, at least for a single exceptional moment, seem to some the best option or perhaps a necessary one? Where did these ideas come from? What events, experiences, and conditions nurtured them and honed them to the point of action?

It took a dying man with nothing to lose to defiantly reveal a glimpse of the true anarchist spirit. Gerhardt Lizius had earned a reputation as one of the most extreme and intransigent contributors to both the *Alarm* and the *Arbeiter-Zeitung*. It was Lizius who penned the famous paean to explosives, "Dynamite! Of all the good stuff, this is the stuff." At the time of the bombing, Lizius was the city editor of the *Arbeiter-Zeitung*. When Albert Parsons quietly arrived at the courtroom to turn himself in, Lizius was spotted riding in the carriage with him.[38]

By the time he was brought into the grand jury room, it was clear to all that Lizius was a dying man. Reporters described him as being in the last stages of consumption. Likely Lizius had been in poor health for many years. In 1879, while working as a printer in Indianapolis, Lizius had been struck by a bullet meant for his boss when a drunken rival editor burst into the office and wildly emptied his revolver. The bullet entered his hip, passed through his groin, and lodged dangerously close to his spine. Doctors at first thought his chances for survival were poor; however, he rallied and later moved to Chicago but never fully recovered. Long suffering, deeply committed, and with little to lose, Lizius used his moment in the witness box to denounce the law, God, bourgeois justice, and the failure of his comrades to toss more than one bomb.[39]

Lizius, though fiery and defiant, chose not to reveal anything of value to the prosecution of his friends, but used his moments on the witness stand to praise the employment of revolutionary violence. "You," Lizius said to the jurors, "do not and will not understand the excuse for the Haymarket slaughter. You measure your grievance by what you know. Were you to give the theory of Socialism an impartial investigation you would then understand that the achievement of its purposes and the enjoyment of its benefits warrant a thousand times as much bloodshed as you now seek to revenge yourselves for."[40]

The dying Lizius was one of the last of his kind. An unrepentant revolutionary, he was unwilling to deny his beliefs in the face of the state's retribution. Most others did, either to save their own skin or out of solidarity with those captured with them. The Haymarket bomb atomized Lizius's pure faith in revolution.

CHAPTER TWO

FROM RED TO BLACK

Some deep change occurred in the thinking of Chicago's radicals over the span of one decade. While the men who were huddled in Greif's basement hoped to spark a riotous uprising of workers in 1886, nine years earlier Chicago's radicals had acted to prevent one.

On Monday, July 23, 1877, the greatest strike wave in U.S. history rolled into Chicago when a group of switchmen for the Michigan Central Railroad resolved to strike. Two months earlier the Pennsylvania Railroad had announced a 10 percent pay cut for all workers earning more than one dollar per day. Other rail lines followed suit, and workers responded in mid-July by throwing down their tools, damping the fires of locomotives, and holding mass meetings. Clashes between urban crowds and police or state militia intensified as the strike wore on: ten people were killed in Baltimore; a peaceful crowd was attacked and clubbed by police in New York City; three were shot and killed in Scranton; ten in Reading; and rioters and strikers were shot dead in Buffalo, Martinsburg (West Virginia), and Philadelphia. Just before the strike wave arrived in Chicago, railroad managers, shocked at the news that riots had left at least two dozen dead in Pittsburgh and the great Pittsburgh depot aflame—including dozens of warehouses, roundhouses, 104 locomotives, and 2,152 freight cars—began to move their rolling stock out of the city and empty their freight houses.

That night the Workingmen's Party, routinely referred to in the daily papers as "communists," announced they were holding a "monster meeting" on Market Street. Fearing the prospect of Chicago's becoming another Pittsburgh in flames, the conservative press pushed Chicago mayor Monroe Heath to prohibit the rally, but he allowed it on free speech grounds and likely felt vindicated when that night's speeches were tame. Speakers included Albert Parsons, who denounced the "money lords" but also urged the workers to act peacefully and legally. This was the second time that anxious weekend that Parsons had spoken out against violent actions. Two days earlier he was reported to have "told his hearers how, in his opinion, they might organize into trades-unions and bring an amicable settlement of the differences between capital and labor, and did not allude to carnage and incendiarism as a means of accomplishing their end."[1] Even the *Chicago Tribune*, usually loudest among dailies in its full-throated denunciation of the "communists," observed that "the meeting . . . was held under the auspices of the Socialists, who, contrary to general expectation, counseled (at least openly) moderation, and deprecated any resort to violence." Police superintendent Michael Hickey, in his report to the mayor, wrote, "A mass meeting of workingmen was . . . addressed by several speakers who rather counseled prudence and moderation rather than violence, and although some speeches were made by noted communists, and a few at times became somewhat boisterous, the meeting adjourned in a quiet and orderly manner . . . all went peaceably to their homes."[2]

By the next morning the vast shipping warehouses that lined the tracks snaking through Chicago's congested core were struck. A crowd of men and boys—some employees of the railroads, but many not—seized upon the occasion to express their frustrations with the cruel economy and the corrupt railroad barons and marched from building to building calling others out. By mid-afternoon the mob was sizable. A group broke off and commandeered an engine and drove it to outlying yards to rally workers there. Other crowds formed on the city's southwest side and moved up Blue Island Avenue, along where timber was off-loaded from a spur canal and woodworking factories turned the logs into everything from billiard tables to matchsticks. Several meatpacking plants shut down as roving strikers reached them. Factories on Goose Island fell silent. Sailors on lake boats threw down their lines. Mayor Heath issued an order closing all saloons and had the city's fire bells rung in a sequence that summoned the militia to the armory. Marshall Field armed his clerks and stationed them in defense of his department store. Several hundred "special policemen" were deputized and assigned to station houses. The commander of the U.S. Army for that district, Assistant Adjutant General R. C. Drum, telegraphed the War Department alerting it to "serious trouble" brewing in Chicago. Washington ordered the Twenty-second Infantry, already entrained and traveling east from its station in Bismarck, South Dakota, where it had been fighting the Sioux people, to pause and await orders once it reached Chicago. Six other companies of infantry were ordered from Omaha to Rock Island, where they would be less than a day's ride from the city.

The moderate tone that Parsons and other suspected communist leaders had taken throughout the weekend did little to allay suspicions that they were somehow orchestrating the mobs. Reports in the *Tribune* alleged that the office of the *Vorbote*, the German-language official Workingmen's Party press, was the nerve center of the riots and that runners carried orders from it to subordinate captains of groups of strikers. (In an era when retractions were a rarity, later that week the *Tribune* corrected itself and reported that party leaders had not ordered or led the riots.) Almost immediately detectives arrived at the *Vorbote* and accompanied Parsons and Philip Van Patten, the head of the Workingmen's Party, to the "Rookery," the city office building, where Mayor Heath waited for them along with his police superintendent, his city attorney, and the commander of the local militia. Heath sat quietly as his cabinet interrogated the so-called communists about their involvement in planning trouble and browbeat them to do what they were already doing: encouraging workers to act peacefully. Superintendent Hickey threatened Parsons directly, telling him as he opened the door and let him out, that he would be held accountable for any violence that might erupt and that "those Board of Trade men would as leave hang you to a lamp-post as not."[3]

Mayor Heath and his officials, who seemed to believe that the riots that had broken out in eastern cities had been planned and coordinated by a secret cabal of communists, were proven wrong the next day. At numerous points around the city, stone-throwing spontaneously escalated to gunfire. A clash between police and strikers at the Michigan Central rail yards on the north side ended with many laid out in the dirt from the blows of police clubs. Police fired on a mob near the Halsted Street viaduct and killed at least one switchman. Later that night police broke up another mass meeting of the Workingmen's Party at Market Square, but despite the serious police provocation, which included overturning their speakers stand and shooting a volley over their heads, those who were gathered offered little resistance and went home.[4]

Fighting intensified the next day as a large crowd formed again around the Halsted Street viaduct with first light and police attempted to chase them away. Shooting, stone throwing, and clubbing continued sporadically throughout the day, leaving several rioters dead. For the first time, militia units charged out from their armories and engaged mobs alongside police. By day's end at least eighteen civilians had been killed. As the riots intensified, the leaders of the Workingmen's Party in Chicago, whose executive committee included Albert Parsons, issued a statement that was notable for its calming intentions: "The success of our honest efforts to increase wages depends entirely upon your good conduct and peaceful though firm behavior. We hereby declare that any riotous action in our meetings will be immediately put down by us. The grand principles of humanity and popular sovereignty need no violence to sustain them. For the sake of the Cause we hold most dear, let every honest workingman help us to preserve order."[5] Reporters noted that some hotheaded workers grumbled about the cowardice of their leaders. They wondered openly if the workers might not have been able to take hold of the city had their leaders fought rather than simply urged their followers to join unions.[6]

Though there were many reports of "incendiary speakers" whipping up the rabble during the riots that broke out throughout the week, none of these outbursts were ever associated with known leaders of the movement. A month later this leadership continued to work to dampen tensions rather than exacerbate them, canceling a planned "grand procession of laboring men" to city hall because "it was thought unwise to irritate the city fathers too much at that time."[7]

Somehow over the course of a decade, Chicago's "communists" went from counseling their followers to avoid violent confrontations to planning them. This evolution of tactics rested on an even more fundamental shift in outlook and social theory. In 1877 when leaders of the Workingmen's Party acted to restrain mob violence, they did so in the belief that industrial change would come about through the steady growth of trade unions and the gradual raising of the working class's consciousness. In 1886 the men in Greif's basement were skeptical that trade unions could ever deliver more than a few extra crumbs to the workingman's table and had come to believe that workers were ready for violent class struggle. Between the one outlook and the other was a wholesale shift in the socialist movement that began in Europe and swept into America.

The Invention of Revolutionary Anarchism

The industrial revolutions of the early nineteenth century spawned numerous radical anticapitalist and antistatist ideologies that varied wildly in their principles and utopian hopes. Though diverse in their schemes for reform, they all generally relied upon one of four paths to change: education, electoral competition, communal or cooperative experimentation, or labor organization. Many, like the high-minded followers of Karl Marx, thought of themselves as revolutionaries, but revolution was a distant step, predicated upon the slow work of education or labor organization. Few were so reckless (especially those who suffered the failure of the liberal uprisings of 1848) as to advocate taking up arms. Those few who were bold enough to value blades over books eventually evolved a fifth option: a distinct school of radical thought that directed its efforts to fomenting violent insurrection, a branch of radicalism that would come to be known as *nihilism* or *anarchism*.

Marx was cautious about endorsing revolution as a near-term strategy, because he understood that a "true revolution" was as much a culmination of historical processes as it was a maker of them. Marx conceived of revolution as consisting of not just the seizure of the state by "the people" but also the overthrowing of one class by another. While this might sound like a distinction without a difference, for Marx it was not, for according to his theory, in order to have a true revolution, a society must first have developed well-defined and self-conscious classes. Any sort of revolt or rebellion that occurred before antagonistic classes were properly constituted could not attain the "universal human emancipation" Marx envisioned and was doomed to be just "a partial, merely political revolution which leaves the pillars of the building standing." Note that according to this formula, the success of a true revolution depended on not just waiting for the working class to constitute itself as a self-conscious "general representative of . . . society," a difficult enough task, but also on the fullness of the maturation of the ruling class, upon the ruling class concentrating "in itself all the evils of society." Dimming even further the prospects for a successful revolution was the problem that it depended upon the full maturation of capitalism itself. "For the oppressed class to be able to emancipate itself," Marx asserted, "it is necessary that the productive powers already acquired and the existing social relations should no longer be capable of existing side by side . . . The organization of revolutionary elements as a class supposes the existence of all the productive forces which could be engendered in the bosom of the old society." Or as he put it in another article: "The conditions of life, which different generations find in existence, decide also whether or not the periodically recurring revolutionary convulsion will be strong enough to overthrow the basis of the entire existing system. And if these material elements of a complete revolution are not present . . . then . . . it is absolutely immaterial whether the *idea* of this revolution has been expressed a hundred times already."[8]

In his most philosophical moments, Marx thought of revolution as awaiting not just the full formation of classes and the development of proper political and economic systems but also the creation of a new type of person. Marx's philosophical materialism was a complicated mechanism—a slow and uneven development of technology; the accumulation of tools, property, storehouses, civil arrangements, social relationships—that worked to change not only the path of history but also the nature of man. In one of his more famous aphorisms, Marx opined, "Circumstances make men just as much as men make circumstances," and this phrase has largely been appreciated for its revolutionary promise: the world can be made over, perhaps even perfected, and with it and by it, mankind too will improve. But this formulation also narrowed the possible circumstances under which a "true revolution" could occur, for the revolution had to wait for sufficient time, class organization, and socioeconomic change to mold a new type of man whose outlook nurtured the values of the coming socialist order.

At times, Marx's historical materialism seemed almost deterministic, as though the machine of history rattled on by itself without regard to the actions of individuals at all. In one famous passage in his first volume of *Das Kapital* (*Capital*), Marx describes the process of revolution in a way that, though envisioning the revolt of the working class as one of the processes of revolution, also places such a great emphasis on the dialectical development of political economy that the actions of actual people become almost inconsequential:

> Along with the constant decrease in the number of capitalist magnates, who usurp and monopolize all the advantages of this process of transformation, the mass of misery, oppression, slavery, degradation, and exploitation grows; but with this there also grows the revolt of the working class, a class constantly increasing in numbers, and trained, united and organized by the very mechanism of the capitalist process of production. The monopoly of capital becomes a fetter upon the mode of production which has flourished alongside and under it. The centralization of the means of production and the socialization of labour reach a point at which they become incompatible with their capitalist integument. This integument is burst asunder. The knell of capitalist private property sounds. The expropriators are expropriated.[9]

Marx's theory of revolution proved most discouraging to radicals in the least industrialized and politically advanced corners of Europe, such as Italy, Spain, and Russia, for though stark class divisions between peasants and landlords existed in these countries, their premodern societies and agricultural economies simply disqualified them from the promise of Marxist revolution. Such backward peoples would have to suffer through the evolution of proper capitalist dynamics first. It was from these areas, exiled by implication to the periphery of the socialist movement, that the anarchist challenge to Marx's theory of revolution first developed.

In the winter of 1864, a fifty-year-old Russian nobleman, Mikhail Bakunin, who had survived six years in Czar Alexander II's prisons for his revolutionary activities in Prague, Dresden, and Russia and had recently tried to join an uprising in Poland, crossed the Alps into Italy hoping to find allies for his crusade to liberate Slavs from under the Austrian Hapsburg heel. He lived for two years in Naples and Florence, where he developed close associations with veterans of Giuseppe Garibaldi's army, brigands, and other *carbonari*. During this time Bakunin moved beyond a nationalist commitment to Slavic liberation and developed a more international and class-oriented outlook. More significantly, he broke with his friend Karl Marx, disagreeing that the revolution was distant and most effectively spread through public congresses, meetings, and resolutions. Bakunin had come to believe that the revolution need not wait, that all that was lacking in any historical situation was the daring to act.

Bakunin's more optimistic belief in the prospects for revolution arose from his different view of human nature. Unlike Marx, who held that the new revolutionary man had yet to be wrought by the forge of history, Bakunin was certain that the rudiments of a new socialist morality were already rooted in the daily lives of workers, peasants, and even the criminal castoffs of society. Bakunin wrote of a widely held "socialist instinct," a yearning for justice, and an "instinct to revolt" that was an accomplished fact of capitalism's exploitative work. So fully interwoven into the lives of peasants and workers were such values that they were not even conscious thoughts; they were "innate" views of the world. "The great mass of workers," Bakunin wrote in 1869, are "exhausted by daily drudgery, are miserable and ignorant. Yet this mass, despite its political and social prejudices, is socialistic without knowing it. Because of its social position, it is more truly socialist than all the scientific and bourgeois socialists combined." In Bakunin's thinking, all the essential ingredients for revolution existed. History simply awaited its cooks.[10]

Bakunin's faith in the deep revolutionary instincts of the masses allowed him to formulate very different strategies from the slow and steady work of organization and agitation required of Marx's view of history. To Bakunin, the people did not need to be converted, tutored, or even much organized, merely led once the latent revolutionary energies of the people burst forth. This meant that for Bakunin successful organizing did not mean enlisting the great masses of workers into a single united organization as Marx planned, but instead required only a few committed members who could assume leadership when the revolutionary moment arrived. A few hundred revolutionaries, "strongly and earnestly allied," were all that was needed, Bakunin thought, because "all that a well-organized society can do is, first, to assist at the birth of a revolution by spreading among the masses ideas which give expression to their instincts, and to organize, not the army of the Revolution—the people alone should always be that army—but a sort of revolutionary general staff, composed of dedicated, energetic, intelligent individuals, sincere friends of the people above all, men neither vain nor ambitious, but capable of serving as intermediaries between the revolutionary idea and the instincts of the people."[11]

While for Marx the test of any workers party was its doctrines, for Bakunin it was its strength of organization. For Marx the role of the radical intelligentsia and of socialist organizations was to tutor the benighted masses about the true nature of their exploitation, to make them aware of their true class interests, class consciousness, and class solidarity through building up workers parties and trade unions. This view of social change placed a premium on ideology and analyses, for the working class, ignorant and disorganized, could be easily misled into any of a number of philosophical cul-de-sacs—utopianism, republicanism, nationalism—or worse, goaded into premature revolutionary adventurism. Marx saw his role and that of the organization he founded in 1864, the International Workingmen's Association (IWA, also known as "the International"), as guarding the working class from these ideological dead ends and shepherding them toward their destiny. In contrast, Bakunin's belief in the revolutionary instinct of the people afforded him the luxury of not worrying much about the ideological purity of the movement. Action, not doctrines, was what mattered to those who had faith in the innate socialist and rebellious nature of the masses.[12]

If revolution was possible immediately, then the question of the character of revolutionary organization moved from the realm of the abstract to the practical. Marx had long envisioned, and even tried to organize, a single centralized mass organization that could coordinate political, industrial, and educational efforts throughout the capitalist world. To Marx, for whom revolution was a distant goal, such an organization was a necessary means of defending the rights of workers and honing their class consciousness. But to those who believed the revolution was truly immanent, the form of their organization was the future in embryo. To Bakunin, the centralized character of Marx's International doomed the equalitarian and democratic principles it hoped to establish through revolution.[13]

Bakunin's alternative to forming all workers into a single mass party was to create small, autonomous secret organizations that had the discipline and will to undertake revolutionary actions that could expose the hypocrisy and violence that were latent within the existing order, and to provoke confrontations that would lead society toward a crisis that would bring classes into open conflict. At that moment of crisis, the dedicated revolutionaries would take a leadership role, but being a situational position of command rather than an institutionalized one, the leveling socialist values would be sustained. "You want a popular revolution," Bakunin wrote, "consequently there is no need to recruit an army, since your army is the people. What you must form are general staffs, a network well organized and inspired by the leaders of the popular movement. For this purpose you do not, in fact, need to have a large number of people initiated into the secret organizations."[14]

Never one to be accused of not putting his theories to work, in 1868 Bakunin and his followers organized a secretive organization, the International Alliance of Social Democracy, and applied for affiliation with Marx's IWA. Marx's camp quickly vetoed their membership on the grounds that the International could not have another "International" organization within it. Bakunin then offered to drop the name and have each of the alliance's sections apply as representative sections from their countries of origin. This led Marx to maneuver for several years to block the accession of Bakuninist sections to the IWA.[15]

Bakunin's theory of revolution seemed vindicated in 1871 with the spontaneous uprising known as the Paris Commune. In the wake of France's disastrous defeat by Prussia, a siege of Paris, and the flight of the government out of the city to nearby Versailles, Parisian workers rebelled and seized control. For two months a central committee of Paris workers ran the city's government, toppling a few hated monuments and executing a handful of "enemies of the people," including the archbishop. In May, after the national army had stormed the last barricade, thousands of communards were executed.

For Bakunin, as for socialists around the world, the Paris Commune provided inspiration and many practical lessons. It revealed the murderous brutality of the state. It demonstrated the importance of individual acts of courage and leadership. It also seemed to confirm Bakunin's critique of Marx's slow, methodical, and intellectually coordinated route to revolution. Though the Paris Commune had been defeated, its lesson seemed to be that only by uncorking the innate but unrealized revolutionary power of the masses could real change occur. As Bakunin explained, "Contrary to the belief of authoritarian communists—which I deem completely wrong—that a social revolution must be decreed and organized either by a dictatorship or by a constituent assembly emerging from a political revolution, our friends, the Paris socialists, believed that revolution could neither be made nor brought to its full development except by the spontaneous and continued action of the masses, the groups and associations of the people."[16]

Propaganda by the Deed

Bakunin's intellectual contributions to the theory of revolution still failed to answer a critical question for revolutionaries: how does one go about starting a revolutionary insurrection? There was nothing new about advocacy of individual violent acts as a revolutionary tactic. A strain of Jacobin writing in the French Revolution extolled political violence. Auguste Blanqui, whose ideas were accused of animating the exaggerated excesses of the Paris Communards, advocated coups, secret cabals, and political assassinations as means of restoring the French Republic. Throughout history assassins had long stalked crowned heads and were often lauded for their heroic actions. But no one had a clear theory as to how assassinations or other acts of political violence could push the working class to realize its historic destiny and rise to fight its class oppressors.

However, in the 1870s another new idea emerged that recast acts of violence in an entirely different light. This idea was that in addition to their immediate material effect, the value of violent attacks upon the symbols or institutions of class oppression had a secondary and potentially greater impact: such deeds educated the workers as to their true situation and the true path to socialist salvation. In effect, well-chosen violent initiatives had the force of propaganda. Actually, they were seen as better than written manifestos or rousing speeches, because they could reach the great illiterate masses and created lessons no one could ignore, and because these lessons were reality—they were facts, not theories. By this way of thinking, armed actions could be viewed as succeeding even if they failed to so much as wobble the workings of the government or slow the gears of the capitalist system.

The earliest example of this type of thinking came from an Italian nationalist and socialist, Carlo Pisacane, who had served as Giuseppe Mazzini's lieutenant and head of the republican army. In 1857, as Pisacane was preparing to invade the kingdom of Naples with a small force and hopefully foment a peasant uprising against the crown, he sketched out his political philosophy in a work later published as *Testamento politico*. In this manifesto Pisacane derided those revolutionary intellectuals who patiently thought their insights would make revolutions happen: "Propaganda of the idea is a chimera, the education of the people is an absurdity. Ideas result from deeds, not the latter from the former, and the people will not be free when they are educated, but will be educated when they are free. The only work a citizen can do for the good of the country is that of cooperating with the material revolution: therefore, conspiracies, plots, attempts, etc."[17]

Pisacane lived out his ideals and pressed on in his hopeless campaign only to perish on a Calabrian field. His *Testamento* was not published until twenty years after his death, but his doctrine of action and deeds influenced other Italian revolutionaries close to him. How influential Pisacane was remains a matter of heated dispute among scholars of the period, though the issue of how much authorship of anarchist ideas he should be credited with seems misplaced, as the conditions and environment that influenced him were the same ones that nurtured a uniquely brash brand of Italian anarchism.[18]

From the peasant countryside of southern Italy, these ideas found their most famous champion in Mikhail Bakunin, who began expressing similar sentiments soon after his sojourn there in the late 1860s. Bakunin began writing of actions as a form of propaganda as early as 1870. Among the many pieces of unsolicited advice he offered in his "Letters to a Frenchman," written to the people of France on the occasion of their defeat by Prussia, was to urge them to begin to value their actions more than their slogans and to see actions as slogans in another form. "All of us must now embark on stormy revolutionary seas, and from this very moment we must spread our principles, not with words but with deeds, for this is the most popular, the most potent, and the most irresistible form of propaganda."[19]

This idea spread quickly among the Italian and Spanish socialist leadership, for whom this new strategy promised to overcome their most daunting obstacle: how to proselytize and organize among the illiterate peasant masses of these least urbanized and industrialized areas of Western Europe. By the time the Seventh Congress of the International Workingmen's Association was held in Brussels in the fall of 1874, Italian and Spanish delegates proclaimed "propaganda by deed" to be their policy of action. Enrico Malatesta and Carlo Cafiero elaborated these policies in December 1876 in the *Bulletin de la Fédération jurassienne*, the organ of the Swiss IWA, writing that their Italian federation "believes that the insurrectionary deed, destined to affirm the socialist principles by means of action, is the most effective means of propaganda and the only one which, without tricking and corrupting the masses, can penetrate to the deepest social strata and draw the living forces of humanity into the struggle."[20]

Malatesta and Cafiero were willing to put these ideas to the test a few months later by attempting to seize a government building and burn its archives of tax records in the city of Benevento, though to little effect but their own swift arrest. Though Malatesta's small band of poorly armed revolutionaries knew in advance that they were no match for the government's regiments, their mission was not as quixotic as it appeared, for their belief in the propaganda value of such attacks gave them faith that they would advance their cause even as they were defeated on the battle-ground. As one participant in their raid later wrote, "We could not hope to win, since we knew that a few tens of individuals armed with almost unserviceable rifles cannot win battles against regiments . . . Partisans of the propaganda of deeds, we wanted to commit an act of propaganda . . . [an act] that cannot and must not count on anything but the echo it might find in the populations."[21]

A similar belief in the propaganda value of violent action advanced among a small but influential circle of German socialists led by a locksmith, Erich Otto Rinke, and a pair of newspaper compositors, Emil-August Werner and, most famously, August Reinsdorf, who would become an anarchist martyr after his execution for attempting to dynamite Kaiser Wilhelm I and his royal family in 1885. Together in October 1875 Rinke, Werner, and Reinsdorf formed a secret organization in Switzerland that they simply called "the Association" and composed a manifesto that differed little from other Marxist programs in its analysis of society but laid more emphasis on the role of violence in overcoming capitalism. "Instructed by the lessons of history . . . that in order to achieve the transition from the unjust society which is in decline, to the just society of the future whose establishment is taking place before our eyes in the form of trade unions and local groups, a violent solution will be necessary, which will be a social revolution."[22]

At this transitional moment the Germans of the Association did not de-clare themselves devoted to the tactics of propaganda by deed, but merely to the centrality of the "social-revolutionary principle, which all members support to advance." On first thought this seems to be only a minor shift from the reigning socialist doctrines of the major socialist parties then in existence. But though it was a small alteration, a slightly greater emphasis on one particular aspect of socialist strategy, this minor change effected a great transcendence of long-standing and bitter debates. By reorienting their focus from the means of achieving a revolution to the revolution itself, the leaders of the Association sidestepped the bitter arguments about whether socialists' time and efforts were better devoted to competing in elections or organizing trade unions. Their answer to the question of electoral versus trade union struggle, the burning issue that divided socialist Marxist and Lassallean groups in Germany, was that the question was not a matter of principle but one of tactical opportunity. To these social revolutionaries, who believed that the unjust system teetered on the edge of collapse (a decline "taking place before our eyes"), the deciding push could come from any direction. The important question was not from where to push but whether to push at all.[23]

A more systematic theory of violent propaganda was elaborated in a new journal launched in Berne, Switzerland, in 1876 for the purpose of carrying these emerging doctrines of revolutionary anarchism into Germany. Though this journal, *Arbeiter-Zeitung,* was published in German, it was the work of a cosmopolitan group of radicals: it was financed by a Russian, edited by a Frenchman, and directed by the three Germans who made up the core of the Association: Werner, Rinke, and Reinsdorf. Its editor, Paul Brousse—a young French physician, who had escaped a prison sentence in France for his role in the Paris Commune and other subversive activities only to make his own attempt at propaganda by deed by attacking Barcelona's city hall in 1873 and then fleeing from Spain to Switzerland—filled the *Arbeiter-Zeitung*'s pages with arguments for propagandizing by deeds. Brousse attempted to elevate this doctrine from a mere call to violence to a more reasoned and calculated tactic: "We are primarily supporters of propaganda by the deed, of propaganda through action, always provided of course that this be treated seriously and not in an infantile fashion." Though the *Arbeiter-Zeitung*'s run continued through just thirty-three issues, ceasing publication in October 1877, it carried the substance of this new idea far among German radicals in both Europe and America.[24]

Up to this point in the development of the idea of "propaganda by deed," the sort of actions contemplated were collective, not individual, as were their objects. Communards throwing up their barricades, Malatesta's band burning property records, Brousse and Spanish anarchists attacking Barcelona's city hall—all of these actions were undertaken by groups and directed at public institutions. But could individual acts of violence achieve the same purpose? And while government buildings and records were obviously useful and instructive symbols to attack, were representatives of government also legitimate targets? In other words, could a private act of violence against another individual also be considered a blow that would raise revolutionary consciousness?

It was probably inevitable that older justifications of regicide and murder would combine with the concept of propaganda by deed to justify individual acts of revolutionary violence. The most unique offspring of this union was the joining of an ancient ethics of regicide to the new anarchist justification for attacks that had no chance of leading to any immediate social change, no chance of success by the ordinary standards in which this is measured.

All of the older ideas of the justice or necessity of using violence judged the morality of violence in balance with its chance of success and therefore its power to fight injustice. Revolutionary violence was clearly justified in killing the tyrant, hatching the well-planned coup, or as part of a general uprising; whether it was ethically permissible to assassinate a lower official or a wealthy burgher, however, depended on the degree to which their removal would materially slow the machinery of exploitation. But the unknowable benefits of action suddenly opened a door to justifying all manner of indiscriminate violence. By viewing the value of a violent act as being primarily didactic, anarchist thinking abstracted the effects of violence from the real to an immeasurable, almost metaphysical realm. How could one measure how much education flowed from a bombing? How many consciousnesses were raised by an assassination? Ironically, the idea that began in the quest to find a form of propaganda that was more real than words ended up creating a system of thought that allowed any act of violence to be transcendently justified by its imaginary benefits.[25]

Such logic can be seen in some of Brousse's writings in the *Arbeiter-Zeitung* where he indicated that violent deeds did not need to immediately lead to mass uprisings in order to be successful. Well-aimed acts of violence inevitably hastened the revolution by forcing everyone to consider the idea of socialism and their place in the social order. Brousse turned to the Paris Commune, a tragic failure, for an example of how this worked:

> A social upheaval like that of the Paris Commune does not leave any worker indifferent. You have to hunt around for a book, you have to buy a newspaper, but revolutionary action comes right into your own home, into the midst of the family, and forces itself on your attention. Who is not forced to reflect when faced with the terrible questions raised in the public arena? . . . Who to-day, now that the communalist question has been raised in the full glare of daylight, has reached the Hotel de Ville . . . [with] its heroes and martyrs, would dare to admit that he does not know about it? Everyone has taken sides for or against. Two months of fighting have done more than twenty-three years of propaganda.[26]

In this way every terrorist was converted into a martyr, as every act, no matter what its consequences, could be seen as a brave step forward for the movement. Brousse wrote, "Let us act, if only from the point of view of propaganda. Perhaps victory will crown our efforts, and if it is martyrdom let us remember that the idea does not perish by the sword, does not fall beneath bullets. Let us never forget that it is the blood of the people which nourishes and makes fertile the ground of Revolutions."[27]

Peter Kropotkin's journal, *Le Révolté*, a journal published in the tolerant city of Geneva but read by radicals throughout Europe and in the United States, marched down a similar path. The old testament of Carlo Pisacane extolling propaganda by deed was quoted approvingly in December 1880 in an article by Carlo Cafiero discussing the doctrine of "L'action," which concluded that "our action must be permanent revolt, by word, by writing, by the dagger, rifles, dynamite."[28] One of the more eloquent appeals to propaganda by deed was published later that spring. Kropotkin's "The Spirit of Revolt" made the case for the necessity of individual action by posing the timeless question, What moves masses of people to suddenly defy authority and risk everything for a principle or a slim hope? How was it that "men who only yesterday were complaining quietly of their lot as they smoked their pipes, and the next moment were humbly saluting the local guard and *gendarme* whom they had just been abusing,—how is it that these same men a few days later were capable of seizing their scythes and their iron-shod pikes and attacking in his castle the lord who only yesterday was so formidable?" Kropotkin's answer was simple and unequivocal: "Action!" It took only a few courageous men to stand up to encourage the rest to rise. "Courage, devotion, the spirit of sacrifice, are as contagious as cowardice, submission, and panic." Stylistically avoiding details of what actions he thought represented such courage, Kropotkin instead kept his essay on an abstract but unambiguous plane that celebrated the actor and not the act. Action, he wrote, would be "sometimes tragic, sometimes humorous, but always daring; sometimes collective, sometimes purely individual, this policy of action will neglect none of the means at hand." Every revolution required its heroes to go forward: "Men of courage, not satisfied with words, but ever searching for the means to transform them into action—men of integrity for whom the act is one with the idea, for whom prison, exile, and death are preferable to a life contrary to their principles—intrepid souls who know that it is necessary to *dare* in order to succeed—these are the lonely sentinels who enter the battle long before the masses are sufficiently roused to raise openly the banner of insurrection." In the end it was the lone man or small party of action upon whose shoulders rested the burden of history: "One courageous act has sufficed to upset in a few days the entire governmental machinery, to make the colossus tremble." Kropotkin's romantic appeal to the power of demonstrative violence was a prime example of how far these ideas had come to define anarchism at this time.[29]

Propaganda by deed's slide from collective direct actions to individual acts of terrorism seems to have been completed by the spring of 1882 when a striking worker, Charles Fournier, approached his employer in the factory town of Roanne and fired a shot at him but missed. Fournier's attempt to kill his boss was just one among a number of violent episodes in a violent labor conflict, but his brazen daylight assault struck a chord with French anarchists. While striking textile workers immediately held a meeting to denounce Fournier, anarchists in Lyon organized a public meeting for the purpose of presenting him with a new revolver. His act was praised in the pages of Kropotkin's *Le Révolté,* which referred to his attempt as "propaganda by the deed, the most fecund, the most popular." Shortly after Kropotkin and other anarchist leaders in France were tried for belonging to a banned organization, and more bombs went off in and around Lyon, including one in a music hall, the "groupe parisien de propaganda anarchiste" plastered posters on walls around Paris that defiantly claimed the right to undertake any terrorist actions: "Yes, we are guilty of applying our theories by all means: by word, by the pen, BY THE DEED—that is to say, by revolutionary acts, whatever these may be. Yes, we acknowledge them loudly. We claim them as ours. We delight in them."[30]

Red versus Black

Marx and Friedrich Engels finally swept out of the International all the Bakuninist elements at the Fifth General Congress of the IWA held at the Hague in 1872. Marx and his allies combed Bakunin's manifestos and flung every seemingly heretical idea they could find at the Bakuninists in their midst. For their part, Bakunin's partisans denounced what they saw as the increasingly dictatorial behavior of Marx and the general council of the IWA, which he controlled through his proxies. During the week in which this convention met, a great pile of philosophical and tactical disagreements accumulated between the two camps.

Digging down through this doctrinal debris and finding the foundation of their differences has proven troublesome to most scholars, who have overlooked the simplest basis of their argument—Marx and Bakunin's different theories of revolution—and instead have been attracted to the shinier and more sophisticated philosophical conflicts, like those over the role of the state in a postrevolutionary society. But in reading through the extant minutes of The Hague Congress, there are interesting moments when the delegates themselves perceived the plain contrast in their views of revolution as being central to their disagreements. After the credentials of several Bakuninist-aligned groups were rejected by the Marxists, and as most of the Spanish federation was shown the door, a Spanish delegate, Rafael Farga-Pelicer, defended his comrades by saying, "The Spanish sections are quite active in the struggle against capital which they hope to destroy possibly soon." Later, in another debate that broke down along Marxist and antiauthoritarian lines,

Adolf Hepner, who with Wilhelm Liebknecht edited the flagship Marxist paper in Germany, denounced "the nonsense of the antiauthoritarians . . . charge against the General Council of not having made a revolution. Are these good people so unscientific as to believe that one can make revolutions? Do they still not know that revolutions arise only in a natural way and are stages of historical development? Have these people not even surpassed the barricadology?" At this the shouting between sides became so intense that the chairman, Friedrich Sorge, warned everyone that he was going to suspend the session and clear the hall unless they quieted down.[31]

James Guillaume, a Swiss schoolmaster, rose to defend the antiauthoritarians, saying they were misunderstood: "We are adherents of a definite policy, of social revolution, of the destruction of bourgeois politics, of the state." It is interesting to note in this quote how Guillaume placed destruction of the state as the last in this series, indicating, perhaps, the primary stress placed on revolution. Later, in his report on the congress to his German friends in New York, Sorge noted that fighting raged with the Bakuninists. "These people," Sorge complained, "preach revolution without organization . . . fight without leaders."[32]

Bakunin lost his fight with Marx in the International, but his optimistic theories of revolution continued to appeal to many radicals who were impatient with Marxism's cautious, intellectual, and dogmatic leadership of international socialism. These new ideas promised not only a shorter and more direct path to the promised land on the other side of revolution, but they also offered a way out of the doctrinal infighting that divided the socialist movement into two great warring factions: Marxists, headed in Germany by Wilhelm Liebknecht, and Lassalleans, followers of Ferdinand Lassalle, led after Lassalle's death in 1864 by Johann Baptist von Schweitzer. If actions were more important than words, if formulating the correct doctrine was less important than organizing and doing, then the great questions that divided Lassalleans and Marxists—the role of the state, the usefulness of elections, the economic laws governing wages—none of these mattered so much. By the early 1870s, as the factional infighting among German socialists reached its most vicious and disruptive point, Bakunin's revolutionary faith became most attractive.

Bakunin's revolutionary idea found room to grow in the midst of the ideological drift and confusion of the established German left. The two great rival parties of German socialism, the Allgemeiner Deutscher Arbeiterverein (ADAV) and the Sozialdemokratische Arbeiterpartei (SDAP), were both in turmoil: the authoritarian leader of the ADAV, Johann Baptiste von Schweitzer, resigned from the party in March 1871, and in the following year the two towering leaders of the SDAP, August Bebel and Wilhelm Liebknecht, were imprisoned for their principled opposition to the Franco-Prussian War. During this rudderless time, the German socialist parties vacillated between attacking each other and proposing various terms of marriage while purist factions within each intrigued to forestall any merger. Meanwhile the ever resourceful chancellor Otto von Bismarck seized on the disunity and weakness of the socialists and intensified his political repression. In 1874 alone, eighty-seven socialists in Berlin were sentenced to a total of twenty years in prison, and both the ADAV and the SDAP were banned in a half dozen other major centers of activity. According to historian and contemporary observer Hermann Schlüter, this turmoil and "confusion" in Germany bred what he derisively termed "revolutionary romanticism."[33]

This new revolutionary anarchist romanticism, with its belief that the revolution was about to break out at any time, grew up first in London, Paris, Berlin, St. Petersburg, and Geneva but spread quickly to America. Radicals on both sides of the Atlantic were closely connected; they corresponded with one another extensively, moved freely between Europe and America, and shared the main journals of radical opinion: *Freiheit* (London and Zürich), *Le Révolté* (Geneva and Paris), *L'Avant-Garde* (Berne), and *Arbeiter-Zeitung* (Berne). Indeed, it is a mistake to think of radical communities on either side of the ocean as being separate. Radicalism was divided not by geography but by ideological schools, and radicals of the same mind on either continent were more closely associated with one another than they were with their factional rivals across town.[34]

This was especially true in the burgeoning American cities whose rapid influx of immigrants lent them a particularly international character. German immigrants in particular congregated in urban areas that were fully culturally German: *Kleindeutschland* districts that allowed them to maintain old world customs and connections. With their massive foreign-born populations, highly developed ethnic institutions, and segregated ethnic spaces, Chicago and New York were less alien to these immigrants than were common European destinations for political ex-patriots like London or Paris. In the 1880s Chicago's German-born population outnumbered all other ethnic groups in the city and made German the most commonly spoken language in the city. It was said that Chicago was the fifth-largest German city in the world. German American labor newspapers tended to carry far more news from Europe than they did notices of American events. No wonder, then, that many socialist immigrants, though they became active in American politics, union organizations, and publishing, looked first to trends and events in Europe.[35]

The ideological proximity of Chicago to central Europe can be traced through the careers of the city's radical editors. More than the party office or the union hall, the editorial office exerted the most powerful influence over movement policies in this era. Editors of workers newspapers not only established the terms of debate and the strategic direction of the movement through their editorial columns, but they also were usually the most popular public speakers and the most influential party leaders. As the *Vorbote* observed, a bit too grandiosely, in 1880, "The history of the workers' movement in the United States is at the same time the history of the workers' press."[36]

In the case of Chicago's succession of radical editors, they tended to be recent immigrants who brought with them the latest political ideas and orientations of the continental movements they left behind. According to the daily commercial press of Chicago, the "incendiary" ideas in the socialist movement were supplied through the new German-language weekly newspaper, the *Vorbote* (the closest translation would be "herald" or "harbinger"), founded in 1874. The *Vorbote*'s first editor was Carl Klings, a knife sharpener who arrived from Germany in 1869. Klings had once been a leader of socialists in Germany and a trusted correspondent of both Ferdinand Lassalle and Karl Marx. His experience, international connections, and reputation allowed him to quickly emerge as a leading socialist organizer in the city, speaking at early gatherings of the city's chapter of the International Workingmen's Association (also known as the "First International"), serving on the general committee of the Allgemeiner Deutscher Arbeiterverein and its successor, the Social-Politische Arbeiter Verein, and editing the *Deutsche Arbeiter*, one of many short-lived labor weeklies. Naturally, Klings was the choice of Chicago's socialists to be founding editor of the socialist *Vorbote*, a name copied from the organ of the German-language federation of the First International based in Geneva and edited by Klings's friend Johann Philip Becker until its failure in 1871. In 1875 Klings put aside his grinding wheel in favor of a dish towel and opened a dingy saloon on South Market Street that also served as *Vorbote*'s editorial offices and was reputed to be the watering hole for the city's German radicals. After a sensation-seeking reporter printed a spurious story about how Klings regaled his barroom listeners with a plan to seize the city's waterworks, pump the mains full of petroleum, and thereby ignite the fine houses of capitalists from within, the mayor refused Klings a liquor license. Klings moved his bar to Blue Island Avenue, where it was again said to be the headquarters of the "Chicago Commune."[37]

Klings was typical of a surprising number of German political refugees who secured appointments as socialist newspaper editors almost immediately upon reaching American shores. He was succeeded at the *Vorbote* by Conrad Conzett, a printer who was active in the First International in Switzerland before coming to Chicago in 1869. Conzett's chair was then filled by another refugee, Gustav Lyser. Lyser was born into a literary and progressive Dresden family and as a young man joined a circle of like-minded progressives gathered around a socialist paper published in Braunschweig, the *Volksfreund*. Lyser's radicalism quickly exceeded the patience of both the SDAP and the authorities, and he was expelled from the party and reportedly imprisoned in Frankfurt before fleeing to New York in 1874. About the same time as Lyser settled in the Chicago area, Paul Gelaff, "a man of ordinary abilities and education . . . (but) a fanatic for the socialistic cause," one of the founders of the socialist movement in Denmark and editor of a socialist newspaper in Denmark associated with the First International in 1871, also arrived and founded *Dye Nye Tid* (The New Age), which was soon designated the official Danish organ of the Socialist Labor Party. Another German socialist leader, Paul Grottkau, took over as editor of the *Vorbote* in 1878, the same year that he set foot in America.[38]

The growing community of recent socialist immigrants in America should be understood as being as much a part of the movements they left behind in Germany, Austria, Bohemia, or Denmark as they were leaders of any sort of separate or independent American left. When the editor's chair of the *Vorbote* was vacated in 1875, the paper's manager, Jacob Winnen, turned to socialist leaders in Germany for a replacement, sending a pleading letter that suggested, "Perhaps a party member with prior experience in the party press who would make for a capable editor might be willing to emigrate." Nor were such transatlantic postings viewed as permanent. Conrad Conzett, who edited both the *Arbeiter-Zeitung* and the *Vorbote* in the mid-1870s, later returned to Switzerland and edited the *Sozialdemokrat*. Socialist author August Otto-Walster edited the St. Louis labor paper *Volkstimme des Westens* from 1877 to 1880 and then returned to Europe and succeeded Conzett in editing the *Sozialdemokrat*. Hermann Schlüter immigrated to Chicago in the 1870s, where he was one of the founders of the *Vorbote*, returned to Germany in the 1880s, and then came back to New York in 1890, where he assumed the editorship of the *New Yorker Volkszeitung*. Besides the fact that all of these socialist activists lived in U.S. communities that functioned as fully in German as those they had left in the old country, the expectation that their postings would be temporary probably contributed to the reason why many of these journalists did not endeavor to learn English. After living in Chicago for six years, Carl Klings was reported to be still unable to speak English. Paul Grottkau, the editor of *Vorbote* on and off from 1878 to 1888, was reported to be ignorant of English as late as 1887. Some socialist intellectuals saw their compatriots' insularity as a barrier to their mission in America. Friedrich Engels, for example, criticized German American socialists for their clannishness and urged them to "doff every remnant of their foreign garb . . . become out and out American" and "above all things learn English."[39]

The active ideological and institutional ties between the old and new worlds of German radicalism are not difficult to uncover when the timeline of German socialist development is placed alongside that of its American counterpart. Well documented is how the rise and fall of the International Workingmen's Association in the decade after the Civil War occurred in tandem and coordination with Karl Marx in London and his associates throughout Europe. Just as the IWA began to grow in America in 1868, Marxists in Germany led by Wilhelm Liebknecht declared socialist unity as their priority (though these efforts were unsuccessful at this time). Almost simultaneously, German socialists in America extended a fraternal hand to their Yankee counterparts even while they privately objected to their seemingly petty-bourgeois concerns such as women's rights. Ultimately, though, rather than adapting their theories to American conditions as their Yankee partners advocated, the IWA's German American leaders upheld their doctrines in the face of evident failure, purged their English-speaking elements, and were happy to bury a purified party rather than live with a compromised one. Less well established is how subsequent developments in Germany influenced the direction of parallel American socialist policies.[40]

In May 1875 the two German socialist parties, the SDAP and the ADAV, agreed to merge at the historic Gotha Congress and formed the Sozialistische Arbeiterpartei Deutschlands (SAPD). Suddenly the cry of unity became the ideological priority of the moment, and socialists in America, most of them German and many still corresponding with associates in Deutschland, followed suit.

In July 1876 representatives of the three existing socialist organizations met in Philadelphia and combined to form the Workingmen's Party (WP). Quite contrary to type and prior experience, the least controversial event of their four days of convention was the adoption of their platform of principles. While more than one socialist organization in the past had torn themselves apart fighting over the shades of meaning in the wording of single planks in their platforms, there, fittingly in the City of Brotherly Love, representatives from three ideologically separate socialist groups adopted a detailed eleven-point platform with almost no debate. In what may be the only such entry of its kind in the history of the American left, the minutes of that day's session read: "The discussion of the declaration of principles did not occupy much time."[41]

Just as the newly merged German SAPD pledged that it would pursue a legal, gradual, and peaceful road to socialism, in the United States the Workingmen's Party and its successor, the Socialist Labor Party (the name was changed in 1877), also stressed lawful electoral change. When these two movements' founding platforms are examined side by side, they are nearly identical. Of the eleven demands listed by the Workingmen's Party in 1876, nine are present in the SAPD's founding *protokolls* in nearly the same wording. (The two that were absent—the demand for railroads and telegraphs to be operated by the government and the demand for the establishment of bureaus of labor—were less appropriate to conditions in Germany, where railroads were more tightly regulated and the Prussian bureaucracy was something to be feared, not expanded.[42])

In adopting the strategy of unity and fusion of their German compatriots, German American socialists were forced to venture out from their ethnic enclaves and seek American partners. In the wake of the great railroad strikes that rolled across America the previous July and the electoral success of the Workingmen's Party in Chicago and elsewhere in the fall elections, German American leaders came to the conclusion that working with the Yankees was unavoidable, given their overwhelming demographic and cultural power. But these ethnic groups never saw eye-to-eye. Many German American leaders regarded "Anglo-Saxons" as being "superficial thinkers," haters of "higher thoughts," and persons of "simple habits," according to a typical article in the *Vorbote*.[43]

German American Marxists, who took their cues directly from the old bookish sage in London, thought electoral politics were a bourgeois trap and especially hated the Yankee reformers who brought into the socialist movement the remnants of their older commitments to abolition, women's rights, land reform, spiritualism, and cooperative schemes of many kinds. German Lassalleans, when they were not battling German Marxists, were more comfortable with the Yankees' republicanism but found their application of democratic principles to their own organizations and subsequent rejection of centralized party authority and discipline maddening. Neither German-speaking faction ever fully understood that many of those same Yankee reformers whom they denounced as bourgeois faddists were deeply radical in the lengths to which they were willing to contemplate structural changes to society, or that they were also militants who believed that arms were necessary to enforce and preserve their democratic rights. Both ethnic factions proclaimed that the nation had a choice between the ballot and the bullet, but only the Yankees had faith that the ballot would ultimately prevail (though where constitutional rights were denied, the Yankees were in favor of revolutionary change by mass insurrection, just as many of them were when they resisted slavery before the war). The German socialists, imbued with a theory of history that taught them that the only meaningful change was wrought by violent revolution, viewed the ballot merely as a stepping-stone to higher levels of radical thought. Both were patient: for Yankees there was always an upcoming election, an evil to reform, an unwashed horde to educate, while German Marxists actually took a longer view of social change and held that the working class must be educated, organized, and empowered before going to the barricades.[44]

Cautiously, some German socialists began to make awkward efforts to appeal to English-speaking Americans. Judson Grenell was a Michigan native who, with his friend Joseph Labadie, recalled being the "first distinctively American English-speaking wage workers in Detroit to be known as Socialists." Grenell remembered how he was first introduced to socialism by a German socialist group in Detroit that was just then making its first effort to reach Americans. Grenell's fifty-year-old memory of the scene begins with him walking along Michigan Avenue and seeing a sign on a door that read "Social Democrats meet at 3 pm: Everybody Welcome." Curious, he walked up a flight of stairs: "Several small groups stood around, most if not all of those composing the audience talking in German. However, when the meeting opened, the chairman made his address in English. It was an attempt of German-born and German-speaking social democrats to introduce the English-speaking wage workers of Detroit [to] the economic theories of Karl Marx."[45]

In pursuit of English-speaking supporters when the newly unified Socialist Labor Party assembled in Newark, New Jersey, in December 1877, the party conducted business in both German and English for the first time, a sore point with some delegates who complained of how the proceedings were slowed down by having to repeat every little point in English. At Newark the party platform was changed, made more "imprecise" in the words of one observer, to make it more comprehensible to the "English" workers. Unlike the founding convention of the party, which published its proceedings only in German, the Newark assembly published the report of its business in both languages. A native-born bilingual activist, Philip Van Patten, was chosen to be the party secretary. Most importantly, the party dropped many of its rigid Marxist restrictions on political action and revamped the organizational structure to mandate that although separate ethnic sections may exist, their members must combine to conduct essential party business in a "main section" meeting. In both Chicago and New York this provision allowed for later de facto control of the party machinery by a minority of Yankee reformers who were able to monopolize the main section meetings, which were conducted in the English language.[46]

In the end, such efforts did little to attract Yankees. Laurence Gronlund, a Danish American socialist author, then a Socialist Labor Party activist in St. Louis, claimed a year or two later that he could count the number of American socialists on the fingers of one hand. Local groups of socialists commonly wrote in to these papers saying they might have some success in organizing American workers if only they had good public speakers who spoke English. In Chicago or New York, where sizable socialist meetings were organized, ethnic divisions were maintained by setting up separate podiums at opposite ends of the hall or the public square to accommodate speechmaking in different languages. The *New York Tribune* estimated in mid-1878 that of the one thousand socialists in the city, fewer than one hundred of them were English-speakers. Based on the party's own records, such estimates were overly generous, as the one American section in New York never enrolled more than fifty members and in May 1878 appealed to all English-speaking Germans in the party to join the American section because it had so few members and was in danger of collapsing.[47]

Any strategically minded observer viewing such conditions would have concluded that the prospects for socialist success were near hopeless. Neither the old Lassalleans, who as a German minority could never win a meaningful election beyond the scale of the neighborhood, nor the Marxists, who had utterly failed to make any inroads in the ranks of American labor unions, was any closer to its goal than the other. Some never really tried to recruit outside of their ethnic enclaves, as socialism to them was more a cultural habit than a crusade. One critic described the old German socialists in Boston as listlessly using socialism as "a good thing to pass a Sunday evening with—behind several glasses of lager."[48]

Initially the party's unity strategy appeared particularly promising in Chicago, where the party seemed to be led by a multiethnic coterie of leaders. In the spring of 1878 the Socialist Labor Party (SLP) held a nominating convention that expressed the party's new approach. Breaking with local socialist practice, journalists from the "capitalist" newspapers were admitted to observe the proceedings. Three chairmen were selected—one German, one Bohemian, and one American. All motions and resolutions were repeated three times, being translated into each language. A full slate of candidates was nominated, and one of them, Frank Stauber, was elected to the city council with another missing the mark by just twenty votes, leaving the socialists "a little jubilant" at the outcome of the SLP's first election. Later that November the party increased its vote and elected three men to state assembly: Leo Meilbeck, a Moravian cabinet maker who left carpentry in 1875 to work for the public library because of his mastery of languages and his fine penmanship; Charles Ehrhardt, a German garment cutter who once kept a restaurant near the corner of Clark and Lake but lost it in the Great Fire; and Christian Meier, a German brush maker who immigrated when he was four years old and had been working at his trade since he was thirteen. The SLP also won a seat in the Illinois state senate, electing a thirty-one-year-old Pennsylvania-born picture-frame maker named Sylvester Artley.[49]

The Chicago party's first foray into city politics in April 1878 was well marred by the customary levels of dishonesty. A reporter wryly noted on the day of the election, "No matter how trivial the office that is contested, there are always rumors of attempted frauds and ballot-box stuffing, and the cry of forged tickets is heard on every side." He went on to document many such incidents, including one knife fight in a polling booth, but thought overall that the day at the polls "passed off very quietly."[50] At an SLP meeting where the results of the election were first discussed, aldermanic candidate Albert Parsons said he had proof that in the fifth voting precinct at least nine votes were cast for him but only five were reported. Henry Stahl, corresponding secretary of the furniture workers union, who ran for city council in the Eighth Ward, complained that at least forty-eight votes for his opponent were "crowded into the box." Stahl charged that many more unspecified "outrageous frauds" were carried out throughout the city.

Uncharacteristically for a group that supposedly would be so disheartened two years later by ballot-box stuffing that they lost all hope in the progressive possibilities of electoral politics, once Parsons and Stahl had finished recounting their list of election frauds, meeting chair Thomas Morgan moved that the party "let the matter drop," and his motion was adopted without further debate. Apparently, routine ballot-box stuffing was not considered worth pursuing unless it provided a clear opportunity for protest and organizing. Garden-variety voter intimidation (then known as "bulldozing"), repeat voting, ballot-box stuffing, mistakes in ballot tallying, and a long list of creative dirty tricks were regular features of every Chicago election in the Gilded Age.[51]

The following spring of 1879 the SLP further expanded its power in the city council by adding three more aldermen to their caucus and draining off enough Republican votes to elect a liberal Democrat mayor, Carter Harrison, who most importantly understood his debt to them. In his inaugural speech Harrison defended his erstwhile socialist allies from what he saw as unfounded public fears: "Some persons fear an organized resistance to authority in Chicago. I do not. I do not believe that there is in our midst any considerable body of men mad enough to attempt such folly, for they must know that they would be as chaff compared to the solid masses who love our institutions and are determined that law and order shall reign."[52] Harrison appointed Frank Stauber to the powerful city finance committee, handed several SLP leaders patronage appointments, and swung a contract for printing city notices to the *Arbeiter-Zeitung*. The SLP had successfully leveraged its small numbers (best estimates are that there were fewer than one thousand party members in the city) into a disproportionate share of the city and even the state's political power.[53]

This taste of political power was fleeting. By the time the next statewide election rolled around that fall, the socialist vote had plummeted by two-thirds and the party lost all of its seats in the state legislature. Likewise in the next spring municipal election of 1880, three of the four socialist incumbents lost their seats, and the fourth, Stauber, was denied his reelection by vote fraud, though this too was a symptom of socialist decline. Stauber's opponent's retail ballot-box stuffing proved an effective margin only because the socialist vote had plummeted eighteen points from the previous election. Over the next year the number of Chicagoans dropping a red socialist ballot in their polling boxes declined to just 1,999 from a peak of 11,858 two years before.[54]

Something significant had changed between 1879 and 1881 that rapidly and thoroughly destroyed this promising political movement. Whatever happened could not have been primarily blamed on the disillusioning political corruption that was rampant in Chicago. For those with a dim view of the efficacy of the ballot box to begin with, the efforts of machine politicians to steal elections did not suddenly come as a shock in 1878 or 1879. Rather, the "militant element" within the SLP that despaired of the power of the ballot box was swayed by a sudden shift of ideological trends and political events occurring in Europe. Not only did these Chicago militants have their radical tendencies deepened by the international circulation of publications and news, but their numbers suddenly leaped at this very moment by the arrival of militant socialists exiled from Germany. What happened to the SLP in the wilds of Chicago politics had not changed the party, but instead a new way of thinking about social change that began in Europe quickly shifted the way that Chicago radicals perceived and interpreted their misfortunes.[55]

The German Revolutionary Turn

While anarchist ideas quickly spread around Europe and into the United States, their most swift and powerful impact appeared on the course of events in Germany. The spread of this doctrine of violent action through socialist ranks in Germany indirectly changed the entire course of the German socialist movement.

By the mid-1870s, the SADP had established a flourishing institutional base of party newspapers, offices, Reichstag (German parliament) seats, and affiliated clubs and unions. Carefully balancing both Marxist and Lassallean ideologies, the SAPD declared itself the party of the working class, refused to disavow its revolutionary aims, but also mandated adherence to law and electoral reform as party orthodoxy. Just as the SAPD's strategy of lawful gradualism seemed to be succeeding, judging by the growth in party membership and votes, the ideas coalescing around the tactic of direct violence were seized by those who were impatient with the SAPD's slow, nonconfrontational road. Most famously, such a conversion seized one of the most popular leaders of the SAPD, Johann Most, turning him from party stalwart to leader of its militant opposition.

Most's ideological journey was a slow but steady one. In June 1876, Most—then an editor of the SAPD party newspaper, the *Berliner Freie Presse*, and a delegate to the Reichstag, whose term was interrupted by his arrest two years earlier for a provocative speech he had made on the second anniversary of the Paris Commune—had just been released from prison. It was his second stint behind Kaiser Wilhelm's bars. He served eight months in Zwickau Prison for a speech he made in 1873, time he spent productively writing a popular adaptation of Marx's *Das Kapital* and his own *Die Loesung der Socialen Frage* (The Solution of the Social Question), in which he blasted utopians like Charles Fourier and Robert Owen, called Pierre-Joseph Proudhon "the most confused among the third-rate social quacks," and denounced advocates of violent revolution, saying, "I want not your fists but your minds! . . . Only think and the idea shall triumph." Enjoying a stroll along the capital city's main boulevard with his friend August Reinsdorf, Most was taken aback when Reinsdorf challenged his commitment to socialism. Reinsdorf dismissed the SAPD, calling it "eine Stimmzettel- und Zeitungslesser-Parte" (a ballot- and newspaper-reading party). Most defended his party's revolutionary nature, while Reinsdorf shook him with his argument that only by taking the next step of heroic action, of a violent campaign against the state and its minions, would the revolution be achieved. Their argument grew so loud that they attracted the attention of a nearby policeman. Most later remembered this day as planting the idea of propaganda by deed in his mind, an idea that caused him to increasingly question his party's law-abiding strategies for change. He had begun to reconsider whether he wanted his follower's minds or their fists.[56]

Meanwhile, the circle of budding anarchists that had produced the *Arbeiter-Zeitung* and included Paul Brousse, August Reinsdorf, and Emil Werner began to radicalize a second tier of less learned and talented activists who were not able to leave their mark in print as their leaders could but instead acted out their ideas in more physical ways. Emil Hödel, a twenty-year-old tinsmith, the unwanted son of an unwed teenage mother, a youth with a reformatory upbringing and a police record for theft and assault, discovered a new purpose for his life after spending time in the company of Reinsdorf, Werner, and others. Hödel threw over what was becoming a comfortable life as an occasionally paid organizer for the SAPD by his increasingly militant statements and was officially expelled from the party in April 1878. On May 14 Hödel jostled his way through a crowd watching the elderly Kaiser Wilhelm and his daughter pass by in an open carriage, pulled out a revolver, fired three errant shots at the kaiser, and emptied his remaining three chambers toward the bystanders who tried to tackle him.

Two weeks later the eighty-one-year-old kaiser, who stubbornly refused pleas to alter his daily route or ride in a closed carriage, passed again down the Unter den Linden and was struck by two blasts from a shotgun aimed out a third-story window by a professor of agricultural economics, Dr. Carl Eduard Nobiling. Nobiling's aim was steady, and Wilhelm surely would have been killed were it not for the army regulations that required the wearing of helmets in public on Sunday, a practice the old soldier never gave up. Nobiling was accomplished with his revolver, and as an angry mob burst into his room, he shot the first man, an innkeeper, in the face. However, somehow the would-be assassin missed his mark when he aimed at his own temple as the group tackled him. Nobiling was not as close to the anarchists of the *Arbeiter-Zeitung* as was Hödel, although he knew Emil Werner and was influenced by anarchist beliefs.[57]

While the SAPD scrambled to distance itself from Hödel and Nobiling, Germany's nascent anarchist movement defended their attacks. Paul Brousse, now editing *L'Avant-Garde,* filled the June issue with discussion of the act of regicide. One article praised Nobiling's act in principle: "We cannot call the man who wants to get rid of an emperor, even the German Emperor, crazy, any more than we called [Felice] Orsini and [Giuseppe] Fieschi madmen in France; and then there are forms of homicide that we do not condemn and even approve: regicide, the vengeance of the worker against his boss, all these are cases in point." However, other contributors criticized Nobiling for acting alone rather than as part of a broader movement. "We did not load Hödel's pistol or slide the pellet into Nobiling's carbine, because we knew at the outset that regicide is a purely republican act of propaganda, where afterwards it is too easy to misrepresent the intentions of the perpetrators." Johann Most, not yet a full-blown advocate of violent deeds but fast drifting in that direction, responded to Hödel's act with articles in the *Freie Presse* disclaiming any connection to the would-be assassin and a speech that skirted close enough to an endorsement of his action to land him in jail for another seven-month stint. At the time Most made this speech, he was probably unaware that among the items found in Hödel's pockets was a picture of Most himself.[58]

Chancellor Bismarck seized upon Hödel and Nobiling's deeds as a lever to destroy the Socialist Party and weaken the National Liberal Party, thereby allowing him to push through his own legislative agenda. Conveniently, police detectives did not follow up many leads connecting Hödel and Nobiling to the Werner, Reinsdorf, Rinke, Brousse secret society of anarchists, presumably because proving the would-be assassin's linkages to the anarchists would have relieved the social democrats of guilt by association. Berlin police did not even pick up Werner for questioning after intercepting a letter from Werner to Brousse indicating that Werner knew Nobiling personally. But politics trumped justice, and Bismarck skillfully exploited Hödel's and Nobiling's trials, shifting the public mood against the SAPD on the eve of critical Reichstag elections. The SAPD lost a third of their seats. With fewer socialist allies returned to Berlin and a 10 percent decline in their own votes, the Liberals acquiesced and approved an antisocialist law that banned all the activities of the SAPD while allowing the party to continue to exist in name only. In one of the most miscalculated forms of protest in socialist history, SAPD leaders voted to dissolve their party in advance of the law's taking effect. In a letter to Friedrich Engels, SAPD leader Wilhelm Liebknecht explained how if the party bent over backward to comply with the law, it would prove its loyalty to the German people and overcome the repression quickly, concluding, "We want to kill them with our lawfulness."[59]

Many German social democrats found the violent rhetoric of the growing anarchist movement more appealing with Bismarck's opportunistic banning of most socialist newspapers and political activities after the assassination attempts on the kaiser in 1878. The emergency antisocialist law was vigorously enforced, throwing many of the leaders of Germany's socialist movement into jail and forcing others to emigrate. Immediately upon the law's passage, the government suppressed thirty-five newspapers and ordered the dissolution of hundreds of the socialist party's affiliated organizations, including twenty-one labor unions, fifty-five political associations, ten educational organizations, seven cooperatives, four performing troupes, and thirty-six singing clubs. Many socialists left their belief in the worker's ultimate triumph through parliamentary means behind them as they entered a cell or a steamship. A few managed to avoid the repression—some by lawyerly skirting around the edges of the law, others by hiding their activities completely from official view. By driving socialist activities underground, Bismarck forced previously democratic and parliamentary activists to adopt the conspiratorial tactics of the very political theorists, such as August Blanqui and Giuseppe Mazzini, that they had long denounced as adventurism. A movement once based on open meetings, party newspapers, and elections had turned into one characterized by code names, safe houses, hiding places for forbidden tracts, and men watching doors—the sort of things Russian radicals had always lived with. Such an environment bred a militant state of mind, greater toleration of violent expressions, and extreme plans.[60]

For a handful of loyal party leaders this strategy of capitulation went too far, and they recoiled into the arms of the militants. Johann Most, the bookbinder whose fearless oratory in a vernacular style had earned him both fame and frequent prison terms, was given twenty-four hours to leave Berlin upon being released from prison. Most fled to London, where he joined a growing cohort of German exiles bubbling over with revolutionary braggadocio and launched an opposition newspaper, the *Freiheit,* which he smuggled back into Germany stuffed inside mattresses and distributed through a network that included Reinsdorf, Brousse, and the other hard-boiled anarchists.[61]

Another uncompromising party leader, Wilhelm Hasselmann, a chemist turned labor spokesman, one of nine deputies who survived the party's decline in the polls, defiantly took the floor of the Reichstag on October 10, 1878, and for two hours railed against the state, against capitalism, and urged his comrades to use every means at their disposal to fight this unjust law. "I am not personally in favor of revolution; I prefer pacific means. But if we are forced to fight, we shall know how to fight; and I shall be proud to lay down my life and die on the field of honor. Let Prince Bismarck remember the 18th of March, 1848." Hasselmann was ordered to leave Berlin the following month and moved to Hamburg, where he published an innocuous family weekly newspaper filled with light entertainment while secretly continuing to write anonymously for banned journals like Most's *Freiheit.* Though prohibited from residing in Berlin, as a Reichstag deputy he was entitled to travel there for official sessions, where his speeches calling on the workers to resist the antisocialist oppression made him a hero to the party's old base and an enemy of the cowed party leaders, who hoped they could quietly bide their time but watched as the initiative was seized by the radicals. When the Reichstag took up the antisocialist bill again in early May 1880, Hasselmann stood alone in his party in trying to arouse the people to action, announcing, "The time for parliamentary chatter is past and the time for deeds begins."[62]

Johann Most's *Freiheit* was a bellwether of the sharpening mood of radicalism in the early 1880s. Through its inaugural issues in the winter of 1878–1879, *Freiheit* followed the program of the Social Democratic Party and merely called for the restoration of political and civil rights in Germany. It renounced violence and conspiracies and upheld the ballot as the workers' best hope. But beginning in the spring of 1879, a few outbursts of more violent rhetoric broke into its pages: A report of a speech Most gave on the anniversary of the Paris Commune concluded with the statement that the social question could be resolved only through violent revolution. In April and May a series of articles appeared critiquing the opportunistic policies of the SAPD and especially its distortion of socialist theory that claimed revolution could be brought about by words instead of deeds. In September the *Freiheit* declared that "only a revolutionary act" could save Germany. Throughout the next year the *Freiheit*'s sharper tone complicated matters for SAPD leaders in the Reichstag, where the paper's more exciting issues were being waved about by the conservatives as evidence of the dire threat of socialism to the public order and, in consequence, the need to maintain the antisocialist laws that had to be renewed each legislative session. At the SAPD's secret summer 1880 conference at Wyden Castle, Most and Hasselmann were formally tossed out of the party.[63]

Almost immediately after word of their party expulsion reached London, the *Freiheit* veered away from its former official advocacy of socialist political action and trumpeted the doctrines of insurrection, violence, and propaganda by deed. In September 1880, a month after he and Hasselmann were expelled from the SAPD, Most translated and published a version of Sergei Nechaev and Mikhail Bakunin's fiery *Catechism of the Revolutionist*. Through that winter and spring *Freiheit* ran several articles on its front page extolling the power of the individual act of revolutionary violence. One of these articles, "The Tactics of the Revolutionary Party," appeared on the eve of a gathering of revolutionaries in London that would establish the doctrine of propaganda by deed as the core strategy of the movement.[64]

One clear sign of the *Freiheit*'s new direction was its featuring of contributions by August Reinsdorf, the militant who had planted the seed of anarchism in Most's head some years earlier. These articles detailed proper revolutionary tactics, including the organization of militant cells that should each operate independently and attack bourgeois society with whatever weapons they had available. Reinsdorf was not prone to idle talk. Soon after he corresponded with Most and revealed his plan to murder the police chief of Berlin, he was arrested near chief inspector Carl Otto von Madai's home with a dagger in his coat pocket. While it seems Reinsdorf's plan to blow up the Reichstag building never got past the dreaming stage, this may have been because of the effectiveness of the spy network that kept officials informed of his every move and the fact that over the next two years, Reinsdorf was arrested and imprisoned for a few months at a time on a succession of charges, including engaging in suspicious activities, distributing banned materials, and using false identification papers (although a judge overturned his more serious conviction for raping the ten-year-old daughter of a family he was staying with). He then fled to Paris, working odd jobs and contributing more articles to *Freiheit* and making plans with accomplices to blow up the entire German royal family at the dedication of the massive Niederwald monument in the Rhine valley then being erected in celebration of the unification of the German empire. By November 1881 the transformation of *Freiheit* was complete, and anarchist Sebastian Trunk noted this milestone gleefully, writing fellow uncompromiser Victor Dave, "Today *Freiheit* is what it should be. A newspaper that is completely for the revolutionary worker."[65]

The Revolutionary Diaspora

At first German socialist refugees trickled individually into the United States. Then groups of exiles arrived en masse. In December 1880 a delegation of New York's German socialists watched as a steamship docked. When their comrades appeared at the top of the gangplank, they waved their red flags and cheered. Thirty-one socialist refugees from Germany had arrived. Before leaving Hamburg each of these men was given a sealed letter by an SAPD party delegate and told not to read its contents until they were at sea. The letter urged each comrade to remain true to the cause: to "uphold the old flag" and to find new comrades in the New World while supporting the old ones. The letters reminded each man that they were "apostles" in a new land but must keep in mind those who remained at home.[66]

Chicago's German American socialists followed these developments closely by reading the party press and pamphlets and by direct connections to the leaders involved. Also, the ranks of the advocates of force within the American SLP grew with the arrival of a few influential socialists from Germany who were already convinced of the importance of force and imbued with the latest doctrines of revolutionary anarchism. As the proportion of militants in the American movement increased, the doctrine of unity and the party's patience with the few idealistic Yankees in their midst was put to the test. Clearly, as they had in experimenting with ethnic and ideological unity by following the example of the SAPD and the Gotha Congress, German American socialists again set their policies and agenda according to events in the fatherland.

The American socialist movement was profoundly affected by the infusion of German political refugees who were recently embittered by the failure of democratic politics to protect their fundamental rights and the betrayal of liberal politicians in the Reichstag. Initially both the arrival of radicalized immigrants and lessons of their experiences hardened German American socialists' opposition to political compromise both with other parties and within their own ranks.

German sections in New York City that had once embraced a policy of unity with their Yankee comrades now demanded the right to nominate political candidates independently from the Yankee-dominated main section of the city, which, under the existing party constitution, was the only body given such power. The leaders of the main section successfully protested to the national office, saying that the Germans' plan "divides the party into factions based on distinctions of race." William West, one of the oldest Yankee members of the party, wrote: "The one thing that divides the members is the form Political Organization should take . . . [I, however, believe] that all distinctions of race should be abolished . . . when the party meets as one body only the English language should be spoken. Germans and other so-called foreigners learn to speak English in their business transactions, because they must, they must learn to do so in their political operations, for the same reasons, or they will never secure the co-operation of the American (English-speaking) population."[67]

In mid-January 1879, SLP leaders began to weaken in the face of German determination to control the party, in which they were an overwhelming majority. A committee charged with devising a plan of permanent political organization proposed allowing the creation of separate language sections within single assembly districts. West was disgusted, saying, "Nothing better devised to break up and destroy the party could have been devised, even by Bismarck or the Pope. You will see in each Assembly District from three to six [party] candidates running for the same office, which would of course result in defeat of the party at the election." New York's American section raised the ethnic stakes by countering with a proposal to bar "half-citizens" from voting on party nominations. (A "half-citizen" was a legal resident who had declared his or her intention to become a citizen but for whom the requisite waiting period had not yet expired.)[68]

Such political wrangling damaged the reputations of both ethnic factions in the SLP but buoyed the position of that smaller group of radicals who opposed political action altogether. Opponents of electoral politics in principle gathered around the charismatic saloon keeper Justus Schwab. Schwab was blunt and uncompromising in his opposition to the idea that socialism could be drawn out of a ballot box: "The right to vote without the right to work is a chimera, a farce, a delusion, and a snare."[69] What had been merely a spirited debate escalated into a physical confrontation between advocates of force and democratic socialists at a main section meeting in March 1879 when Schwab objected to something Charles Sotheran, a leader of the American faction said, and smashed him over the head with a chair. Schwab's German section then refused the demands of the English section to drum him out of the party.[70]

Just as the rift between ethnic factions in New York City widened, the most famous and radical Bismarckian exile of them all landed in New York City. Wilhelm Hasselmann, a former editor of the socialist newspaper and a two-term member of the Reichstag (indeed, Hasselmann's term as an elected Reichstag member ran through the remainder of that year), was actually a double refugee, expelled from the German SAPD for ultra-radicalism and hounded out of Germany for his increasingly militant speeches.[71]

Hasselmann was an odd product of modernizing Germany. When he was a young boy, his father abandoned his family for America. After the death of his mother, young Hasselmann was taken in by rich relatives who treated him more as a servant than a member of the family. A precocious student, he entered a polytechnic school and studied chemistry and engineering, but after discovering radical politics he took a post as an assistant editor for a Lassallean newspaper, *Neue Social-Demokrat*, where he developed a highly emotional style of prose that appealed more broadly than the stilted hairsplitting that was typical of socialist publications of the day. In 1876 Hasselmann stood for election to the Reichstag, and, to advance his candidacy, started a little weekly called the *Die rote Fahne* (the Red Flag), whose vehement rhetoric and popular style so disconcerted the socialists gathered at the Gotha Congress that they demanded he fold it. Hasselmann defied the party not only in persisting in his publication efforts but also in his conduct in the Reichstag. After the assassination attempt on the kaiser, SAPD leaders decided their best course of action was not to directly oppose the legislation but to prove their national loyalty by behaving within the confines of the law and quietly regrouping for another election.[72]

In London Hasselman was a member of Most's inner circle, dining at Madame Audinet's restaurant with Most, former Paris Communard Édouard Vaillant, and the terrorist August Reinsdorf. Such friendships and dinner conversations pushed him further toward a faith in the transformative power of violence. Just before sailing for America, Hasselmann contributed an essay to *Freiheit* titled "An Honest Word to the German Workers." In it Hasselmann addressed the crushing of Germany's SAPD and appealed to the German workers for a "rescuing deed," concluding that only armed resistance to the state could possibly change the existing political order. Such expressions preceded Hasselmann across the Atlantic and further established his popularity among the most radical elements in New York before his arrival.[73]

Within weeks of arriving in New York City, Hasselmann seems to have been the catalyst for the founding of the Social Revolutionary Club, the first organization in America explicitly focused on arming for and provoking the coming workers' revolution. Its two dozen or so founding members included Justus Schwab, the flamboyant saloon keeper who was as renowned for his fists as for his vocal cords. One of the things that distinguished the Social Revolutionary Club from other socialist parties and clubs was that included among its standing committees was a weapons committee.[74]

At first the members of the Social Revolutionary Club attempted to maintain their ties to the wider socialist movement. They continued to attend Socialist Labor Party meetings, though to what purpose is unclear, as it became more evident with each passing meeting that they shared less common ground. In January 1881 another row erupted at an SLP meeting when a leader of the "compromiser" faction moved that members of the Social Revolutionary Club should be expelled from the party. The vote carried, but Moritz Bachmann, a well-known radical journalist, shouted for the social revolutionaries to remain in the hall. Over a chorus of shouts, Schwab was acclaimed chair of the protest meeting and organized the signing of a petition denouncing the "compromisers'" actions. After fifty or so signatures had been recorded, a "compromiser" by the name of Fred Meine stepped forward to take his turn with the pen, but once within reach of the document, he snatched it up and ran for the door, throwing the room into pandemonium. Meine later claimed that Schwab hit him with a chair (clearly Schwab's preferred weapon), while another "compromiser," Fred Ackerman, swore out a warrant against social revolutionary Carl Seelig for smacking him with some other piece of the hall's furnishings. The Chicago *Vorbote* later published a letter celebrating the fight, the correspondent writing how pleased he was at how far the New York party leaders had progressed and how they had finally chosen not to be bossed by "wishy-washy" socialists (*süßwassersozialisten*) and party "parasites." Meine and Ackerman, the *Vorbote* correspondent reported, were the most injured in the melee but "deserved what they got." Seelig and Schwab were arrested for assault, and Schwab posted both their bonds.[75]

One month later the rival socialists of New York City could not even drown their mutual hatred long enough to gather for their traditional yearly commemoration of the Paris Commune. On the evening of March 20, 1881, radicals in New York could choose to attend either of two competing commune memorial meetings, each, of course, claiming to be the authentic one.[76]

Likewise, Chicago's socialist movement was also fractured by the arrival of the new and more militant German socialist refugees. One of the earliest exiles from Bismarck's crackdown, Paul Grottkau, brought with him to Chicago a militant outlook and a penchant for factional infighting. Grottkau had been a young bricklayer in Berlin when he was taken on as the political apprentice of Johann Baptiste von Schweitzer, leader of the Allgemeiner Deutscher Arbeiterverein, and tutored in the arts of factional infighting. Grottkau took part in the great Gotha Congress of 1877 and was a rising leader in socialist ranks until he was jailed for running afoul of censorship laws as an editor and then exiled from Germany.

Paul Grottkau's militancy appealed to a growing faction of socialists, and this, combined with his experience in party maneuvering, got him rapidly promoted to a position of leadership within Chicago's socialist movement. Within a few months of his arrival in Chicago in 1878, Grottkau took over the editorial reins of the *Arbeiter-Zeitung* and steered it away from support for the SLP's unity platform and its electoral strategy, instead adopting a more orthodox Marxist focus on trade unions and worker organization. Grottkau likened political socialists to Don Quixote tilting at windmills.

On the eve of local Chicago's elections in the spring of 1878, militants in the SLP split the party along ethnic lines by announcing their intention to parade their socialist militia, the Lehr und Wehr Verein, through the city and out to the picnic grounds as part of their upcoming summer festival. Fearing that this news would undermine the party's electoral support, the SLP National Executive Committee issued a statement declaring that the party had no armed affiliates and no official association with such groups and advising its members to not participate in any such events that misrepresented the legal character of the party. Seizing the opportunity to roil the factional waters, Grottkau published a spurious translation of the text of the SLP's executive committee's telegram. He translated the words "request" and "urge" as the stronger word "prohibit" (*untersagen*) and created the impression that a committee in Cincinnati made up largely of Americans had assumed the right to order Chicago's socialists to leave their rifles at home, infuriating many German-speaking party members.[77]

Chicago's German militants ignored the requests of the party leadership and positioned the 136 armed members of the Lehr und Wehr Verein in the front of the parade that snaked through the city and to the picnic grounds. Grottkau ascended the speakers platform dressed in a soldier's uniform and closed with the thought, "We want peace but if someone wants war we are equipped to stand up for our rights." He soon earned a reputation as one of the more militant socialists in the city. His speeches at the SLP's evening mass meetings were typically recognized in the morning papers as being the "most violent," as they advocated "the taking up of arms and the shedding of blood if the demands of the Socialists were not immediately complied with."[78]

In the wake of these events, an anonymous member of the English-speaking section in Chicago complained of Grottkau's leadership in a manner that revealed he understood that the controversy was not really about party policies over the public display of arms, but was really between those who believed in the path of unity and elections and revolutionaries who did not:

> It seems strange that the Chicago membership, which reached its present strength only through the liberal policy of political and industrial organization of the Socialistic Party, should allow those who openly declare their hostility to political action to pack their business meetings and adopt resolutions which the whole section fears is contrary to their honest belief. Especially is it ridiculous that Paul Grottkau, a person who has no knowledge of the Party history, having just arrived from Germany, should don the blue blouse of the military Lehr and Wehr Verein and presume to sneer at the ballot box in a country, where, above all others, the ballot box, properly used, is a power irresistible and indisputable. Our English-speaking Chicago membership . . . if they properly understood the malicious purpose of the Vorbote plotters, they would teach them that our long struggle to build up in Chicago a reasonable political and trade union movement has not been in vain.[79]

Grottkau continued to toss wrenches into the party machinery. In July 1878 Grottkau's *Arbeiter-Zeitung* charged that SLP national secretary Philip Van Patten was actually an agent of the rival Greenback Party and was using his office to steer the socialists into supporting Greenbacker ambitions. The SLP responded by revoking the *Arbeiter-Zeitung*'s status as an official party newspaper, though it later reconsidered and granted the paper partial recognition in the "interest of party unity." From that time on,

Chicago's SLP was essentially two separate organizations split along ethnic lines. Only a handful of activists had feet in both camps. Albert Parsons, partly because he found work as assistant editor of a new English-language paper published from editorial offices shared with the *Vorbote* and the *Arbeiter-Zeitung*, increasingly caucused with the German section. George Schilling, largely because of his involvement with the Irish-dominated city-wide trade union federation, the Trades and Labor Assembly, remained a member in good standing with the main section but also maintained ties with his German compatriots.[80]

Later that fall the intensifying repression of socialists in Germany became an issue of particular concern to the German wing of the party and the German sections of the SLP in Chicago. German party members did not view these developments in Germany as distant events. Apparently, neither did German authorities, who in November included in a list of thirty-two banned publications both the *Arbeiter-Zeitung* and the *Vorbote*.[81] In one of its last displays of ideological and ethnic unity, New York's SLP organized a huge public meeting to oppose Bismarck's repression on January 22 at Chickering Hall on Fifth Avenue. The event drew a crowd estimated at five thousand and featured speakers from all positions on the socialist spectrum, from labor reformers like keynote speaker John Swinton (then managing editor of the *New York Sun* but soon to be publisher of *John Swinton's Paper*, a national labor newspaper); the ancient Yankee Internationalist William West, who occupied a seat of honor on the stage; and proponents of force Victor Drury and Justus Schwab. All joined hands along with Adolph Douai and Charles Sotheran, leaders of the SLP conservatives, who Schwab and Drury would later denounce as "compromisers." In March, Chicago's Turner Hall was the site of a similar event, where the guest of honor was Ludwig Ecks, a recently arrived exiled organizer of the SAPD from Berlin.[82]

Chicago's German sections tapped Grottkau to chair a special committee to raise funds for the relief of socialists in Germany. Grottkau went beyond the idea of raising funds to support the resistance of the SAPD and called for the party to provide passage to America and find jobs in America for outlawed German radicals. However, his plan went too far for the leaders of the SLP, who probably feared it would augment the militants' power in the party, and the SLP National Executive Committee flatly rejected it, writing, "Refugees and exiles are recommended to the sympathy and practical as-sistance of all members . . . We are, however, of the opinion that emigration of German Socialists should not be encouraged, for if there was ever a time when they should be at their posts, it is now."[83]

Chicago's SLP contained its schisms long enough to hold the largest political rally in the city's history in March 1879, though even there the ethnic and ideological cracks were exposed. One of the highlights of the massive political rally was a joint parade and drill of the city's three socialist militia groups, but this fell apart when one of the militias, the Jaeger Guards, refused to follow an order from the commander of another, the Lehr und Wehr Verein, because the order had been given in English.

Though all factions dampened their ethnic hostilities in the interest of the spring municipal election, once it was over the factional fights continued. A month after electing four socialists to city council, tempers flared at an open meeting as several members denounced Grottkau for his "rule or ruin" leadership of the *Arbeiter-Zeitung*. Meanwhile, charges were flung at a meeting of the main section that party leader Thomas J. Morgan had secretly maneuvered the party to aid the Democrats, including distributing "smooth-bore ballots" that contained the names of both Socialist and Democratic candidates.[84]

This was enough for Benjamin Sibley, one of the Yankee leaders and most popular Socialist candidates in Chicago, who resigned from the party and threw his hat in with the labor wing of the Democrats. Sibley blamed his disillusionment on the "German clique," with their "imported theories" of "sudden and violent change," who kept aloof from Americans, particularly Grottkau, "who has exerted a fearfully bad influence on the German socialists." Sibley's defection was the first of several Yankee political socialists who left the party at that point. The handful of Yankees who remained were increasingly isolated as English- and German-speaking factions retreated into their own sections.[85]

What had begun as a dispute over the wisdom of parading a socialist militia on the eve of an election campaign had widened into a more fundamental philosophical disagreement over the purpose and potential of electoral activity. Not very long before, there was a moment when political ideals and ethnicity did not seem to align. Just before the spring municipal election of 1878, the labor wing of Chicago's Democratic party sent a delegation composed of its most bona fide working-class leaders bearing an olive branch to SLP headquarters. The Democrats mistakenly thought that because the "tin pail" faction had recently deposed the "silk stocking faction" of Chicago's democracy, they might find common ground with the socialists upon which to bargain. Instead, the SLP executive committee "sat down upon them" and "emphatically gave the gentlemen to understand that the day when the workingmen could be bought over to the old parties by political tricksters who had not a tithe of sincerity about them had passed."[86] These confused Democratic politicians had probably never before encountered a political organization for whom winning or losing any particular office was less important than upholding the consistency of their principles.

The experience of the frustrated "tin pail" Democrats highlighted the original point of agreement among all the members of the SLP: that the party must maintain its independence and avoid entanglements with corrupt capitalist parties so as to uphold the purity of its socialist platform. Repeatedly party members from both sides of the ethnic divide acted on these precepts as they policed the behavior of their leaders and candidates. Thomas Morgan, perhaps the man who most firmly cemented the ties between the party and the city's trade union movement, was on several occasions publicly grilled over charges he tried to maneuver the nomination process to aid the Democratic Party. Sylvester Artley, the frame maker who represented the party in the Illinois state senate, the highest office ever reached by a socialist up to that time, became the subject of a party investigation because on one occasion he caucused with the Republican Party in Springfield and reportedly had pledged his vote to a Republican candidate for the U.S. Senate if needed, though in the end he cast his vote for a fellow socialist. Throughout this controversy apparently no one brought up in Artley's defense the fact that he had single-handedly managed to secure passage of a law creating Illinois' first Bureau of Labor Statistics. Rather, further objections were raised to his having introduced such legislation without having first consulted the party.

Commitment to the principle of party independence and socialist ideals was widespread at first in the SLP regardless of what language was spoken in meetings. But as disillusionment with parliamentary politics spread, occasioned by the passage of Bismarck's antisocialist laws and the sudden influx of socialist refugees from Germany, a new view of political action took root exclusively in German circles. Influential German socialists, such as Paul Grottkau, August Spies, and Justus Schwab, reversed their view of elections. They came to see them not as an expression of the people's will, nor as a mechanism for change or reform, but rather as an opportunity to demonstrate that the ballot box was a dead end. Quietly, covertly, these leaders had arrived at a new view of social change that rejected the idea that real meaningful change could ever occur in a peaceful, orderly, or legal manner. The forces of capitalism were too entrenched, too corrupt, and too powerful to ever allow their overthrow by pieces of paper counted out at an election or tallied in a legislature. Their apostasy from SLP orthodoxy was not appreciated at the time it occurred, because formally these leaders continued to participate in the electoral process, though in the expectation and the hope that their efforts would show to the masses the error of their mistaken faith in democracy.

By the start of 1880, the main section no longer attracted any German-speaking members except for George Schilling. The Yankee faction retained just enough power to hang on to the national party machinery through the contentious election of 1880 as another factional fight erupted over the question of endorsing General James Weaver, the Greenback Labor Party's nominee for president. Later that year when two delegates from the English-speaking section visited the German section, one was denied the right to participate in the proceedings, and the other was threatened and run out of the meeting hall. Chicago's English section quietly informed the party secretary that the reason they were months behind in paying their party dues was that the German section had stolen its funds to pay their own campaign debts. English-camp leaders for the first time described the Grottkau faction as "anarchists."[87]

Later that summer, provoked by a slew of editorials that accused English-speaking members of being corrupt tools of other parties and interests, Chicago's English-speaking main section censored the *Arbeiter-Zeitung* and voted to throw its editor, Grottkau, out of the party. In response, German leaders held a rump meeting, declared themselves the new main section, and repealed the previous meeting's action. This meeting was chaired by a young, up-and-coming leader of the German section, a future Haymarket martyr by the name of August Spies, who was also elected the recording secretary. Both the French and English sections of the Chicago SLP formally protested the coup, the French politely issuing "a protest against the ... meeting which was called and attended by Germans only," declaring they "do not recognize the officers elected by said meeting." Thomas Morgan, the organizer of the Chicago SLP, wrote to the party secretary saying simply, "Speiss [*sic*] cannot be trusted ... What I desire is to through [*sic*] out all action of our section until the question of Presidential campaign is settled or until Grotkau [*sic*] has had time to kill himself."[88]

In less than two years since arriving in Chicago, Grottkau had succeeded in solidifying his control of the militant faction of the SLP and driving those who remained committed to peaceful and electoral labor reform to either go over to the smaller "American" faction or to leave the party altogether.

The policy of unity, which had been launched with such goodwill and hopes three years earlier, a program that showed great promise a year earlier by polling one out of five of the votes in the city, was dead.[89]

A new faith in the coming of the workers' revolution had spread far on both sides of the Atlantic by 1880, and this belief had transformed Chicago's and New York's socialist movements from being girded to travel the long, slow road to communism into groups expecting the revolutionary upheaval to arrive any day. Chicago's German revolutionaries had swept aside those who clung to their ballot boxes and trade union gradualism and had taken control of the party, its press, and its allied labor organizations. But in so doing they had opened the door to a new set of leaders who were so eager for the revolutionary break that they were not willing to wait for it to happen on its own. It was natural, after all, for a few hard-boiled radicals to take the next step beyond preparing for revolution and wonder what sorts of actions they could take as individuals that might hasten its arrival.

CHAPTER THREE

THE BLACK INTERNATIONAL

St. Petersburg's cobblestone streets were blanketed in snow on March 13, 1881, as the iron carriage bearing Czar Alexander II lumbered toward the Winter Palace surrounded by a mounted guard of six Cossacks. The czar no longer traveled in open sleighs like his brother, the Grand Duke, who followed behind, as assassination attempts had grown both closer and more frequent. In 1878 someone had managed to bomb a dining hall in the Winter Palace, killing a handful of soldiers and servants. The following year a well-dressed schoolteacher named Alexander Sokoloff approached within arm's reach of the czar's open carriage and got off four errant shots before he was subdued. A few months later a mine exploded along the route the royal train had just passed. Letter bombs arrived with troubling regularity.

Late for an afternoon appointment, the czar's driver turned off the prescribed route and took a shortcut along the Catherine Canal. Sofya Perovskaya, a petite twenty-seven-year-old granddaughter of the governor general of the city, stood watch and flung a white handkerchief when she saw the royal carriage turn off the main boulevard. This was a signal to the bombers positioned farther up the road. As the carriage neared, a man stepped into the street and threw what appeared to be a cake in front of its trotting horses. The blast came a tad late after the armored carriage had passed, but the charge had sufficient force to splinter its tail boards and throw several outriders to the ground. A young boy who had passed nearby lay in a pool of blood. Broken glass from a row of gas lamps tinkled to the stone like noisy snowflakes.

Ignoring the pleas of his guards to stay in the carriage, Alexander stepped down to check on the wounded. Guards reached for the bomber, who drew a pistol from his coat but was subdued before he could get off a shot. Amid this confusion a second person in the crowd drew a glass jar filled with nitroglycerin from his coat and with cool aim tossed it squarely at the monarch's feet. The explosion tore through a crowd of officials and bystanders, leaving a dozen dead or dying, including the bomber himself. Alexander was flung on his back, belly ripped open, his right leg hanging by a thread of flesh, his left shattered from his ankle to his knee, and one eye dangling from its socket. The force of the detonation was so great it shattered the czar's wedding ring and drove the pieces into his hand. He was taken by sleigh to the palace, where physicians worked furiously, stitching closed arteries, amputating the czar's shattered legs, but he died within the hour.[1]

News of the assassination and the identity of the "Nihilist" perpetrators zipped around the world on transoceanic telegraph cables and appeared in American newspapers the following morning, shocking conservatives and exhilarating radicals. Justus Schwab festooned his New York City saloon with bunting in celebration, and it quickly filled with self-proclaimed revolutionaries celebrating the deed. While rejoicing over the regicide, Schwab told a reporter, "In America the fate that has overtaken Alexander has a point. There are those in the United States who should heed the warning, for it bodes disaster to some among us in high places . . . the heads of American monopolies have cause to tremble. They are oppressing the people of the land and for just such oppression Alexander was killed." When asked to name such monopolists as he meant, Schwab said, "Well, I am willing to mention Jay Gould and William H. Vanderbilt as representatives of the class to whom I refer." They, Schwab said, "had better consider well their future actions."[2]

New York's Social Revolutionary Club hastily organized a mass meeting to celebrate the assassination. One club member, Joseph Hoffeldt, was arrested for pasting red handbills on telegraph poles around New York announcing "a public meeting of all sympathizers with the aims of revolution" and headlined: "Sic Semper Tyrannis! Russia's Despot Killed By Our Friends!" A hat was passed around Schwab's saloon to pay poor Hoffeldt's fine. The Bowery's Steuben Hall overflowed on the appointed night, and its stage was festooned with red banners, most notably one that expressed a newer idea of the movement, praising the transformative power of the heroic individual: "The spirit of the Commune expands as the axe of the executioner falls on the necks of the martyrs." Schwab opened the gala, saying, "We assemble today to rejoice over the death of a great tyrant who had checked all progress in Russia." Others followed in similar spirits until William Hasselmann, the exiled radical Reichstag deputy, concluded the evening by calling the group's attention to the fact that Alexander was not the only tyrant in the world, arousing great peals of huzzahs.[3]

Revolutionary socialists throughout the country crowed over the czar's death. Paul Grottkau and Albert Parsons expressed their pleasure at the murders before a crowd of two thousand in Chicago. Though the national SLP office issued a statement condemning the assassination and declaring that socialism could not be ushered in by the decapitation of aristocratic leaders, Chicago's own dwindling English section of the SLP approved a resolution condemning President James Garfield for offering official condolences to the people of Russia and further declared, "Our only regret in connection with the execution of the Czar of Russia is that the destructive force of the explosion that destroyed his miserable life did not include within its destructive scope every tyrant whose existence imperils or prevents free speech, free press, free ballot, and the legitimate progress of human freedom." In St. Louis militants circulated a call for a mass meeting at the courthouse that was illustrated with a death's head and crossbones and signed by the "friends of progress and the children of the goddess of liberty."[4]

Many elements of this particular regicide were heartening to revolutionaries, not least of which being that the murder was accomplished by a dynamite bomb. At the time, this was viewed as a very modern and sophisticated technology that promised to equalize the imbalance of power between governments and their people. The populist conspirators were lionized as champions of the people and perfect examples of revolutionary self-sacrifice. French radical Jean Grave recalled that this event convinced him that dynamite was preferable to printing in spreading revolutionary principles. Johann Most was ecstatic, writing on the front page of *Freiheit* in a column framed in a red border, "At Last! Triumph! Triumph!" What followed was a celebratory article noting that the killing of one vile beast was but a moral victory and that to achieve real change one monarch a month must be slain so that no one would want to be a king anymore. In return for this outburst, British authorities jailed Most for sixteen months.[5]

Czar Alexander II's assassination fired the minds of American revolutionary socialists because it seemed to validate the new revolutionary ideas spreading quickly on both sides of the Atlantic, including the idea that violent actions were valuable not only for their direct effects, such as removing a tyrant, but also for their educational power. And that true revolutionaries did not allow their actions to be impeded by the sentiments of a false bourgeois morality.

The Russian nihilists' thinking arose from a challenge to the conventional ethics that viewed violence as being justifiable only in certain circumstances, such as self-defense, resistance to great oppression or usurpation, or when carefully balanced between means and ends. Enlightenment thought sanctioned the violence of the rioting crowd as the natural verdict of the people against tyranny but was less supportive of individual acts of violence. For the revolutionary generation of Montesquieu and Thomas Jefferson, the justice of one's cause could be judged by its ability to stir the hearts of the people. The great republican era of the late eighteenth century that witnessed the French and American Revolutions, that lopped off the head of one absolute monarch and shook thrones throughout Europe, that launched decades of wars both imperial and civil, was nevertheless an age characterized by a great concern for moral philosophy and, in particular, concepts of natural rights, justice, and humanitarianism. Taken together, this tradition acted to limit the circumstances, degree, and kind of actions that could be justified by the new doctrines of the anarchist movement. Republicans were just as fond of secret societies as were the anarchists, but their ethics of violence were directly opposite that of the anarchists: republicans conspired to rouse the people to violence, whereas the anarchists plotted violence to rouse the people.

It is difficult to trace the roots of anarchist ethics too deeply into the past without finding them tangled with many other philosophical and theological traditions, but certainly the disillusionment felt by supporters of the failed liberal revolutions throughout Europe in 1848 represents a watershed between Enlightenment ethics of the eighteenth century and the rise of a new nihilist negation of them. The democratic revolutions of 1848 were crushed by monarchical governments and by the betrayal of working-class demands by bourgeois reformers. The failure of liberal reform drove several influential writers to not only rethink their strategies of reform but to also question the liberal tradition entirely. Mikhail Bakunin could certainly be counted in this group, but he was predated and overshadowed by Alexander Herzen, who is rightly considered the grandfather of Russian revolutionary thinking.

Herzen was one of the first authors to not only attack liberal theories of government, which he dismissed as "the last dream of the old world," but to also reject the whole Enlightenment apparatus of rights, morality, and progress. Progress was an oppressive idea that shackled the living for the betterment of a promised future, which is often an illusion. Herzen rejected the idea that any eternal moral ideals existed apart from the needs and aspirations of living people. Ethics could not be derived from laws of historical development, as Jean-Jacques Rousseau so famously attempted to do, because history obeyed no laws. Therefore, morality was only what people made of it, and the highest—perhaps the only—value was liberty; as Herzen put it, "The truly free man creates his own morality." Herzen had no sympathy for any existing institutions and was one of the first to celebrate ruination as a liberating and creative force. "Let all the world perish! Long live chaos and destruction!"[6]

Herzen's striking opposition to moral precepts and values ran directly against the Enlightenment winds that had been blowing for a century. Remarkably, Herzen's unique amorality surfaced at the same moment in the writing of the German thinker Karl Heinzen, who also overthrew what he considered to be the sentimental and overly tenderhearted idealists of the republican tradition. In 1849 Heinzen published an essay that provided a most novel justification for political violence. Appropriately titled "Der Mord" (Murder), it was written soon after Heinzen's immigration to America and his disillusionment with the crushed democratic revolutions of 1848. In it Heinzen flayed liberals who had placed their faith in the power of their righteous principles, people who "said so often that the freedom party has no need to concern itself with numbers, that its principles alone is sufficient assurance of victory, that ultimately it will overcome any enemy no matter how powerful, etc." Heinzen failed to see by what actual mechanism such goodness would prevail: "This mere vague belief in the moral force and ultimate victory of . . . freedom over that of barbarism is merely a soporific, an instrument of self-destruction." Like Marx, who was just then penning *The Communist Manifesto*, Heinzen believed that actual things and actions, not ideas, moved history. Though unlike Marx, who preferred to paint a broader canvas and to speak more figuratively of classes, conflict, and struggle, Heinzen minced no words about what history showed him to be the mainspring of change. "Murder," Heinzen wrote, "is the principal agent of historical progress." Such a simple and plain equation between violence and social advancement reoriented the ethical imperatives of those seeking freedom, for to not act in the face of the possibility of advancing liberty through one's actions now was to condemn society to continuing oppression. As Heinzen put it, "To have a conscience with regard to the murdering of reactionaries is to be totally unprincipled. They wreak destruction, in any way they can, thereby obliging us to respond in kind as defenders of justice and humanity." The question became not whether to act violently but how to employ violence most effectively. Heinzen indicated how unbounded his theories of murder were and foreshadowed the later anarchists' celebration of Alfred Nobel as the greatest liberator of mankind through his invention of dynamite when he concluded: "The greatest benefactor of mankind will be he who makes it possible for a few men to wipe out thousands."[7]

Heinzen's reasoned defense of murder proved very popular with the anarchists of the 1880s, who reprinted it frequently in their newspapers and wrote paeans to Heinzen crediting their debt to him as one of their intellectual forebears. Dr. Edward Nathan-Ganz, one of the anarchists most directly responsible for spreading revolutionary anarchist ideology to America (see chapter 4), hailed Heinzen's influence in the pages of Chicago's *Vorbote*. Robert Reitzel, the most literary-minded of German American anarchists in the late nineteenth century, wrote poetry to Heinzen's memory. The famed anarchist Johann Most was arrested in New York after he had the unfortunate timing of republishing Heinzen's essay on the very day that Leon Czolgosz assassinated President William McKinley in 1901, adding in a preface that the article "was true yet today."[8]

A new ethics of violence also arose in Russia, particularly among the "Generation of the Sixties," which was led by student radicals whose protests closed St. Petersburg University in 1861. Outlawry and political violence had long been seen as natural, and even progressive forces among Russian intellectuals and revolutionaries from the Decembrists onward were deeply enamored of the Russian tradition of peasant brigands and populist bandits and adapted their antiauthoritarian courage to the language of modern politics. Student radical Peter Zaichnevsky and his pamphlet *Young Russia* (1862), a tract that called for a "bloody and pitiless" campaign against Russia's monarchy in which "rivers of blood will flow and that perhaps even innocent victims will perish," marked the beginning of a new era in which small underground groups attempted to rouse the slumbering masses against the czarist government.[9]

This generation of radicals would adopt a thorough materialism; their intellectual hero was not Marx but Ludwig Büchner, whose 1864 book, *Force and Matter*, rejected all spiritualism, idealism, and romanticism on the grounds that nothing but matter and forces exist. Such absolute reduction of all philosophical problems to atoms and vectors appealed to the Russian "Generation of the Sixties" not only because it provided a clear, rational basis for uprooting a thousand years of encrusted traditions sanctioned by God, crown, and custom, but also because it provided the grounds for a new revolutionary ethics. Büchner's conclusion was pitiless in its iconoclasm: "We must finally be permitted to leave all questions about morality and utility out of sight. The chief and indeed the sole object which concerned us in these researches is truth. Nature exists neither for religion, for morality, nor for human beings; but it exists for itself. What else can we do but take it as it is? Would it not be ridiculous in us to cry like little children because our bread is not sufficiently buttered?" Russian student radicals began calling themselves "Nihilists" in recognition of their hard materialism and the willingness to question all values, traditions, and institutions that fidelity to a single truth, the truth of natural facts alone, required. Nicholas Chernyshevsky, one of the first of this generation to be persecuted for his views, extolled such ascetic virtues as the true calling of the revolutionary in his 1862 novel, *What Is to Be Done?* while wasting away in his cell in St. Petersburg's Peter and Paul Fortress.[10]

What Is to Be Done? was a work that, despite its ponderous plot and its coded references, inspired generations of Russian radicals with its portrait of a new revolutionary hero, Rakhmetov, a young man who happily sacrificed all the pleasures of normal life for the cause. Rakhmetov focused all of his energies on steeling himself for the revolutionary struggle to come: he built his muscles, abstained from liquor and sex, slept on a thin mat, and cut himself off from all close human relationships. The greatest test of Rakhmetov's devotion to the people was not the bed of nails he slept on one night to prove to himself he could withstand torture, but the young woman caught in a runaway carriage whom he saved by grabbing the rear axle as it passed and wrestling it to a stop. Torn and bruised, he was taken back to the young widow's dacha to recover from his wounds, and after a fortnight the woman confessed her love and urged him to marry her. Rakhmetov refused, saying:

> "You see, such people as I have no right to unite the fate of any one else with their own."
> "Yes, that is true," she said; "you have no right to marry. But till the time when you must renounce me, love me."
> "No, I cannot accept that," he said. "I must suppress love in my heart; to love you would tie my hands. Even as it is, they cannot be free so soon, for they are already tied. But I shall untie them. I must not love."[11]

Soon a secret student organization calling itself Hell adopted a personal code of revolutionary asceticism modeled on Chernyshevsky's hero that required abstinence from all luxuries, celibacy, and the separation of the revolutionary from all social connections, including one's family. On April 4, 1866, Hell member Dmitry Karakozov approached Czar Alexander II as he was climbing into his carriage at the Summer Palace, aimed a double-barreled pistol at his head, and fired, though his shot was jostled off target by a drunken worker who stumbled against his elbow. After his execution, Karakozov was hailed as a martyr by revolutionaries everywhere, but his standing as a revolutionary hero soared with the publication of Alexander Herzen's exposé of the Russian secret police in 1867 titled "The White Terror." In it Herzen described Karakozov's unflinching resolve under indescribable torture, his determination not to confess or beg pardon, turning Karakozov into the embodiment of the heroic ascetic revolutionary. (Of course,

Herzen's story was untrue—Karakozov actually recanted, found religion, and apologized for his act before being sentenced to hang—but his sympathizers refused to believe Russian accounts of his appeal for clemency.)[12]

Karakozov's daring to take matters into his own hands inspired many others to consider how much impact the act of a single person could have. A young dropout from the University of Moscow, Sergei Gannadevich Nechaev, took these ideas furthest and ended up codifying the substance of a nihilist ethics in a notorious essay titled *Catechism of the Revolutionist*. Nechaev's *Catechism* was so extreme that even his friend and one-time collaborator, Mikhail Bakunin, distanced himself from it as soon as it became public. Nechaev was well aware of its incriminating ferocity, hiding his copy with a secret code that the Russian state police could not crack without help from Nechaev's associates. *Catechism of the Revolutionist* was so shocking that the Russian prosecutors, eager to uproot the underground network of student revolutionaries, found it an irresistible piece of evidence to introduce to the court at the trial of Nechaev and his comrades. No one outside of these secret radical circles had seen the manuscript until the czarist state published the transcript of the trial in a government report in 1871.

The *Catechism*'s power derived from its synthesis of all the previous threads of extreme revolutionary thought. It combined the tactics of propaganda by deed with Chernyshevsky's revolutionary asceticism and overlay the whole with the nihilist's rejection of all moral precepts as empty bourgeois sentimentality. "All tender, effeminizing feelings of kinship, friendship, love, gratitude, and even of honor itself must be suppressed in him by a total cold passion for the revolutionary cause." Hanging over Nechaev's prose, like the mist over a graveyard, is a chilling longing for destruction, blood, and death. So pervasive was this sense of doom that in the end Nechaev defined a heroism that was based less on the revolutionaries' millennial goals than on their stoic martyrdom. The *Catechism*'s opening line was, "The revolutionary is a doomed man."[13]

Catechism of the Revolutionist was a work that not only defied and negated all moral feelings and values but also constructed a consistent nihilist ethics that defined as moral anything that advanced the triumph of the revolution: "Everything that facilitates the victory of the revolution is moral . . . Everything that hinders it is immoral and criminal." Such expressions were not really new, as Karl Heinzen had written of murder in a similar way more than a decade earlier. But Nechaev took the next step and detailed the sorts of actions that revolutionaries had to be willing to take in order to best achieve their goals, such as drawing up lists of names of the enemies of the people who must be killed.

Perhaps most eye-opening was that Nechaev applied the same revolutionary ethics that permitted all manner of actions against bourgeois society to the internal operations of the revolutionary movement itself. Revolutionaries, Nechaev demanded, had to be ruthless and duplicitous in their treatment even of members of their own organizations. Nechaev recommended that a revolutionary cultivate followers whom he could take advantage of and exploit as needed: "He has to look upon them as part of the general revolutionary capital placed at his disposal." (Nechaev later proved himself true to his own precepts when he organized the strangulation of one of his young followers whom he felt had become unreliable.) Revolutionaries had to use the full arsenal of human deceit available to them to undermine bourgeois society—for Nechaev, people were nothing other than material to be orchestrated and exploited for the cause. This is the reason for severing all close relationships, for Nechaev recognized that any genuine feelings of compassion or connection with others threatened a revolutionary's ability to lie, cheat, and manipulate. Love and friendship were dangerous because they had the power to "stay his hand."[14]

Some passages of the *Catechism* were prophetic in their recommendations as to how a revolutionary group should operate. In part 2, "The Attitude of the Revolutionary toward His Revolutionary Comrades," Nechaev directs revolutionary groups to make collective decisions and plans but with the understanding that such plans would be carried out by individual initiative. "Comrade-revolutionaries . . . must, insofar as possible, discuss all major matters together and decide them as one man. In fulfilling the plan determined in this manner, each must count on himself, insofar as possible. In the fulfillment of a series of destructive actions each must act himself." This sounds eerily like the theory introduced by the prosecution at the trial of the Haymarket anarchists in 1886, in which it was alleged that a general plan had been agreed upon at a secret meeting of the armed groups on Monday, May 3, which was then to be carried out the following night by each member's own individual initiative. Moreover, the real revolutionaries were also given specific advice about what to do with the "doctrinaires, the conspirators . . . idly prating . . . on paper." They needed to be thrust to the front and put in danger, where they might, by their actions or their sacrifice, do some real good. "One must ceaselessly push and drag them forward, into real skull-cracking commitments, as a consequence of which the majority will perish without a trace and a few will yield some genuine revolutionary results." (It is intriguing to wonder if such advice might not have been followed in the case of the Haymarket riot when the most rabid radicals somehow happened to be miles away when the bomb was thrown, but the more moderate anarchists—August Spies, Albert Parsons, and Samuel Fielden—were all on the scene because they had been asked by the others to speak at the rally.)

The *Catechism*'s revolutionary ethics proved to be a mixture that was as intoxicating to the revolutionaries of this age as it was repulsive to all others. After being published by the Russian government, it was regularly reprinted in anarchist journals in various forms for the next few decades. Johann Most, probably the most influential anarchist of his generation, published portions of it in his London journal, *Freiheit*, in 1880 and reprinted it again after he moved his paper to New York. Albert Parsons published sections of the *Catechism* in his Chicago newspaper, the *Alarm*, twice "by request" in the months leading up to the Haymarket bombing.[15]

Nevertheless, the ferocity and totality of the *Catechism*'s amorality was more than most social revolutionaries could stomach. Few anarchist leaders, with the possible exception of Johann Most, repeated its most troubling call to all revolutionaries to wring out of their beings all human compassion and affections. But the romanticism of the image of the totally dedicated revolutionary had its appeal. Even Yankee labor reform journals were swept up in it: the San Francisco *Truth* and Denver's *Labor Enquirer* published a paean to the totally dedicated activist that concluded, "The Revolutionist seeks the happiness of others at whatever cost, sacrificing for it his own. His ideal is a life full of suffering, and a martyr's death." Apparently others drew from these ideas a clear and convincing justification for using violence, even attacks against ordinary individuals, in pursuit of revolutionary change.[16]

These ideas filtered into the United States slowly. Publications like *Le Révolté* were passed from hand to hand, and choice articles were reprinted in American publications like Chicago's *Vorbote*. But they did not begin to take deep root until a forceful and single-minded man arrived in America to advocate them. Dr. Edward Nathan-Ganz was the first public advocate in America of a new revolutionary creed with an almost magical belief in the power of individual acts of violence and a moral philosophy that excused them.

Edward Nathan-Ganz and Anarchist Morals

In the summer of 1880, a short, dark-complexioned, bespectacled man calling himself Alexander Rodenow boarded a steamer in Liverpool, arrived in New York, and was promptly naturalized with the name Dr. Edward Nathan-Ganz (it was not uncommon at this time for Europeans fresh off the boats to be taken before a local judge and granted citizenship). Nathan-Ganz's background is murky. On the Continent he used various other aliases, including Bernhardt Wyprecht and the surname de Costa. Various sources describe him as either a German or a Russian. When arrested in London in December 1881 on an extradition warrant from The Hague, Nathan-Ganz claimed to have been born in Budapest, Hungary, a country that conveniently had no extradition treaty in force with Holland. He may have been from an aristocratic family, for he had much formal education and was reputed to be conversant in a dozen languages. (His extant writings do indicate that he was an elegant writer in both English and German.) Other sources indicate he had previously lived in France and was associated with a Parisian social revolutionary club.[17] According to an early chronicler of anarchism, Nathan-Ganz had worked with Johann Most publishing the *Freiheit* in London. Most's newspaper *Freiheit* was a bellwether of the sharpening mood of radicalism at that very moment.[18]

Nathan-Ganz was a rare sort of true internationalist and revolutionary. He regularly traveled between England, America, and the European continent, apparently supporting his activities through various fraudulent sales schemes. A reporter for a London daily found Nathan-Ganz holed up in The Hague, Netherlands, in 1881 and interviewed him in a "very comfortable" suite of rooms he had rented. On the wall were two pictures, one of Nathan-Ganz's mother and the other of a pretty young woman who had been sent to Siberia for her nihilist activities. The reporter noted that the table in the room was covered with books, newspapers, postal cards, and a revolver. When asked if he was planning to travel on through Europe, Nathan-Ganz told the reporter that he had been banned from entering France and several other nations, though he did not say why.[19]

If Nathan-Ganz arrived in America as Most's apostle of direct action, his earliest activities did not leave much of a mark on the historical record. It is said that he founded New York City's Social Revolutionary Club, but soon after doing so it seems that Nathan-Ganz trekked north to that great cradle of reform, Boston. Likely his trip was a pilgrimage to visit one of the greatest German radical essayists of his generation, Karl Heinzen, who had immigrated to the States in 1847. In America Heinzen edited and published one of the longer-lived radical journals, *Der Pioneer*, but enthusiasts of direct action such as Nathan-Ganz probably knew him best as the author of "Der Mord," one of the seminal works of revolutionary anarchism in that it laid a firm philosophical basis for tyrannicide. Heinzen had lived in Boston since 1858 and died there on November 12, 1880, just about the time that Nathan-Ganz may have arrived. His interest in Heinzen was evident, as his first writing to appear in an American publication was an homage to Karl Heinzen on the occasion of his death, published in Chicago's *Vorbote*. Nathan-Ganz's eulogy was pained by the knowledge that Heinzen did not live to see the fruit of his labors: "Poor friend . . . you weren't able to see the moment when a new time started. Your spirit will be with us and you will be looked upon as our idol for new deeds."[20]

Nathan-Ganz stayed in Boston and picked up Heinzen's fallen pen. Less than a month after Heinzen's death, Nathan-Ganz launched the first revolutionary anarchist journal in America in the English language. Appearing in December 1880, the *An-Archist: Socialistic Revolutionary Review* was not the usual fly-by-night sheet that Boston's lively intellectual and social community regularly sent off into the world. Nathan-Ganz had ambitious plans and told fellow radical publishers in his prospectus that his journal would be a "magazine in large format (28 pages)" with an initial printing of twenty thousand copies. Moreover, it was to be established with well-known agents (whom Nathan-Ganz referred to as "collaborators") in leading centers of anarchist agitation: Felix Pyat in Paris; the aging lion of the Italian civil war, Giuseppe Garibaldi, in Rome; the infamous Russian nihilist Leo Hartmann; Adhemar Schwitzguebel in Geneva, Switzerland; and, of course, Johann Most in London. Assisting Nathan-Ganz in Boston was the well-known and respected labor essayist W. G. H. Smart. Dispelling his investors' and supporters' skepticism about his ability to finance such an operation, Nathan-Ganz posed as an independently wealthy man: "Ample means and the exclusion of a personal gain, put me in a state of sacrificing for my ideas and the cause I defend."[21]

In his advance-sheet prospectus, Nathan-Ganz laid out for his journal the task of serving as "a rallying point and an assembling ground of the till now scattered socialistic army on this continent." Except for the fact that the journal was to be written in English and aimed at an American readership, its stated principles were similar to those of Johann Most's *Freiheit*. Like Most, Nathan-Ganz seemed clearer about what he did not want his journal to contain than what principles he stood for. "We will not proclaim this review to be a 'Bible' of Socialism, nor will we make it a vehicle for *dogmas*. We will not advance any utopian theories, having for their object an ultimate fixed state—to be the climax of all social evolution . . . We will not load our pages with dry theoretical abstractions, indigestible by common understanding." At bottom the *An-Archist* rested on the idea that "*force* has since the beginning of history been the *accoucher* ("birth") of any serious reform; we have the sincere conviction, and will strain our efforts to impart it to the masses, that their only salvation is in *Revolution*."[22]

Judging by the only full issue that exists along with a list of the highlights of a second issue that is lost, the *An-Archist* lived up to its promises. It was not dogmatic, giving room to both local Boston reformer W. G. H. Smart, who led off one column by admitting that he "does not pretend to be an an-archist in the sense explained on a preceding page," though he was in agreement "with the anarchic wing of the Socialistic Movement in believing that the first step towards the attainment of economic revolution . . . is the overthrow of all existing political institutions." Nor was it dry; one article by a "Dr. Medicus" advised against the use of one's sexual organs for pleasure alone. It was a spread-eagled advocate of force, reprinting in its first issue Felix Pyat's essay on "Revolutionary War Science." ("For the good of the people, iron and fire—all arms are human, all forces legitimate, and all means sacred . . . Killing, burning—all means are justifiable. Use them; then will be peace!") Practical measures were detailed in "Col. N . . . Z['s]" (surely Nathan-Ganz) explanation of the proper use of street barricades. Its second issue featured Bakunin's essay "The Principles of Revolution," an article by Johann Most on the current state of socialism in Germany, and another contribution from "Col. N . . . Z" on "Revolutionary War Science," this installment dealing with the use of explosives.[23]

Nathan-Ganz's newspaper survived long enough to publish only two issues. Just as he was printing his second number, in March 1881, he was arrested for fraud—for selling through newspaper advertisements expensive watches that he never delivered. His newspaper was an inadvertent casualty of his arrest. Nathan-Ganz was put on trial in late March and released later that week. A few months later he turned up in London as a delegate to the London Congress that established the anarchist version of the International Workingmen's Association, commonly known as the Black International.[24]

The Spread of the Black International

Most's imprisonment for praising the assassination of the czar kept him from participating in the most important international revolutionary congress of his life: its secret sessions held in a back room of the Fitzroy Arms on Euston Road, just a couple of miles from his cell in Coldbath Fields, Clerkenwall. There the bones of the old International Workingmen's Association (IWA) were disinterred, and this venerable name, once belonging to an organization headed by Karl Marx himself but since dead for five years, was updated to the more inclusive International Working People's Association (IWPA). The London Congress of July 14–19, 1881, resurrected the idea of an international socialist organization, but more importantly it marked the beginning of a new phase of the revolutionary movement, for it was in that sweltering London pub that this new organization decided that propaganda by deed was its defining strategy.

Here was the opportunity that many German American advocates of force had been waiting for: a new departure that afforded them the opportunity to define themselves and their movement more clearly, to ally themselves with a new international movement, and to finally step out from the shadow of the toothless and doddering SLP. Eagerly they appointed members to represent them in London or, lacking funds to send someone to England, arranged to be formally represented by proxy.

Every major grouping of revolutionary socialism on the continent—Parisian communards, Jura Mountain artisans of Switzerland, German political refugees, Basque cells, Italian plotters, Russian nihilists, and others—were represented. Three delegates traveled directly from the United States with credentials from New York, Philadelphia, Chicago, Boston, and Mexico City. In attendance were a number of leading revolutionaries, most famously the anarchist philosopher Peter Kropotkin, but also including a number of individuals who had already taken up arms in their struggle for socialism: Italian firebrand Enrico Malatesta and his comrade Vito Solieri had fought with Carlo Cafiero in the failed attempt to spark a peasant uprising four years earlier. French anarchist and schoolteacher Louise Michel had been one of the last defenders of the last barricade at Montmartre as the Paris Commune fell. Validating their importance was the presence of a French police agent, one Monsieur Serreaux, whose identity was uncovered years later.[25]

The Social Revolutionary Club of New York City sent one of its own founding (and apparently pugnacious) members, Carl Seelig, to represent it in London. Two members of a Boston Revolutionary Club voyaged to England: Marie Le Compte and Dr. Edward Nathan-Ganz, though Nathan-Ganz officially represented a Mexican labor federation. Two other American groups were represented by proxy. In all, the United States was one of the best-represented countries at the congress, having a total of five out of forty-five delegates, the third largest representation after the host nation England and nearby France.[26]

Boston's delegate Marie Le Compte, though portrayed by historians of anarchism as a flighty romantic, was a remarkable woman. She was an associate editor of the *New York Labor Standard* and translated key works of

Bakunin and Kropotkin into English and delivered speeches on the revolutionary potential of beggars, tramps, and outlaws in half a dozen countries. She not only took part in the Paris bread riot of March 1883 with famed communard Louis Michel, but also was, as she later recalled, "the 'Anglaise' who wore the red scarf, and 'led,' as they call it, the rioters to pillage the bake-shops and knock the heads off the 'St. Josephs,' 'Virgin Marys,' and 'Infant Jesuses,'" which she called "horrible monstrosities in plaster." She was then wounded in a skirmish with the police and had to flee to Switzerland to escape arrest.[27]

Even before the congress commenced, the seriousness of its revolutionary purpose was proclaimed by Kropotkin, who distributed a circular stating that the upcoming meeting was for the purpose of establishing two organizations: one a public association to represent workers and the other an underground society for the purpose of coordinating the activities of small groups of conspirators. Within the anarchist movement, the heightened feeling of many that they held the fate of society in their hands was intensified even further by the conspiratorial and secret methods of organizing encouraged by these new anarchist principles. When anarchists met in London for an international conference in 1881, delegates arrived not knowing where the meeting was to take place. Each conferee was met individually and guided to a secret location, where they were assigned a code number that was used in place of their names for all business. During the meeting the delegates agreed not to elect any chairpersons, speakers, or officers who by their leadership would be at greater risk of prosecution, and no formal votes on matters of policy were tallied. It took three days for the group to work through the preliminaries of reports, statements of solidarity, and lengthy debates over whether or not to publish "official" proceedings (it was decided this was too undemocratic, and every delegate was free to tell the newspapers whatever they wished), and whether to appoint a central committee (this idea was shot down in favor of designating corresponding secretaries without official powers). While such precautions were not the product of unfounded paranoia—years later it was discovered that there were at least two police agents in attendance—they were also less effective at protecting the secrets of the movement than they were in offsetting the gathering's sparse attendance with a sense that their numbers meant less than their resolve.

When the autonomy of all groups involved was duly endorsed by all, the discussion turned to the ever-present revolutionary question of "What is to be done?" Edward Nathan-Ganz, recently arrived from Boston, gave his answer in the plainest terms. He suggested using the funds already collected for the purpose of publishing instruction manuals to train their followers how to make bombs. If there was enough money, Nathan-Ganz thought, the best use of it would be to found a secret military school where modern principles of chemistry could be taught. His Boston colleague Marie Le Compte supported him with a compromise, ditching the chemistry school but supporting the idea of having local groups publish secret bomb-making manuals in many languages. There was little opposition to such incendiary proposals, and the recorded debates dealt more with the question of which group was drier tinder for the revolutionary spark, peasants or industrial workers. On the necessity of killing people there was great unanimity.[28]

Despite the antipathy of the leading members toward hierarchy, authority, and the entanglements of laws, the congress did finally agree upon a "federative compact," which was issued with the admonition: "The Congress, recognizing that it has no other right than to indicate a general outline of what it considers the best form of revolutionary socialistic organization, leaves the groups to initiate such organizations, secret or not, as may seem to them useful in effecting the triumph of the Social Revolution." This quasi-platform was quickly published in slightly varying forms in many radical journals, most notably *Le Révolté* in Paris, the *Freiheit* in London, *Liberty* in Boston, and *Vorbote* in Chicago. Brimming with revolutionary fervor, the London Congress "compact" is striking in that it is mostly concerned with questions of method rather than principle. It details the best means of igniting the revolutionary fires rather than bothering to itemize the evils to be abolished or even to draw the outlines of the paradise to be won. Central to its plans was a willingness to employ violence as a propaganda tactic:

> Whereas the International Workingmen's Association deems it necessary to add "Propaganda by Deed" to oral and written propaganda; and, furthermore, whereas the moment of a general conflagration is not far distant, and the revolutionary elements of all countries will be called upon to do their utmost—the congress urges all organizations affiliated with the International Workingmen's Association to heed the following proposals:
>
> It is absolutely necessary to exert every effort towards propagating, by deeds, the revolutionary idea and to arouse the spirit of revolt in those sections of the popular masses who still harbor illusions about the effectiveness of legal methods.
>
> Those who no longer believe that legality will bring about the revolution will have to use methods that are in conformity with that belief . . . it is absolutely necessary . . . to keep in mind that a deed performed against the existing institutions appeals to the masses much more than thousands of leaflets and torrents of words.[29]

Such a clarion call for immediate violent action had never before been so openly and directly made outside of Russia. Apparently, however, even this rhetoric was the tame public version of darker plots discussed behind the closed doors of that Charrington Street tavern. The report of the "Compact" written by one delegate (probably Le Compte) and published in Benjamin Tucker's Boston *Liberty*, began with the offhand remark, "Of course, the Congress could not declare publicly its full opinion regarding revolutionary methods of action, but in the following resolutions it expressed a few ideas on this point."[30]

The seriousness with which these words were taken marked a new phase of the movement, and more than a few intrepid activists drew up their courage and followed their principles. The decade that followed the London declaration was one filled with a dramatic series of political robberies, murders, and bombings across Europe, all linked to individuals just one or two degrees removed from those present at the London Congress.[31] *Liberty* recognized the deadly seriousness of this innovation and warned, "Only the future can determine how far the Congress was wise in subordinating propagandism by voice and pen to what it calls 'propagandism by fact.'"[32]

Though many novel elements were expressed in its lengthy declaration, the point of greatest significance was that for the first time an international socialist organization had established that armed revolutionary activity was its primary strategy and that propaganda by deed was a useful tactic toward this end.[33] To Nathan-Ganz and the other Americans quaffing their pints amid the bellicose speeches of their comrades, this coming epoch was one to be swept in a socialist apocalypse of nearly biblical dimensions. Nathan-Ganz wrote of the congress:

> I am sure that the London Congress will in future history mark the beginning of a new period, the period of the solution of the social question, the only question worthy of the attention of *men*, the only question truly existing, which, like the Gordian knot, admits no other resolution than the sword. The London Congress means the beginning of the *Social Revolution* of that inevitable, sublime-terrible hurricane, purifying the present heavy-laden atmosphere and dispersing the clouds from that divine picture: *Universal Happiness and Universal Freedom.*[34]

Nathan-Ganz's view of the importance of the London Congress was endorsed in certain circles of American radicals, especially the German socialists in New York City and Chicago who not only shared his millennial vision, enthusiasm for chemistry and the propaganda by deed, but also organized as quickly as they could to ratify the London Congress's means and methods as their own.

The Chicago Conference

The London Congress that founded the Black International the second week of July 1881 was followed shortly by a similar gathering held in Chicago that October. The organizers of the American conference explicitly linked their meeting to the one in London. An early announcement of the Chicago meeting stated, "A National Socialistic-Revolutionary Congress is to be held in Chicago, beginning October 21, for the purpose of forming an American federation of the International Working-People's Association recently reorganized at London. The initiative in calling the congress is taken by those groups which sent delegates from this country to the recent London congress."[35]

Nineteen delegates carrying credentials from fourteen cities assembled in Chicago's north-side Turnverein Hall and opened their first session by debating whether to proceed in secrecy or in the open. It was quickly resolved to keep the meeting open to the public. Without much discussion the delegates agreed to endorse the platform of the London Congress that had met earlier that year.

There was some wrangling over the wording of a resolution dealing with elections, though this question was not nearly as contentious an issue as has been supposed. August Spies drafted the call for the convention, and his wording made clear his own skepticism about the usefulness of voting: "Socialistic groups and sections of all shades, provided they are weary of compromise and desire to accomplish the social revolution by means other than political action, are invited to send delegates to Chicago."[36] Rather, the issue moved through the assembly with little drama. According to one participant's account of the conference, "one of the hardest contests" that arose over the three days of meetings was not that of elections but a disagreement over what to call the new organization: should it be the "International Working People's Association" or the "Revolutionary Socialistic Party"? But even this fight aroused little bitterness as this same observer recorded that by the end of the last day's proceedings, "It was the general opinion that no congress of the kind was ever so harmonious."[37]

Some diversity in views of political action were evident as the conference opened and delegates read the instructions they were given by the groups they represented. A. F. Hoffman, representing the Socialistic Educational Society of Milwaukee, stated that his group insisted that he oppose all alliances with capitalistic political parties they deemed a "decisive factor to achieve success." John P. Dusey, holding the proxy of the Social Revolutionary Club of Paterson, New Jersey, was instructed to oppose cooperation with all political parties except socialist ones, because they were all "reactionary weapons." Chicagoan Peter Peterson, representing a Kansas City group, declared his client's demand that all socialist candidates must be members in good standing for one year prior to their nominations. The Boston Liberty Club, whose delegate Joseph Swain traveled to Chicago to attend in person, drafted the longest list of resolutions, which included the club's desire to abandon appeals "to legislative and other political persons and bodies" and to sweep away "the great American superstition, that for the redress of social wrongs the ballot is the only and infallible instrument or agency." Understanding that the word "only" provided a sliver of redemption for the ballot in this instruction, no group sent explicit instructions to the congress demanding the new party's complete rejection of participation in elections. After all the proxies had been read, August Spies, representing the Chicago section, commented that he had been provided with written instructions but that these coincided with the others. Thus, by the conclusion of the first day's discussions, there was general agreement that the party might enter politics, but only when endorsing party members on a purely socialist platform and with a healthy skepticism about the possibility that socialism could ever be elected.[38]

Both August Spies and Albert Parsons were elected to the most important committee of the conference, the committee on resolutions, winning two of the five seats that seven delegates vied for. Peter Peterson and Joseph Swain were accepted, while two delegates both representing armed groups, Theodore Blum of the Jaeger Verein and Theodore Polling representing the Lehr und Wehr Verein, fell short and did not win their seats. Historians have generally characterized the committee's fifth member, Justus Schwab of New York City, as having taken the opposite position on the political question from Parsons and Spies, but the record fails to support this contention.

Before the resolutions committee retired into executive session, several of the committee members stated their views on the electoral question. Schwab opened the debate by delivering what was described as a long speech in which he argued that political campaigns were not worth the effort they required. He pointed to Massachusetts, where laws protecting workers had passed but were then ignored. More threatening was the fact that once socialists entered a political contest, politicians from capitalist parties attempted to exert control and brought their money and corruption into their ranks. Schwab pointed to the unhappy experiences of socialists in California who had been captured by anti-Chinese populists to illustrate this point. Rather, he concluded, it was simply a better use of their time to put all their efforts toward spreading their ideas and principles and to work for the "mass revolution."

If the excerpt of Schwab's speech preserved in the pages of the *Vorbote* is an accurate summary of his views, and if Schwab represented the toughest position on the resolutions committee, then whatever disagreement there was over the question of voting was simply a matter of tactics and expediency rather than a more fundamental one of principle. Schwab, at least at this time, was not opposed to liberal democratic institutions. The day before the conference convened he was interviewed by a reporter, and when asked how he hoped to achieve his goal of overthrowing the capitalist system, he said, "by all means," including elections. "We intend to uphold the political institutions which our forefathers fought for, and, if violence is used against us, we will go further." Ultimately, Schwab did not oppose political participation because it was contrary to socialist or anarchist doctrines but because it was a waste of their meager resources.[39]

In his response, August Spies agreed with Schwab that even when they won elections the party did not achieve much for socialism and that the point of their efforts should be to spread their ideals. Standing on the same understanding of politics as Schwab, Spies did not actually disagree with Schwab's criticism of political campaigns but rather wished to broaden his definition of what constituted agitation. Spies argued that elections were in fact one of the most effective methods of agitation and education of the masses. As the *Vorbote* summarized his argument, "Spies, however, spoke with great warmth in favor of participation in elections and could not see why the workers should not make use of their voting rights. One ought to go to the ballot box and there make the principles of the party clear to the people." This was especially true because when workers' representatives pass laws that are not executed, then the party has a uniquely effective issue to organize around. It is at that moment, Spies explained, that "we have something which is concrete and we can then fight with the law book in one hand and the weapon in the other."[40]

Albert Parsons, while not disputing any of the points raised by either Schwab or Spies, spoke from his greater understanding of the native population of American workers, reminding them that "we live in America" and that they had to accept the fact that Americans believed everything could be achieved through elections. Parsons asked if the party should not prove to the people that this idea was wrong and in that way win them to their cause. Parsons, Spies, and Schwab constituted a majority of the resolutions committee and pushed through a statement over the objections of Peterson and Swain. Given their agreement on fundamental principles, it was not that difficult to arrive at a plank that encompassed all their views by favoring "independent political action whenever such may be deemed advisable for the purpose of demonstrating to the workingmen the utter wrongfulness and inefficiency of our political institutions and the so-called free-ballot remedy."[41]

The remaining two members of the committee had little else in common besides their opposition to participating in elections. Joseph Swain, who represented the Boston circle of "individualist" anarchists led by Benjamin Tucker and who blended the thinking of Proudhon with such American proto-anarchists as Josiah Warren, Stephen Pearl Andrews, and William Greene, submitted a minority report that was a paean to individual sovereignty, economic cooperation, and rejection of all authority. Peterson did not sign on to Swain's manifesto, though he stood with him against Spies and Parson's ballot plank simply because he was utterly opposed to electoral politics in all circumstances.

On the last day of the conference the delegates took up the majority report and replaced the resolutions committee's electoral plank with a more specific one that established practical rules for electoral action. The final statement adopted by the congress read: "*Resolved*: That under no circumstances our members are allowed to vote for any person or with any party which does not absolutely approve our platform." In the end, the conference endorsed fighting capitalism through the ballot box, although it chose not to state officially what Parsons and Spies believed: that the only purpose of doing so was to show that capitalist democracy was a fraud. Clearly all the delegates, whether from Chicago or New York, and even the autonomist Joseph Swain, agreed that elections could not do what republican theory claimed it could: implement the people's will. Parsons and Spies, contrary to their depictions by leading scholars, did not stand apart from their revolutionary comrades on this or any other fundamental point; rather, they merely stood for a bit more candor in the party's declaration.[42]

None of these debates were bitter, prolonged, or fought without compromise, because all those who gathered in Chicago were there for the same reason. They were all, as Spies's invitation described them, "weary of compromise" and desiring "to accomplish the social revolution by means other than political action." The one element of the resolution committee's recommendation that passed on to the final draft without alteration of a single word was its most militant. This was a resolution favoring "the organization of the revolutionary propaganda and preparation for an aggressive warfare to be waged against the system, supporters and upholders of exploitation of man by man, and to introduce in its stead free social and industrial cooperation." It seems, then, that the bedrock consensus of the gathering was that the "means other than political action" of the party they founded should prepare the masses for "aggressive warfare" (*angriffskreig*). To this end the group officially recognized "the armed organizations of workingmen who stand ready with the gun to resist the encroachments upon their rights."[43]

A fortnight after the congress adjourned, the German section of the SLP assembled for a meeting to discuss their role in the upcoming fall elections. August Spies was elected chairman and used his bully pulpit to gush with praise for what the Chicago Conference had accomplished. The results of the conference were unexpectedly positive; he was surprised at how fast the platform was assembled and how clear and effective it was. He was glad that the Chicago Conference had officially and uncritically endorsed the resolutions of the London Congress, a program that Spies said he completely agreed with. The only thing he disagreed with was the choice of Revolutionary Socialistic Party (RSP) as the name of the new party; clearly Spies preferred aligning the organization more closely with the revolutionary anarchists of Europe by adopting their same name (the International Working People's Association).[44]

In just one year from the time Dr. Edward Nathan-Ganz and Wilhelm Hasselmann stepped off their gangplanks onto American soil, a new movement of revolutionary anarchism had organized out of the ashes of the Socialist Labor Party. Unlike socialist or anarchist movements in America's past, leaders of this movement viewed neither the ballot box nor the trade union as having the capacity to redeem capitalism. Instead, all practical measures were directed at one end—sparking or aiding the mass insurrection of the working class. Spies, Parsons, and the other Chicago "socialistic revolutionaries" had succeeded in reorienting American socialism away from its libertarianism and its republicanism. Instead they embraced an imported and foreign ideology of direct violent action, distilled in the pressure cooker of European tyranny by conspiratorial alchemists huddled in the free cities of Geneva and London.

Yet despite the enthusiasm and the celebrations for the work that had been accomplished at the Chicago Conference, once the red and black flags, the banners of fighting slogans, and the flowers adorning the dais were taken down, little was done to promote the new Revolutionary Socialistic Party. So little was done in the months after the party's founding that even its least enthusiastic delegate, Joseph Swain, who had been outvoted at every turn, complained, noting that the three-person committee led by August Spies that was charged with publishing the proceedings of the congress had shirked its work. (While Swain was correct and the committee had been dilatory, it may have been that Spies was distracted by personal problems at the time, as he was sued for debts and a property he owned at 10 Marion Place was foreclosed upon later that year.)[45]

The torpid pace of progress of the new Revolutionary Socialistic Party after the Chicago conference was not due to any lack of commitment or ardor on the part of its organizers but was a consequence of the arrival in America of a man widely viewed as the world's greatest prophet of immediate, unblinking, by any means, revolution. When Johann Most landed, he immediately became the movement's most effective organizer and for a time the focus of all the efforts and plans of local RSP organizers.

On December 18, 1882, the steamer *Wisconsin* tied up to a Manhattan pier, and a slight man with a deformed face stepped off. Part of his jaw was missing from a childhood surgery that left all of his features slightly stretched to his left, a fact he tried to hide behind a full beard. Most was a reluctant immigrant: as noted earlier, he had been pushed out of England, where he had been jailed for praising the bombing of Czar Alexander II, and his publishing company had been shut down after he praised the stabbing assassination of Britain's top-ranked minister in Dublin by Irish separatists. He was met by a modest crowd of cheering supporters sporting red ribbons on their hats, lapels, and shirtwaists, who escorted him to Justus Schwab's saloon. That night Most spoke before an immense crowd in Cooper Union.

Most arrived not as a savior but as a symbol for the ideas and slogans that had preceded him and that he shouted from stages across the land. The Revolutionary Socialistic Party had been founded in Chicago, the New York Social Revolutionary Club had broken with Brooklyn's political socialists and become an independent party, and the great residue of Marx's old First International, represented by the hard-knuckled western workers used to fighting strikes with dynamite and fists, had all adopted revolutionary programs. These militants were rapidly being swept up into a movement that invested all of its hopes in a revolutionary whirlwind that would blow away the old order. The duty of every true socialist, then, was to prepare for the coming maelstrom. Educate and organize, to be sure—that was the reason for at least formally continuing to run for office or lead trade unions forward toward their petty demands—but most importantly, arm for the coming class war.[46]

Exploiting the splash of publicity that the arrival of the world's most notorious anarchist provoked from the nation's dailies, Most immediately entrained for a lengthy speaking tour, arriving a week later in Chicago, where he spoke before a capacity audience numbered in the thousands at the Aurora Turner Hall. He reveled in shocking his listeners with his wide embrace of the amoralist ethics of Nechaev: everything must be torn down and demolished, and all governors, priests, ministers, bankers, monopolists, and all opponents must be put to the knife like cattle; though on second thought he reconsidered and believed it might be more useful if they were put to building roads and other public improvements before they were killed. A revolution required funds, and these should be seized from banks and stores, robbed at every opportunity. Most repeated these sentiments in two national tours over the next six months that totaled as many as two hundred speeches.[47]

Journalists loved to report on his speeches, editors fell over one another looking for new ways to revile him, and publishers were content that news of Johann Most sold newspapers. The *Christian Index* ran itself out of metaphors in denouncing him: "He is the hobgoblin of anarchy . . . He deals absolutely in fire and brimstone. His nostrils smoke with wrath. He fairly wallows in allegoric gore. His coming is the avatar of the Demon of Destruction. He is the modern Attilla [*sic*]. He is the 'Giant of the Brocken,' presaging a new Reign of Terror, and a new era of guillotine days."[48]

Somehow Most's marathon speaking tours and the organization of new revolutionary socialistic clubs excited a number of influential Yankee labor reformers who found his muscular socialism stirring, even practical. Two such labor activists with large working-class followings, Burnette G. Haskell, who published *Truth* out of San Francisco and inherited the sandlot crowds from earlier demagogues like Denis Kearney, and Joseph Buchanan, whose Denver *Labor Enquirer* was very influential among western railway men and miners and who sat on the general executive board of the Knights of Labor, moved to join forces with the new revolutionary socialists. Suddenly new possibilities and new fields of agitation seemed to be opening.

At first *Truth* expressed both enthusiasm and a misunderstanding of the core principles of doctrines of force. It celebrated the arrival in New York City of the "fearless" Johann Most but described him as a sort of German Thomas Jefferson, saying that he "advocates the institution of a democratic, or popular Government," although "being embittered by continual persecution, the conviction ripened within him that legislation would never effect the desired ends and he gradually associated himself with the Social-Revolutionists . . . who advocate as means of accomplishment, revolution instead of legislation . . . No doubt California will not be behind in the race to do honor to the man who lives and suffered for a noble principle, and whose actions indicate that he is no less ready thus to sacrifice his very life. A hearty welcome to John Most!"[49]

Judging from the tone of the articles published in *Truth*, there seems to have been a very rapid evolution of Haskell and *his* contributors toward revolutionary force in the spring of 1883. When the year began it was clear that support for the use of bombs and acts of assassination was qualified by the observation that violence was the last resort of people who had no freedom or democratic power. *Truth* reveled in a speech given by Wendell Phillips, the "golden trumpet of abolition," the high point of which was Phillips extolling the righteousness of the nihilists and their tactics, but only for their own nation. Where tyrants and kings ruled, as in Russia, "in such a land dynamite and the dagger are the necessary and only proper substitute for Fanueil Hall . . . This is the only view an American, the child of 1620 and 1776, can take of Nihilism—any other unsettles and perplexes the ethics of our civilization."[50] Before long, clearer glimpses of the doctrines of force broke through the pages of *Truth*. When a letter to the editor agreed with the sentiments of Irish leader Michael Davitt, who urged the use of "moral dynamite" rather than "the chemical compound," Haskell responded cryptically, "How about dynamite for the purpose of propaganda?"[51] On the eve of the international conference that founded the Black International in London, *Truth* proclaimed itself an official organ of the International, among whose listed "objects" were "to eradicate the false impression of the people that redress can be obtained by the ballot."[52]

By the summer of 1883, *Truth* ran a front-page commentary titled "Revolution—Dynamite Will Be Used in America," which argued that the American republic had been taken over by the "money changers of the North," who had "obtained complete mastery over Congress and the Courts" since the Civil War. Monopolies had spread from money to land, transportation, telegraph, and in trade "until the people have been burdened almost beyond endurance by the oppression." By deftly shifting the focus from the denial of political rights, as in Russia, to the lack of liberties, equality, and rights in American industry, the author of the article was able to sidestep the usual objections to anarchist doctrines of force that in America the people have the power through the ballot box to accomplish reform without violence. Democracy, the writer said, was ineffective against such concentrations of money power, and the nation was instead set on a path toward bloody revolution. It would begin with a few "bomb-throwers" whose dynamite would make them the equal of armies. Once conflict had broken out, the masses of workers would "be forced into organization" and then the "Vanderbilts and the Jay Goulds, the Stanfords and the Crockers, the monopolists and big thieves . . . will be summarily disposed of." The current industrial system "must pass away" but will not do so "until washed out in blood."[53] *Truth* backed up its principled support for bombings by providing its readers with detailed instructions for brewing up nitroglycerine and mixing it into dynamite.[54] It also published a full account of the founding congress of the Black International and its resolutions.[55]

Burnette Haskell brought the new revolutionary doctrines to the workers of the West by blending the doctrines of force with traditions of labor reform. Haskell dressed up his new organization in the mantle of the defunct First International by naming it the International Workingmen's Association, Pacific Coast Division. Its bylaws blended doctrines of force with traditional socialist labor unionism. They declared it "the duty of every member . . . to assist and aid the organization of the Knights of Labor, the various Trade Unions, Farmers Alliances and all other forms of organization in which the producers have organized . . . themselves." This duty rested uneasily alongside the stated goals of the association, which included "to eradicate the false impression of the people that redress can be obtained by the ballot" and "to prepare the way for the direction of the coming social revolution by an enlightened and intelligent public thought."[56]

At the same time, the old SLP, which for a time had continued to hold some support among native-born Americans, sank further. In May 1883 the national secretary of the party, Philip Van Patten, went missing. A search of his apartment discovered a suicide note indicating that he took his own life because of the disappointments he had suffered in trying to build the party. Adding to the confusion was the mysterious disappearance of all the party files and records that were in Van Patten's trust, leaving remaining officials without even a list of the names or addresses of the party's members. (Some years later Van Patten resurfaced, having faked his own suicide as a way of making a complete break with the party.)[57]

August Spies and Paul Grottkau embarked on speaking tours that spring of 1883 and upon returning to Chicago reported that revolutionary socialism was gaining in favor everywhere they went. They now established the "Information Bureau" they had pledged to create a year and half before but had never undertaken. Perhaps they now sensed the vacuum that Van Patten's disappearance had created as well as a changed mood among socialists for a bolder and more forceful platform. It was, seemingly, an auspicious time to again organize a national congress of all the scattered groups that had joined their way of thinking: that revolution was near and revolutionary groups must begin preparing for it.[58]

In his official capacity as head of the Information Bureau, Spies issued a circular calling all "Socialists of North America . . . pioneers of Labor in the great Social War" to send delegates to a conference in Pittsburgh in October. The stated purpose of the meeting was to remedy the problem that was keeping socialists only half aware of their historic mission and preventing many from properly preparing "that force which is destined to abolish the infamous institutions of oppression." Perhaps Spies felt a tinge of irony when he identified this problem as "the deplorable dissension . . . of [all] who are working for the same end."[59]

If Spies really hoped that the upcoming Pittsburgh Congress would overcome socialist divisions and mark the beginning of a new era of united revolutionary action, he must have been sadly disappointed at the small and narrow showing of the twenty-six delegates present for its opening day. More than a third of those awarded their credentials were from the two poles of revolutionary agitation, New York and Chicago. All but two representatives were German. But if Spies and his Chicago comrades thought the problem they faced was not one of building the movement in terms of numbers but rather of focusing the thinking and plans of those few who counted, then the Pittsburgh Congress was a tremendous success. In Pittsburgh the socialist revolutionaries spoke out loudly and without the euphemistic wording cautiously adopted at the last conference in Chicago in favor of "energetic, relentless, revolutionary, and international action."[60]

A rare peek inside the thinking of Chicago's rank-and-file revolutionaries was afforded soon after the Pittsburgh Congress was announced. A general meeting of all the anarchist groups was held on Sunday morning, a time guaranteeing that all could attend and that there would be plenty of time to elect delegates and, more importantly, to hammer out a united stance for their representatives to carry to Pittsburgh. Though records of the arguments and debates of that meeting are nonexistent today, the final instructions and principles that were to guide their delegates have survived, and they reveal how Chicago's militants cherished their independence and were oriented toward actions, not principles:

> We, the socialists of Chicago, resolve to authorize our delegates for this year's socialist congress in Pittsburgh, Pa., to act for us in the following way:
>
> It is the duty and task of all socialists in the United States of North America, to unite more closely to avoid party quarrels and to attack jointly and with force our common enemy, the capitalists, because the social battle requires a great determined, and self confident army of trained socialist workers.
>
> The delegates of Chicago for the congress in Pittsburgh are hereby obliged to use their influence to the utmost in maintaining the autonomy of the various socialistic propaganda groups, societies, sections, etc.
>
> The delegates of Chicago are ordered to press at the Congress the recognition of the universal arming of the proletariat as indispensable, presupposition of the emancipation of the exploited, and, at the same time, to urge the workers to get in possession of arms.[61]

Out of their four paragraphs of instructions, there were only three princi-ples: (1) that socialist unity is useful in battling capitalists, (2) that autonomy of groups is a good unto itself, and (3) that all socialists should endeavor to arm the working class for the coming revolution. No one seemed to be troubled at the obvious friction between unity and autonomy; rather, all attention seemed to be aimed toward preparing for the coming class battle.

Besides being the only national meeting that Johann Most, August Spies, and Albert Parsons ever attended together, the Pittsburgh Congress was not all that different from the previous conference in Chicago. With a total of twenty-six delegates, the Pittsburgh Congress was not much better at-tended, nor did it venture any programs or initiatives that varied much from the ideas agreed upon two years before. What distinguishes the Pittsburgh Congress from the earlier meeting in Chicago is the simple fact that there seemed to be more agreement and less debate on fundamental issues than there had been before. Where the Chicago delegates had struggled over the phrasing of their plank rejecting political participation, those in Pittsburgh seem to never have been at serious loggerheads. Albert Parsons reported that the "proceedings were harmonious throughout." No participants had described Chicago's attempt at forging a new revolutionary movement as anything like "harmonious."[62]

The only moment of rancor may have come on the second day of the congress when a "secret session" was held and delegates could not later be persuaded to divulge even the subject that was discussed.[63] Some have specu-lated that the subject of this discussion was a detailed plan put forward by San Francisco editor, lawyer, and radical labor reformer Burnette Haskell to create a fully centralized and quasi-military organization to plan, coordinate, and execute revolutionary activities. Johann Most's personal attendance, the first of the "black," or anarchist, conventions he ever attended, seems to have been key to defeating Haskell's plan, for it was Most's insistence on preserving the sort of loose confederation of autonomous groups favored at the previous conferences that carried the day. But in the end, despite the defeat of his proposal, Haskell praised the work of the congress and con-cluded that the Pittsburgh Congress had succeeded in uniting "Reds" and "Blacks" into one body. He editorialized, "As a matter of fact the honest Anarchists are in reality nothing more or less than Revolutionary Social-ists . . . [who] ought to be combined . . . [and] last week at the Pittsburgh Congress they DID combine."[64]

As with the other revolutionary congresses that came before, the several dozen delegates who assembled in Pittsburgh in October 1883 were noted not for their numbers but for the ferocity of their rhetoric. Johann Most naturally secured a seat on the committee of five charged with drafting the congress' manifesto along with his fellow New Yorker Victor Drury, a French radical representing a section in St. Louis, and two prominent Chicagoans, Spies and Parsons. Together they crafted a document that stands unrivaled as the purest expression of the revolutionary thinking of this era.[65]

Opening with a quote from the U.S. Declaration of Independence and closing on an oddly religious reference to the "Judgment Day," the Pittsburgh proclamation tried hard to establish its American character. But aside from quotes from Jefferson and a reference to the U.S. Census, more of the proclamation relied on European intellectual roots, particularly Karl Marx's *Communist Manifesto*. Echoing the *Communist Manifesto* in first laying out the principle that society is divided into classes, "the exploitation of the propertyless class by the propertied," it described in Marxist terms how capitalist society pulls all but the privileged few down to the level of the proletarian, whose work gradually intensifies and whose wages steadily decline while others are thrown even lower, to the depths of the pauper, the prostitute, the vagabond, and the bandit. Marx would have agreed with the radicals of Pittsburgh up to this point, but would have begged to differ when they condemned capitalism as "unjust, insane and murderous." (Marx may have agreed that capitalism was murderous and unjust, but he also respected its cold economic rationality.) Like Marx's *Communist Manifesto*, the ultimate solution to the current social problem was revolution and abolition of private property and, in the words of the Pittsburgh proclamation "when all implements of labor . . . in short, capital produced by labor, is changed into societary property." But whereas Marx consciously avoided specifying how a revolution was to come about, agnostically allowing for each social movement to grasp the tools and opportunities available to it, Most, Spies, Parsons, and the others on their drafting committee allowed only one route to liberation: violent action. It was, they wrote, "self-evident" that "the struggle of the proletariat with the bourgeoisie must have a violent, revolutionary character."[66]

Violence and force were the only path to socialism because of the powerful forces holding down the working class. Pittsburgh's radicals specifically listed their enemies: political parties that "blind" workers; schools that prepare the "offspring of the wealthy" to "uphold their class domination" while spreading "prejudices, arrogance and servility" among the poor; the church, which makes "complete idiots out of the mass" by making them "forgo the paradise on earth by promising a fictitious heaven"; the "capitalistic press," which sows confusion around everything; and the capitalists who pay and control them all. With so many fundamental institutions working to thwart progress, "peaceful means" of change, particularly by the ballot, are "futile." Quoting Jefferson a second time ("It is, therefore, your right, it is your duty, to arm!"), the proclamation declares, "there remains but one recourse—FORCE!"

Presumably following the instructions given to them by the Chicago sections they represented, Spies and Parsons probably had a hand in the proclamation's peculiar ending that stressed both unity and autonomy. To those who had traveled great distances to sing and drink and debate in Pittsburgh's Turner Hall that weekend, the last lines of the *Manifesto* reflected what they believed to have been their great accomplishment. "There exists now no great obstacle to . . . unity. The work of peaceful education and revolutionary conspiracy well can and ought to run in parallel lines." At the time this meant that trade unions, political parties, and even social clubs were useful cover for the more important underground work of revolutionaries.

Albert Parsons believed that the resolutions and platform adopted in Pittsburgh (which he sent to Burnette Haskell's *Truth* with the comment, "Your paper will be the first and probably the only English paper to publish it") placed the American movement "in perfect unison with the International of Europe which has the single aim of the overthrow of Capitalism." Parsons also sent word to Haskell that his paper, *Truth*, had been "adopted" by the congress and praised it himself as giving "no uncertain sound. It gives, indeed, the plain, unvarnished truth."[67]

Within a short time after the Pittsburgh Congress of 1883, the Chicago SLP was shattered. The small band of die-hard American SLP members in Chicago struggled to keep their ranks from dwindling further while distinguishing themselves from militants. Chicago's electoral socialists found that the ideological terrain had been so shifted by the anarchists that they were forced to continually react to their opponents. Meetings were consumed with denouncing Johann Most and other anarchists' most recent pronouncements rather than organizing their own agenda. Their problems were compounded by their penchant for open meetings at which their ideological opponents attempted to hold the floor. At such a meeting in the spring of 1883, John Dusey was recognized by the chair and denounced the American flag as a "dirty rag," after which some sort of altercation broke out with Dusey shouting that he was an anarchist and the chair gaveling him out of order. Beset both within and without, the Chicago American SLP devoted their first meeting in 1884 to debating the precipitous decline in their membership.[68]

When SLP delegates convened in Cincinnati for their annual convention in 1885, it was happily reported that the number of SLP affiliate sections around the country had grown from thirty to forty-two, but this growth seemed to have completely bypassed Chicago. In fact, though there was mention of some letters received from a section in Chicago, the city was not represented at the convention. None of Chicago's thriving radical newspapers were recognized by the SLP, and indeed the SLP did not at this time even have an English-language organ of its own.[69]

As the *Arbeiter-Zeitung* under Spies championed militant action, more moderate socialists were faced with the dilemma of distancing themselves from the militants' violent tactics but at the same time not appearing to denounce the socialist goals they shared. Frank Stauber, once the most successful socialist in local elections, remained friends with the revolutionaries, particularly Spies, but grew more and more concerned as the earnestness of their revolutionary rhetoric became apparent. After the Haymarket bombing, Stauber publicly revealed that a year earlier he had expressed his grave concerns about the possibility that the anarchists would use the May 1 strikes as an opportunity for violent action and said he had spoken with another socialist politician, Paul Ehmann, about "what we could do to prevent it," but they "came to no agreement."[70] Joseph Gruenhut, a socialist labor organizer who had been appointed factory inspector by Mayor Carter Harrison, arranged for the *Daily News* to interview August Spies so as, Gruenhut explained, "to show the public that I differed from them."[71]

Chicago's electoral socialists did not begin to regroup until their anarchist enemies had been defeated by their own actions. Once the anarchist trial was under way, a new coalition of former SLP politicians and labor reform activists issued a call for a conference of those interested in "independent political action." Two days after the guilty verdicts were handed down in August 1886, a total of 251 delegates gathered and formed the United Labor Party (ULP), whose list of planks looked much like the winning SLP platform of 1879. That fall the ULP scored a huge victory over both the Republicans and Democrats, sending eight candidates to the state capital and missing out on winning a seat in the U.S. Congress by fewer than one hundred votes.[72]

Albert Parsons and his fellow Chicago radicals had come a long way in just five or six years. They had formally abandoned their previous Marxist commitments to the slow and steady work of organizing and party politicking and instead had come to embrace the newer romanticism of violence radiating outward from central Europe. The question now was, Would this small band of revolutionaries act on their promises of forceful resistance? Would they live up to their rhetoric?

CHAPTER FOUR

DYNAMITE

Just before midnight on the last day of March 1882, the two hundred or so inhabitants of Tappan, New York, a village on the west bank of the Hudson River across from White Plains, were jolted awake by a sharp report and a sudden shaking. David Storms awoke to the sound of windows breaking and shutters banging. Most people in the community thought they had suffered an earthquake, and some even ran out of their homes. But when the tremor passed and it was determined that the sound had come from the direction of Traitor's Hill, the villagers realized that someone must have finally blown up the André Monument, so they pulled on boots and overcoats to see for themselves. As they approached they could see that a section of the iron fence surrounding the memorial was twisted and missing cross-members. Inside the enclosure the squat obelisk still stood, though scarred on one face and leaning slightly in an easterly direction. Its granite base had been shattered into pieces that were strewn around the hill. Storms had walked by the monument earlier that night on his way home: "I suppose now that infernal thing must have been there when I passed. I might have been blown up too if I'd come by an hour later."[1]

The damaged monument was just two years old, having been placed on the spot of the execution of British spy Major John André on the centennial of his hanging on George Washington's orders. Major André had the misfortune to be caught by a squad of patriots as he was returning from secretly negotiating the surrender of Fort West Point in return for a bribe of twenty thousand pounds to General Benedict Arnold. André had a sheaf of incriminating papers stuffed in one boot. He was buried in the shadow of the gallows on this hill and mostly forgotten until the Duke of York disinterred his remains and returned them to Westminster Abbey. Some time after that, a New York City merchant, James Lee, who also organized the effort to erect the magnificent equestrian statue of George Washington in Union Square, commissioned the carving of a boulder on the road to Tappan that simply read "Andre—Executed Oct. 2, 1780."

In 1878 the famous Anglican cleric Reverend Arthur P. Stanley, dean of Westminster Abbey, happened to visit America and, while staying at the White Plains estate of the railroad and telegraph tycoon Cyrus W. Field, asked to see any nearby historic sites, including the site of Major André's hanging. The pair crossed the Hudson and tramped through Tappan and found a pair of old-timers who knew the exact spot because when they were children they happened to watch with understandable fascination the exhumation of André's remains. Reverend Stanley was dismayed to find that there was no monument, memorial, or marker of any kind in sight. Even Lee's old carved boulder had since disappeared. Field then and there offered to pay for the erection of an appropriate monument if the distinguished divine would pen its inscription.

On the centennial day and at the exact hour of André's execution, Field gave the signal and the André Monument was unveiled. This must have come as a huge relief to Field, as keeping his promise to Reverend Stanley had taken much more effort and expense than he had ever imagined it would. The wily farmers of Tappan refused to sell just the twenty-foot-square portion of the hill that Field needed for his installation and were even more hesitant to deed access rights to it, forcing Tappan to purchase the entire farm that surrounded it for an exorbitant amount. More galling to Field than the prices he paid for declining orchard lands was the public condemnation he suffered for building a memorial to an enemy of the republic.[2]

Police had a number of leads and a general idea of who may have been behind the bombing of the monument. Two suspicious men, one tall and the other "short and stout," had been seen arriving at the Tappan station from the seven o'clock train out of New York City. One of these men was seen taking the road to Traitor's Hill, and both men were seen boarding the next return train at a quarter to nine. The day after the bombing, a newspaper reporter noted a suspicious man with him on the train from New York and watched as the fat man with small side whiskers and mustache, who "acted like a mechanic" and looked like "a respectable Irishman," walked halfway up Traitor's Hill, spied a group of men gathered around the broken monument, spun on his heels, and headed back toward the station, breaking into a run once he thought he was out of sight. Besides these clues that pointed generally to the vandals having come from New York City, police had good reason to suspect that the bombing may have been organized by the city's anarchists.[3]

Eight days earlier someone had taken a chisel to the monument and spent a good portion of the night chipping away Reverend Stanley's lengthy inscription. The next morning, villagers found an American flag placed upon the defaced obelisk and a broadside plastered onto one of its facets. The broadside included a poem with a particular stanza that connected the royalist André to the capitalist Cyrus Field:

> And they who thus can glorify
>   The traitor and his deeds,
> Themselves high treason would employ
>   If 'twould fulfill their needs.[4]

The chiseling investigation was conducted by New York City detectives, an unusual overreach of their jurisdiction, likely prompted by Field's powerful pull in city government. Within seventy-two hours they had arrested their man, a twenty-seven-year-old Bowery sign painter who went by the name George Hendrix, an alias he adopted to spare his family grief when he began publicly associating with the anarchist movement. There can be little doubt that Hendrix was the culprit: he was identified by the monument's neighbor David Storms, who remembered him coming to his back door and asking for a match the night the stone was defaced. A German commuter named Baer gave a description of a man matching that of Hendrix who had ridden the train with him to New York and boasted of his deed. When he was arrested, Hendrix was reportedly asked by a friend how he was found out and replied, "That———Dutchman told them about it." A Detective Reilly, who took Hendrix into custody, also swore that as they were on their way to the police station, Hendrix asked if they might stop off at a saloon first. Reilly told him it would be better if they waited till after he had gone to the station to get a drink, whereupon Hendrix said, "It may be some time before I get back, as when anyone gets in to the hands of Cyrus Field he don't let up on him very easy." Detective Reilly swore that he had said nothing to Hendrix about the reason for taking him down to the station.[5]

The next week's edition of the sensational *National Police Gazette* celebrated Hendrix's act by publishing his portrait under the heading "Hendrix, The Mutilator" and describing him in populist tones:

> We have already reported how he pounded the inscription in the spy's obelisk to a state of illegibility, how he planted the stars and stripes above it, how he gushed into patriotic verse, and how he blithely beamed on the tap room of a neighboring inn during the rest of the night enjoying the glow of his patriotism. He is now under arrest, and Cyrus W. Field is trying his level best to show him the might of money when it is on the side of the police and the law; so Hendrix

seems likely to find that patriotism without funds to back it isn't of much account in the metropolis now-a-days.[6]

Such cynicism that justice could be purchased seemed confirmed when it was
reported that the Rockland constable first met privately with Cyrus Field's
lawyers before delivering an arrest warrant to a local judge.[7]

Hendrix's relationship to New York's anarchists was well known. The
Times described him as "a little lion in the organization" and "a constant
contributor to Socialist papers." A Jersey City group calling itself a chapter
of the International Working People's Association (the anarchist Black International) issued a series of resolutions protesting the arrest of Hendrix
"on a charge of defacing a monument erected by traitor Field in memory
of spy Andre" and pledged "to give our moral and material support to citizen Hendrix or any other person whomsoever may be imbued with such a
spirit of patriotism." Most tellingly, when Hendrix was first arrested, three
individuals visited him at police headquarters: his roommate, his lawyer,
and Justus Schwab, leader of New York's revolutionary socialists. A week
later, Schwab arrived at court and put up Hendrix's bail.[8]

The André Monument was blown up a fortnight later, just about the time
that Hendrix had escaped the clutches of the law on several technicalities,
each instance involving evidence of the reckless haste with which the police
sought to capture him. The individualist anarchist journal *Liberty* denounced
the bombing and implied that Schwab and his comrades were behind it:

> Our friend Schwab glories in the act. "We have had altogether too much theory,"
> he says, and so rejoices in a little practice. The real trouble is that we have not
> had half enough theory. If the true theory of individual Liberty had ever found
> lodgment in the minds of Mr. Schwab and his friends, the Andre monument
> would still be standing, and there would be one stain less on the radical record
> ... If the dynamite policy is ever forced upon American laborers by utterly
> intolerable trespass upon their rights, it must be used to blow up the Cyrus
> Fields themselves and not their playthings. But till then, no dynamite at all! We
> are engaged in serious business, and have not time for child's play.[9]

Liberty's speculations were confirmed years later by a reporter who bored
deeply into the New York anarchist organization after the Haymarket bombing. He discovered proof to his satisfaction that George Hendrix was the
original vandal of the André Monument and that a secret group of five New
York anarchists were responsible for the bombing.[10]

After the charges against Hendrix were dropped and the monument was
bombed, some journals openly wondered if Field might go beyond the law to
take his revenge. The *National Police Gazette* wondered if they might soon

hear of "Cyrus W. Field advertising for the slaughter of Hendrix." The *New York Times* counseled that if Field "wishes to punish any other and further fiends he must make use of the slow methods of law, which are peculiarly distasteful to him." Such warnings led many in the anarchist movement to believe that Hendrix's death two years later while in police custody might have been just such retribution.[11]

Seven months after Hendrix's death, the André Monument was blown up again soon after it had been repaired and placed on a new plinth. This time when windows shattered and beds shook in the middle of the night, the villagers of Tappan did not fear an earthquake; instead they thought to themselves, "Somebody has been blowing up the André Monument again." The charge used was substantially more powerful than that used nearly three years before. A dozen houses in the village had windows cracked or glassware broken, including one home a half mile away. One residence nearly caught fire when an oil lamp was shaken off its perch. Hollow iron posts surrounding the monument "as thick as a man's leg" were snapped off. Iron railings were bent outward "like an archer's bow." The main shaft of the obelisk, weighing several tons, was lifted in the air, spun around, and deposited so that Reverend Stanley's inscription lay unreadable facedown in the mud. The obelisk lay on its side for at least a decade until being righted and displayed without a proper plinth.[12]

Again two groups celebrated the act. A New York "friend" of Albert Parsons wrote to the *Alarm*, crowing, "On last election day somebody cast a vote, and one that counted. It was the vote composed of dynamite against a British spy monument, in which it was knocked to hell altogether. Another lesson for Cyrus W. Field."[13]

The improvements in the power and positioning of the explosive used in the bombings between 1882 and 1885 are yet another intriguing clue to the identity of the bomber. All experts agreed that the first bomb was both amateurish and placed in such a way that indicated that the bombers had no understanding or experience with explosives. *Scientific American* pointed out that when explosives are detonated in the open atmosphere, the force of the blast is concentrated in a downward direction. Since this bomb had been placed near the base of the stone and leaning against it, "the vandal must have had but little knowledge of the action of high explosives under such conditions, or he would have placed the cartridge on the top of the monument, thus assuring its destruction." The bombers followed more sound principles the second time, using a more powerful explosive and placing the charge in a channel they laboriously dug under the base of the monument to its center, where the full force of the blast was directed upward.

Assuming the same group bombed the monument in both 1882 and 1885, those responsible had gained access to better explosives or acquired better technical knowledge in the years in between.[14] Two radical groups operating in both New York City and Chicago at this time fit this description: Irish nationalists and revolutionary anarchists.

The Fenian Connection

When revolutionary socialists proclaimed their intent to use all "scientific means" to liberate the working class, a different group of militants had already declared their own right to use dynamite in furtherance of their cause and had even begun actively raising funds and establishing a secret international network to carry out their plans. About the same time that the International Working People's Association was formed in London in 1881, a group that was much larger, more influential, and enjoyed much more publicity used much the same rhetoric but went one step further and blew up a string of famous landmarks. Any nascent anarchists who thought that by talking about bombs they might attract some cheap publicity for their cause must have been sorely disappointed when their thunder was stolen by a bolder and more determined organization. (The fact that the anarchists were not discouraged suggests that perhaps idle talking was not their purpose.)

The group that so overshadowed the anarchists at their own bomb-talking game were Irish American militants who regrouped after the failures and dissipation of the old Fenians into a secret organization called the Clan na Gael. The clan was founded in 1867 in New York City and grew steadily over the next decade. In 1876 it fired the hopes of Irish nationalists everywhere by conducting a daring raid in which Irish prisoners were rescued from a penal colony in Australia. By this time the clan had around eleven thousand members and had raised enough money to construct one of the world's first submarines, which they planned to use to attack British warships in American harbors.

Though from its inception the clan was dedicated to the use of force to end English rule over Ireland, this policy did not at first extend to attacking civilian targets in England proper. Most of the funds collected were repatriated to allied organizations in Ireland. But by the late 1870s, American clan leaders had grown skeptical of their Irish brethren's revolutionary abilities (as well as their probity in handling funds). Meanwhile a land reform movement spread rent strikes throughout the countryside, and Irish parliamentarians extended their caucus to sixty seats in 1880. English prime minister

William Gladstone reacted by prosecuting the Irish parliamentary leader, Charles Stewart Parnell, and more than a dozen other Irish National Land League leaders for conspiracy. Gladstone suspended habeas corpus for good measure. According to Michael Davitt, the founder of the Land League, the arrest of the organization's leaders, along with the intensified suppression of the movement in Ireland, provoked more violent rhetoric from American supporters. "Extremists, who had always decried the League as weak because constitutional, and who had ridiculed the notion that England would ever concede anything to the persuasion of moral force, began to exult in the fulfilment of their predictions, and took the opportunity of the League's suppression in Ireland for a propaganda of terrorism in England by dynamite and destruction."[15]

As 1881 began, a number of important Clan na Gael leaders resolved to take the fight directly to England themselves. Most important among them was Patrick Ford, a printer's devil for abolitionist William Lloyd Garrison's *Liberator* who later became publisher of the *Irish World*, the largest-circulation paper of its kind at the time. Besides being a leading supporter of Irish independence, Ford advocated other radical reforms, such as Henry George's single tax and land reform and the nationalization of the railroads. Constantly raising money for various Irish crusades and causes, Ford was quite aware that a large number of his contributors were poor workers. His detractors claimed that his entire enterprise rested on the pennies collected from Irish maids and laborers who could least afford to spare them. Even those who were sympathetic to Fenian causes noted its disproportionate reliance on the donations of workers. As Chicago's trade union chiefs were struggling to keep their official weekly paper, the *Progressive Age*, solvent, they included among the reasons for their financial distress the problem that "we cannot raise much money among our Irish fellow workers because they send all their available cash savings to Ireland to fight landlordism in its worst form."[16] During the Great Railroad Strikes of 1877, Ford gradually broadened his support to embrace the labor movement and even to flirt with socialism, not only the milder democratic versions but also its more revolutionary brands. In 1879 Ford mused in his paper, "There might arise circumstances in which the ballot-box would need the support of the cartridge-box."[17]

Tellingly, Ford's interest in the labor movement connected him to some of the prominent anarchists of the day. In 1880 he published a lengthy discourse on socialism by Edward Nathan-Ganz. He also published an essay written by Chicago anarchist William Holmes titled "Are Strikes a Benefit?"[18] Soon Ford went from publishing editorials that endorsed wielding all the "resources of civilization" (a euphemism for bombs) against England to publishing in the *Irish World* detailed descriptions of how dynamite was made. In one of these, would-be bomb makers were encouraged by the suggestion that dynamite was "as easy to compound as it is to make griddle cakes."[19]

While Ford was the most influential public spokesman for Irish independence in America, another Irish immigrant, Jeremiah O'Donovan Rossa, was its most famous fire-eater. O'Donovan Rossa was born in County Cork in 1831 and quickly rose to prominence in the nationalist movement. In his twenties he founded a group known as the Phoenix Society and then became an organizer for the Irish Revolutionary Brotherhood. These activities led to his arrest in 1865 for treason, and he was handed a life sentence. O'Donovan Rossa kept up his unbowed resistance in Chatham Prison, so enraging his guards by throwing his chamber pot at the prison's warden that they slapped him in handcuffs for thirty-five consecutive days. He was thrown into solitary confinement and a bread-and-water diet for three days for refusing to remove his cap in the presence of the prison doctor. For most of his years in a cell he was denied usual letter privileges as punishment for his defiance of prison rules. In his fourth year of imprisonment, O'Donovan Rossa was elected to parliament by the citizens of Tipperary. After five years of incarceration, English authorities offered him an early release if he promised to emigrate to the United States and never return.[20]

Upon landing in America, O'Donovan Rossa found many friends in New York's radical community, and within a short time he was put up as the reform candidate against Boss Tweed. He lost to Tweed in an election that was stunning even by Gilded Age standards for its wholesale ballot fraud, with many more votes being cast in several precincts than the total adult male population of the area. Teaming up with Patrick Ford and his newspaper, the *Irish World*, O'Donovan Rossa helped steer Ford toward a policy that paralleled the revolutionary anarchist ideology. The new policy of the *Irish World* was proclaimed in 1875: "We should oppose a general insurrection in Ireland as untimely and ill advised. But we believe in action nonetheless. The Irish cause requires Skirmishers. It requires a little band of heroes who will initiate and keep up without intermission a guerrilla warfare."[21]

O'Donovan Rossa's newspaper, the *United Irishman*, extolled dynamite not only as the solution to English tyranny but also as the key to the liberation of oppressed peoples everywhere. The *United Irishman* openly advocated the use of the "resources of civilization" against England, appropriating a phrase that Prime Minister Gladstone had used when describing the tactics the British colonial army had employed against a rebellion in Egypt.[22]

The paper solicited donations to a "resources of civilisation fund," whose purpose was not clearly stated but was presumably for the purchase of weapons and explosives. It advertised lectures by a "Professor Mezzeroff," who claimed to be a dynamite chemist and operated a dynamite school for the cause. Mezzeroff's lectures, such as one he gave at Cooper Union in September 1882, hewed to the editorial campaign of the newspaper and were titled "The Resources of Science against the Resources of Civilization." His presentation was described by the *United Irishman* as "Professor Mezzeroff's Dynamite Lecture." Mezzeroff charged an admission of twenty-five cents to all those who were curious to see such a dangerous man.[23]

Professor Mezzeroff has been an enigma to scholars of anarchism for a century. He was a "tall, bony, determined-looking man," who boasted of carrying bombs in his pockets on streetcars. Mezzeroff was almost certainly not his real name, as no one by that moniker can be found in the census of New York. On some occasions he claimed to have been born to a Scottish mother and a Russian father. Other times he said he had been born in Edinburgh, Scotland, and as a schoolboy was beaten there by a soldier for the offense of failing to remove his hat when the queen rode by. The professor adopted a number of aliases, including "Dr. Hodges." Police suspected that his real name was either Samuel or James Rogers. In all likelihood, Mezzeroff was Joseph Conrad's model for the bomb-toting "Professor" in his novel *The Secret Agent*.[24]

It is difficult to establish with any precision when Mezzeroff became involved with the Irish dynamite campaign. William Edwin Adams, noted reformer and editor of the *Newcastle Weekly Chronicle*, recalled in his memoirs that New York's Irish revolutionaries established the "Joe Brady Emergency Club" in the early 1880s. Since this club took its name from one of the assassins of Lord Frederick Cavendish in Phoenix Park, Dublin, it must have been founded after Cavendish's murder on May 6, 1882. Among those whom Adams claimed were founding members was Frank Byrne, an alleged co-conspirator with Brady, but one who got away and opened a liquor store in New York City; Robert Blissert, a veteran of the Marxist First International; O'Donovan Rossa, of course; and Mezzeroff.[25]

Mezzeroff soon became a fixture of New York's radical Irish community. By December 1882 he shared the billing and the stage with O'Donovan Rossa; Joseph P. McDonnell, editor of the *Labor Standard*; and several high Fenian officials, including the president of the Ancient Order of Hibernians. His popularity among Fenians was evident when his manifesto, a two-dozen-page pamphlet titled "Dynamite and Other Resources of Civilization," was passed around at the Clan na Gael convention in Philadelphia in 1883.[26]

In addition to being a member of the inner circle of Irish revolutionaries, Professor Mezzeroff was reportedly also a close associate of anarchist leader Johann Most and a member of the revolutionary anarchist club in New York City and therefore a living link between the two revolutionary movements.

Many reporters at the time thought Mezzeroff may have been a crank, but he was taken seriously by those most concerned with the spread of bombs. The British Home Office obtained a copy of one of Mezzeroff's dynamite pamphlets titled "Prescriptions to Students" and sent it to government chemists for their evaluation. Their conclusion was that Mezzeroff had a moderate knowledge of chemistry but was not the expert he claimed to be. In the end they thought he was a greater danger to the "dupes" he sold his pamphlets to than to the empire.[27]

On the other hand, it might not have taken much more than "moderate knowledge" to brew serviceable dynamite or to build workable bombs. Beyond speaking publicly about the wonders and ease of making dynamite, many alleged that Mezzeroff actually taught a number of apprentices the trade. Patrick McGahey, identified as "an enthusiastic and prominent eastern district Fenian," told a Brooklyn reporter that "the Professor taught all the prominent men of our organization how to make it, and we were impressed at how simple it is." Another Irish nationalist, John F. Kearney, who was arrested in Rotterdam by police who claimed to have discovered a bomb-making factory in his house in 1896, was reported to have told many associates that he learned the art of bomb making from Mezzeroff. Likewise, James Gilbert Cunningham, a man arrested for bombing the Tower of London in 1885, was reported to have learned his trade from Mezzeroff in New York.[28]

Reporters throughout the 1880s claimed that Mezzeroff and O'Donovan Rossa ran a bomb factory somewhere in the greater New York area. One enterprising scoop-seeker followed some leads to a shabby workshop in the Williamsburg area of Brooklyn and there, hoping to find a bomb factory, instead found a factory that was being used to "perfume" butter (in other words, to treat rancid butter to remove its odor and resell it). The "chemist" he found there denied he was Mezzeroff. No daily-paper gumshoe ever found the actual bomb factory, if it ever existed.[29]

On several occasions Mezzeroff was reported to have given public demonstrations of his wares. In July 1885 the Fenian Brotherhood of New York City hosted a gala picnic at High Ground Park in Brooklyn. In addition to speechmaking, dancing, and a drill of the Emerald Guards, who were "out in high feather," the day featured a demonstration. Professor Mezzeroff exploded a number of devices for the crowd, including what a reporter described as a "bomb." A couple of months later another Fenian picnic, this time at Harlem River Park, was electrified just after sunset when Jeremiah O'Donovan Rossa arrived accompanied by Professor Mezzeroff, who was carrying a satchel stenciled with the word *DYNAMITE*. A crowd gathered around and Mezzeroff threw a bomb that he announced was filled with one ounce of dynamite at a rock fifty feet away. A loud report and a brilliant flash "caused a chorus of screams." "Gentlemen," Mezzeroff proclaimed to the crowd, "there was only a single ounce there. I will illustrate to you the awful power of a larger quantity. Every Irish farmer should have a dozen or more of these to use in case of visits from evicters or bailiffs. One of them is warranted to mow down half a regiment." One of Mezzeroff's associates who had accompanied him to the picnic, perhaps taking cover behind a tree like O'Donovan Rossa, was none other than anarchist leader Justus Schwab.[30]

Years after the journalistic interest in the Irish dynamiter had passed, a curious crime occurred that sent reporters tracing the bomb factory story once again, and at this remove a number of men with knowledge of the details were willing to talk. It was a clear early August day when Thomas J. Mooney steered his skiff near the English steamer *Queen* and tossed a bottle filled with phosphorus onto the ship's deck, starting a small fire. Mooney was arrested and identified as having had a number of aliases, including William P. Moorhead and "Prof. Armstrong," and was reputed to have been one of Mezzeroff's assistants at his "dynamite school." According to newspaper reports, which unusually took the pains to note that they had obtained confirmation of the story from two different sources, Mooney was an Irish cop who had been recruited into the Irish Brotherhood and then to America in 1882. O'Donovan Rossa placed Mooney with Mezzeroff at a dynamite factory in Greenpoint, Brooklyn. Mooney then distinguished himself as a reliable operative by blowing up the local Government Board offices in Whitehall, London. Supposedly, Mooney quickly outpaced his tutor and caused a factional rift in radical ranks as O'Donovan Rossa attempted to push Mezzeroff aside and put Mooney in charge of the bomb factory and school.[31]

Whether Mezzeroff actually made any of the bombs that exploded in England will probably never be definitively established, but even at more than a century's remove it is not difficult to connect him to the Irish "Invincibles," who were the foot soldiers of the campaign of assassination and bombing. According to secrets revealed by an informer by the name of Carey before he was murdered for his treachery, a "Miss Byrnes" was the accomplice who brought "knives, nitro-glycerin and fire-arms" to the Invincibles. British police sources believed this "Miss Byrnes" was a Miss

Jeannie Byrnes, secretary of the Ladies Land League of New York City. In 1882 Jeannie Byrnes's father, Thomas J. Byrne, a plumber, appeared on stage with Professor Mezzeroff and introduced him as "one of the men who knew most about dynamite" and revealed that "he had been a pupil of Prof. Mezzeroff for several months."[32]

Mezzeroff was not the only radical with a foot in both the anarchist and Fenian camps. In Boston the chief speaker at a rally to raise funds for the families of the Irish martyrs and to carry forward the struggle against England was Dr. J. H. Swain, who a couple of months later would arrive in Chicago as a delegate to the anarchist International Working People's Association conference of 1882. Swain remarked that he had long been known as a peace advocate, but he had come to see that such "moral revolution" was possible only when "passive resistance is possible." Saying that where freedoms are suppressed the use of dynamite is justified, Swain concluded, "When rulers everywhere abandon brute force and appeal only to reason and love . . . they will find the people only too glad to meet them in the same spirit. Until then there can and ought to be no submission, no peace. Peace cannot be purchased at the cost of slavery."[33]

The connection between O'Donovan Rossa's Irish "skirmishers" and anarchist advocates of force surfaced again in early 1885 when a fight broke out during a socialist meeting in New York's inappropriately named Concordia Hall. The meeting had been called by leaders of the Socialist Labor Party to denounce the recent bombings in London. Justus Schwab, Johann Most, and other anarchists who hailed the bombings as a blow for Irish freedom tried to pack the meeting and take it over. As the two factions filled the hall, they quickly escalated from name calling to shoving, throwing chairs, and eventually fists. When police captain John H. McCullagh read the riot act and ordered the pugnacious socialists and anarchists to go home, he and his men were attacked. Justus Schwab reportedly broke a chair over McCullagh's head. Afterward, one of the officers of the anarchist IWPA told a reporter that Schwab had asked O'Donovan Rossa to send a group of "Irish dynamiters to break up the meeting." Whether O'Donovan Rossa actually did so is beside the point; this anarchist's comment points to a friendly relationship between the two leaders and their movements in New York.[34] O'Donovan Rossa and Schwab were longtime associates: Schwab had been a member of the International Workingmen's Association when it organized a reception to greet O'Donovan Rossa when he first landed in America. Benjamin Tucker, an "individualist" anarchist who opposed the force anarchists, alluded to the association of New York's anarchists and "dynamite" Fenians by referring to O'Donovan Rossa as "Herr Most O'Donovan Rossa."[35]

Though both Ford and O'Donovan Rossa were based in New York, it was Chicago that emerged as the capital of Irish radicalism. Although the dynamite strategy was first articulated by these New Yorkers, the organizational muscle came from the Windy City. It was Chicago's most powerful Irish politico, Alexander Sullivan, who engineered the consolidation of all the main Irish reform organizations under a secret cabal of his associates known as "the Triangle." At the 1881 conference of Irish American leaders at Chicago's Palmer House, "dynamite . . . was in the air and in the speeches from start to finish." If there was consideration of dynamite as a policy, it was done for the most part quietly and in back rooms. However, one committee came as close to endorsing dynamite as it could without actually mentioning the weapon: "our [Irish] brothers have established a special department for instruction in engineering, chemicals, draughting, and mining, and other branches of the higher and technical departments of warfare suitable to the advancement and inventions of the age, [and] we earnestly recommend the like course in the V.C. [Clan na Gael]."[36]

It was at this gathering that Sullivan's Triangle both assumed control and allocated more funds for a bombing campaign. Though the deliberations and policies of this inner circle were secret, news continually leaked out, and within a few years local reporters recognized Chicago's radical distinction; as one report noted, "Chicago has always been in the van of Irish revolutionary methods in this country, and to give to this city and to the northwest a boom in the dynamite direction."[37]

O'Donovan Rossa's brand of violent skirmishing was particularly popular among Irish activists in Chicago. In 1883 the appearance of the "Irish John Brown" (as reporters liked to call O'Donovan Rossa) packed the West Twelfth Street Turner Hall to commemorate four revolutionaries who recently had been executed in Ireland. O'Donovan Rossa proclaimed himself a "strong dynamiter." The crowd then acclaimed a number of resolutions, including this one: "As the sense of the Irishmen and women of Chicago, in mass-meeting assembled, That every man who strikes a blow for liberty—in any land, in any manner—is a benefactor of humanity, and deserves the commendation of all friends of human advancement . . . that . . . we believe Irishmen should, if they could, grasp the fires of hell, as well as the lightnings of heaven, and hurl them into the face of the country's enemy." Five hundred dollars was collected that night to "supply sinews of war to the men who mean active work."[38]

According to German spies operating in America, whose reports were compiled and presented to the head of the Prussian police every few months, at the Chicago conference of the "Irish nihilists," a number of "infernal machines" were shown off and their manufacture explained. More troubling to the German authorities, it was reported that German American revolutionary socialists had lively relations with the Fenians and aided them in securing explosives. In June 1882 the spy reports received in Berlin warned that the social revolutionary clubs, of which the most active were in New York and Chicago, while "numerically the weakest" were in fact "the most dangerous," because they were "convinced of the necessity for the beginning of the social revolution," were closely connected to "Fenians . . . and constitute a point of unity of the most extreme elements of all countries."[39]

Though Clan na Gael skirmishers and revolutionary anarchists were both extolling the transformative power of dynamite publicly while at the same time covertly collecting bombs in Chicago, the documented links between these two militant groups are elusive. However, there were a couple of Chicago labor leaders who bridged both ethnic worlds. Myles McPadden, an Irishman by birth and an iron molder by trade, rose to become national secretary of the iron molder's union. In the 1880s McPadden became a leader of the Knights of Labor and settled in Chicago, where he served as the city's general organizer, leading the efforts of the eight other full-time Knights organizers.[40] While playing a prominent role as a labor leader, McPadden was also an active member of the Clan na Gael. His connections to radical Irish nationalism were evident in 1882 when he was prosecuted by the state of Pennsylvania for conspiracy for the crime of attempting to organize miners and the *Irish World* prominently publicized his case.[41] McPadden worked at the McCormick Reaper Works and was a leader of the strike of the plant's iron molders in 1885. When this strike utterly failed and his molders union was largely broken, McPadden made common cause with the German anarchists who were organizing the unskilled workers in the plant through the Metall Arbeiter Verein (metal workers association) that was allied to the Central Labor Union.[42]

Likewise, one of the men who attended the Haymarket meeting was William Gleason, who had arrived from Ireland eight years earlier. A bricklayer and self-proclaimed "Finian" [sic], Gleason was also a high-ranking member of the Knights of Labor and a delegate to the Chicago Trades Assembly. When placed on the witness stand at the anarchists' trial, Gleason denied that he was one of O'Donovan Rossa's "Irish dynamiters," but when asked the same question a second time, he oddly answered, "I belong to no Irish organization at the present time," a reply that held open the possibility that perhaps he had been a dynamiter in the past. Gleason then affirmed he had been a member of a "revolutionary society" at New Castle upon Tyne in

England. He also confirmed that he was acquainted with Albert Parsons, Samuel Fielden, and other members of the anarchist movement.[43]

Other scraps of evidence hint at connections between Clan na Gael and anarchist bombers. According to Henri Le Caron, a British spy based in Chicago who infiltrated the highest levels of Clan na Gael, Irish skirmishers obtained some of their American dynamite from the Repauno Chemical Company of Philadelphia. According to the *Vorbote*, Chicago's anarchists ordered some of their own explosives from the same company.[44]

The Dynamite Panacea

For both Fenians and anarchists, dynamite was used less as an actual weapon than as a powerful symbol, a symbol whose potency was drawn from its being a product of modern science, the culmination of technology that finally equalized the power of the masses against the state. But there is yet another dimension to the symbolism of dynamite that resonated with Chicago's anarchists and may even have emboldened them to act with a rashness and recklessness they would not have otherwise pursued. This was that dynamite was also viewed as a lever by which a small but committed minority could conquer a more numerous foe. Their power, the anarchists came to believe, came not from their numbers but from their ideological fervor, and this combined with the awesome power of dynamite could compensate for their lack of progress in winning adherents. "We are approaching a great revolution," wrote a columnist in Parsons's *Alarm*: "With modern destructives, a half-dozen men can make the crown of all the Russians too hot to be worn ... the truth is, we have arrived at an age when no government can exist if one-tenth of the people decide that they must cease."[45] Thus the idea of dynamite enabled the anarchists to be sanguine about their small numbers and to put their energies into preparing for action rather than building up their groups.

To would-be revolutionaries, dynamite carried an almost mystical aura of invincibility. At the Northwest Side group meeting of Chicago revolutionaries, a "Comrade Kramer" lectured on the industrial conditions of America. He described how "everything points toward the fight" and all "Reform movements were nothing but soap bubbles." Soon "the large masses who have no possessions are driven to fight—they must fight or perish. Against the bayonets of the ruling classes, they will use different weapons in the approaching fight. A single electric machine is capable of destroying whole armies with the turn of hands, and such a machine is in existence." At this his audience erupted with applause.[46]

Kramer's rhapsodic belief in the liberating potential of dynamite was in keeping with the expectations and fears of some of the leading military minds of his day. James Chester, a captain in the Third Artillery wrote a long analysis of dynamite's impact on military strategy for other tacticians and noted how Alfred Nobel's invention decisively shifted the advantage from states to rebels. Science, wrote Captain Chester, "has concocted compounds which develop ten times the destructive force of gunpowder; it has put into human hands the very thunderbolts of Jove."

> They can be carried in quantities about the person; they can be thrown by hand or with a sling. Nicety of aim is unnecessary. Whatever they strike they pulverize, and kill all within a certain radius. They can be manufactured cheaply, secretly, and readily. Any manufacturer of bad smells in the basement of a soap-factory can turn out more means of destruction in a day than Krupp could in a century. Nay, the work can be done in any back-kitchen. If the devil delights in the horrors of war, he must be in ecstasies over these new inventions . . . Is it likely that the block upon the game of rebellion will be continued long? Are the guardians of society justified in ignoring the fact?[47]

Burnette Haskell's newspaper, *Truth,* came out in favor of the use of dynamite as a revolutionary tool just weeks before the opening of the Pittsburgh Congress in 1883. At the end of June 1883, *Truth* carried an "essay carefully prepared by one of the leading scientific workers in the international cause" that provided its readers with detailed instructions for brewing nitroglycerine and mixing it into dynamite.[48] Ominously, *Truth* urged every reader to save the issue and the recipe. "The time is coming when journals like TRUTH will be forcibly suppressed, when meetings of honest citizens will be dispersed at the point of the bayonet, when the producers will be shot down like dogs in every street. When that day does dawn, the hour for using DYNAMITE will have struck."[49]

Given the unusual interconnections between vigilante groups dedicated to attacking Chinese communities and socialist clubs in San Francisco, Haskell's advocacy of dynamite carried unusual weight. In December 1885 San Francisco police, acting on a tip, broke down the door of a boardinghouse and discovered a closet stuffed with ten pounds of dynamite, fuses, blasting caps, alarm clocks, wire, and literature in Russian and German, including Johann Most's *Science of Revolutionary Warfare* and copies of a journal titled the *Nihilist.* On the walls of the apartment were portraits of Mikhail Bakunin and the Russian czar-killer Sofya Perovskaya. Among the papers seized by police was a sheet listing the names of prominent officials and citizens "to be removed," from California senator Leland Stanford and Chinese consul general Frederick A. Bee down to the local police captain. The four occupants who were arrested all had ties to Dr. C. C. O'Donnell, a former leader of the Workingmen's Party of California, an aid to Denis Kearney, and leader of both the Anti-Coolie League and a newly formed "Socialistic Revolutionary Association" that linked back to Haskell. O'Donnell was identified in the press as having distributed an issue of an ephemeral anarchist paper called the *Dynamite*.[50]

The potential of dynamite, the ultimate tool of the tactic of propaganda by deed, was demonstrated early in 1885 with a series of small bombings in England that caused disproportionate fear and concern among citizens and English leaders because they occurred in highly symbolic locations. On January 2 an explosion shattered the windows of a passing train at King's Cross Station in London. Two weeks later the Warminster town hall was bombed. Then on January 24, a tourist descending the steps toward Westminster Hall in the Houses of Parliament noticed what appeared to be a bundle of cloth that was burning and notified a nearby bobby, who inspected the package, recognized it was bomb, and was bravely trying to carry it out of the building when it exploded, badly wounding him and another policeman. Three minutes later an even more powerful blast wrecked the western side of the House of Commons, smashing Prime Minister Gladstone's chair and shattering the chamber's ornate glass ceiling. Luckily, only one person was nearby and seriously wounded at the time of this explosion, a crowd of others having just rushed down the hall to see what had happened at Westminster. Two miles away another bomb went off in an empty second-floor gallery of the Tower of London.[51]

Revolutionaries in both New York and Chicago held public meetings to celebrate these explosive attacks in the inner sanctums of British government. Albert and Lucy Parsons and their colleagues in the American section of the IWPA extolled the bombings as a sign that the pendulum of history was swinging in the direction of the armed working class. An editorial in Parsons's *Alarm* praised the attack for its power as propaganda: "that explosion in London put more sense into the people than all the common schools have accomplished in a quarter of a century. A few blasts in the Hocking Valley have done more educating than all the schools of Ohio." (About this time, as the editorial line of the *Alarm* moved toward open advocacy of propaganda by deed, the newspaper announced that henceforth all editorials would not bear the full names of their authors, only their initials.)[52]

By the mid-1880s New York's anarchists had been experimenting with explosives for several years. Most and Schwab's Social Revolutionary Club had founded a weapons committee and an "Action and Propaganda Fund," the former to stockpile explosives and arms and the latter to pay for it. Most was eager to publicize these activities in the pages of *Freiheit*, writing of the Action and Propaganda Fund that its moneys were to "be used for the active fighters of the social revolution at every practical means of warfare to support the emancipation of the proletariat and also to encourage the revolutionaries for brave deeds and to assist the people left behind during our fight."[53]

Initially, New York anarchists had the benefit of a trained chemist among their leaders: William Hasselmann, who had studied chemistry at a Berlin polytechnic before being thrown out of the country. One of the founders of the Social Revolutionary Club, Hasselmann was reputed to have taught others in the movement the explosive arts. After the Haymarket bombing, a New York anarchist revealed to a reporter who had disguised himself as a fellow anarchist, "We are carefully taught the use of dynamite . . . Two years ago we had a school, and Hasselmann used to teach us how to make it and how to use it."[54] But Hasselmann was pushed aside once Johann Most arrived in New York, and Most proved unable to tolerate any rivals for his leadership. Hasselmann apparently dropped out of the movement as he fell into extreme penury, experimenting on chemical dyes in his shabby room in the worst street in the worst neighborhood in Manhattan and living off the ten dollars a week his wife brought home as a seamstress.[55]

Hasselmann may not have been the only explosive expert who lent his skills to the anarchist movement. The day after New Year's Day 1887, a New York paper ran a sensational story that claimed to reveal the identity of the man who had supplied Chicago's anarchists with dynamite. Charles W. Zaddick, it was claimed, boasted of giving explosives to the Chicago "revolutionists."[56] Zaddick had come to reporters' attention after he accidentally blew himself and two fellow workers into pieces in shaft sixteen of the New Croton Aqueduct, which was then under construction. One of Zaddick's jobs was to prepare the nitroglycerin for blasting, and he apparently allowed his mixture to get too hot. As just another deadly industrial accident in a city used to them, Zaddick's calamity drew only a small one-day mention in the papers, and he would have passed on to obscurity like so many other victims of their jobs had it not been for a number of other curious details about him that surfaced in subsequent weeks.[57]

A number of items claimed about Zaddick piqued at least one reporter's interest: That he was a German Jew who had studied chemistry in Berlin and art in Paris and immigrated to New York in 1882. That around the time of the Haymarket bombing he worked for an explosives manufacturer located in Baychester, New York, a Long Island hamlet a short train ride from Manhattan. That his house was filled with portraits he had painted of anarchists and revolutionaries. That Zaddick's widow had been visited by Lucy Parsons. That Zaddick had once quarreled with his boss at the Baychester dynamite factory after the boss fined Zaddick for stealing explosives, which he thought Zaddick was selling to local farmers but, it turned out, was actually selling in Manhattan. That during this fight with his boss Zaddick pulled a pistol and snapped off a shot and was promptly arrested and jailed in White Plains. The name of the man who arrived to pay Zaddick's bail was Justus Schwab—the leader of Brooklyn's revolutionary anarchists. All of these details took on greater meaning when Zaddick's foreman, who survived the blast in shaft sixteen, told how Zaddick bragged of selling dynamite to revolutionaries and of having provided the explosives that killed the Chicago police.[58]

Such connections mean little without the support of verifying evidence from different sources. In the case of Charles W. Zaddick there are some other tantalizing props to this story. On January 26, 1886, the U.S. Patent Office issued to a Charles W. A. Zadeck Patent No. 335006 for his invention of an "explosive compound" whose primary innovation was in being far less "sensitive to accidental shocks or concussions with other bodies," had "greater elasticity" than normal dynamite, and was "thereby better adapted for torpedoes and projectiles" while being easily "discharged by means of caps containing fulminate of mercury." Zadeck's address on the patent application was Bartow-on-the-Sound, a hamlet adjacent to Baychester, the location of the Dittmar Powder Company, a large manufacturer of explosives in New York.[59]

At ten o'clock in the morning of September 30, 1886, a massive explosion rocked the Long Island town of Baychester. The shock of the explosion broke the windows of a hospital a mile away and shook medicine bottles off the shelves of a drugstore in a nearby town. Four workers had been packing cartridges at the Dittmar Powder Company when two men who claimed to be hunting squirrels shot toward the building, thus causing the accident, according to a foreman. Police could not distinguish among the body parts of the four workers who had been packing sticks of dynamite at the time of the blast, so they gathered them all up into a single box and delivered it to the coroner.

Carl Dittmar, the owner of the dynamite works, later told a coroner's jury that he had earlier fired Charles Padock for being an anarchist and that Padock threatened to burn down the factory. Dittmar told the jury that Padock took a shot at him, an act that got Padock arrested and fined one hundred dollars. Given the creative variety of journalistic spellings of central

European names at this time, it is highly likely that "Padock," "Zadek," and "Zaddick" were one and the same man.[60]

Along with Hasselmann and Zaddick, Johann Most pursued his own practical lessons in energetic chemistry by securing a job at a dynamite factory in Jersey City under the assumed name of Henri Germain. He reportedly smuggled some of his product out of the factory, but where it ended up no one can be sure. Most may have sent some of it to striking miners in Ohio and perhaps some to his friends in Chicago. One of the letters discovered in August Spies's editorial office after the Haymarket bombing was an offer by Most to send him twenty pounds of "medicine": "I am in a condition to furnish '*medicine*,' and the 'genuine' article at that. Directions for use are perhaps not needed with these people. Moreover, they were recently published in the 'Fr.' The appliances I can also send. Now if you consider the address of Buchtell thoroughly reliable I will ship twenty or twenty-five pounds."[61]

Such ties between New York and Chicago were more than ideological. Radicals freely moved between these two centers of radical activity. M. D. Malkoff lived in New York and took his mail at Justus Schwab's saloon before moving to Chicago and living first with future Haymarket defendant Michael Schwab (no relation to Justus) and then with fellow anarchist and worker for the *Arbeiter-Zeitung* Balthasar Rau.[62]

A few Chicago radicals began to openly boast that they were arming themselves with dynamite. American group member O. A. Bishop boasted that there were five thousand men in Chicago who "knew how to manufacture dynamite in their kitchens for the price of a good dinner."[63]

By early 1885, Chicago's anarchists moved from merely advocating dynamite and bombing as the path to the worker's liberation to brandishing their weapons openly. Henry W. Fischer, a former city editor of the *Arbeiter-Zeitung*, later revealed to reporters that dynamite was stockpiled at the newspaper's offices. "We had a whole arsenal in the office at one time," he claimed. Fischer recounted that they kept some explosives just to experiment with, but these tests sometimes went awry, once shattering some windows in the back of the building and another time blowing off the thumb of future Haymarket defendant Oscar Neebe.[64]

In late April 1885 the anarchists organized a protest against the dedication of the new Chicago Board of Trade Building, a protest that was in many ways a dress rehearsal for the Haymarket protest a year later. A knot of men gathered at Market Square, and Albert Parsons climbed atop a salt barrel and led off the speechmaking. Undercover police officer Thomas Treharn recalled Parsons calling on the crowd to "use the gun and dynamite" to convince the "capitalists and robbers" to give them the full rewards of their labor. Just as he did at the Haymarket, Samuel Fielden capped the rally, urging the crowd to march to the Board of Trade and force their place in the grand supper line.[65] A procession formed and was led by Lucy Parsons bearing aloft the red banner, the line breaking into refrains of the *Marseillaise*. Police had cordoned off the streets leading to the grand trading building, and after a tense standoff between August Spies and Lieutenant William Ward, the officer who a year later would command the anarchists in the Haymarket to disperse, the crowd grew even more surely but moved off. Someone threw a brick through the glass window of a fancy carriage leaving the ball, striking Mrs. Kadish, the wife of the owner of the Vienna Restaurant, on the bridge of her nose, causing her to bleed all over her evening gown.

Pausing briefly at another set of police barricades, the marchers turned and moved on to the nearby *Arbeiter-Zeitung* office at 107 Fifth Avenue. Parsons flung open a second-story window and proceeded to regale the crowd below. Again he was followed by Fielden, who spoke while fistfights broke out sporadically between supporters and opponents of the anarchists in the street.[66]

An undercover policeman watched the crowd until reporter Marshall W. Williamson recognized him and grabbed his sleeve, urging him upstairs, saying, "There is something of interest for you people up there, you had better go up."[67] Williamson, with his undercover cop in tow, led the way to the upper-floor editorial offices, where a dozen people, including Albert Spies, Samuel Fielden, Albert and Lucy Parsons, and Lizzie Holmes, were gathered after concluding their protest. Williamson asked Spies to show him "the package" he had shown him a few days earlier, and Spies handed Parsons a foot-long tube with a fuse protruding from one end. Parsons boasted that there was "enough there to blow up the building." The undercover cop asked Parsons why he had not challenged the police barricades and later remembered Parsons saying, "We were not exactly prepared to-night . . . here is a thing I could knock a hundred of them down with like tenpins." Spies brandished a coil of fuse, and Parsons pointed out that a man could blow up the Board of Trade from a block away.[68]

The following day the *Arbeiter-Zeitung,* in its report of the Board of Trade protest, made no secret of its armed preparations. The parade, the paper boasted, was "well armed, and that also the nitro-glycerine pills were not missing. They were prepared for a probable attack and if it had come to a collision there would have been pieces. The cordons of the police could have been quite excellently adapted for experiments with explosives!" Gottfried Waller, a member of the anarchist Northwest Side group, later revealed that at the planning meeting for the Board of Trade demonstration, Adolph Fischer, August Spies's co-defendant and lieutenant, had handed out bombs made from capped sections of lead pipe, telling his comrades to "use it if we would be attacked by the policemen." Fischer's bombs were apparently no bluff, as a couple of weeks later Waller took one that Fischer had given him out to the prairie and exploded it in the crook of a tree.[69]

Anarchist dynamite talk was not taken seriously by the city's authorities until a rash of incidents involving suspicious devices occurred in late 1885. A few days before Christmas a young boy delivered a package to the general offices of the Chicago, Burlington, and Quincy Railroad, a company known as having unusual resolve to hold firm against the demands of its employees for an eight-hour workday. A clerk unwrapped the package to discover a tin cylinder laced with wire, matches, and some sort of clock mechanism. The contraption was turned over to the police, who panicked and tossed it into the Chicago River.[70]

Then, a few days later, the maid and gardener for Judge Lambert Tree, who was then away serving as the ambassador to Belgium, discovered a device on the front porch of his mansion that was later determined to be a small bomb or what people at this time called an "infernal machine." A "powder man" was called in to examine the object, and he declared in his report that it contained "about one-quarter of a pound of nitro-glycerin," though after fusing and exploding it in the snow of the lakeshore, he con-cluded that "there was not enough stuff in the can to do much damage had it exploded on Mr. Tree's steps."[71]

Harry Wilkinson, a cub reporter for the *Chicago Daily News*, was assigned the task of following up on the bombing scare and went to the anarchist editorial offices on Fifth Avenue to see what those who advocated bombings thought of the devices left at Judge Tree's door and at the railroad offices. Wilkinson had been covering anarchist meetings and rallies for months and had spoken with August Spies a number of times. Spies sat down and happily answered Wilkinson's questions. Naturally Spies denied that the city's anarchists had anything to do with these attempted bombings, though the explanation he provided must have surprised the young journalist. An-archists could not have been responsible for those bombs, Spies told him, because anarchist bombs were constructed differently and were known as "czar bombs" because they were the same type used to assassinate Czar Alexander II. Wilkinson told him that he did not believe him and that this all sounded like a "pretty tall tale." Spies seemed offended and rummaged in an adjoining room, returning to hand Wilkinson a round lead bomb. That bomb, Spies told the stunned reporter, was a sample of the sort of bombs made by persons in their movement, and thousands of them had already been manufactured and distributed through the *Arbeiter-Zeitung* office, he added.[72]

Over the next week Wilkinson and Spies met a couple more times, including once when the pair had lunch with Joseph Gruenhut, one of the organizers of the eight-hour-workday movement, at the Chicago Oyster House. Over oysters and wine Spies told Wilkinson about how the social revolutionaries were preparing to engage in street fighting with the police the first weekend in May and how they had scouted the most favorable locations in the city for these battles. At one point he illustrated the ability of a small group of revolutionaries to destroy a company of militia by laying toothpicks across the tablecloth. In the article Wilkinson published about these plans a day or two later, he noted that Market Square and some of the intersections on Randolph between Desplaines and Halsted Streets were favored. Prophetically, Gruenhut told Wilkinson, "I think the great crisis will come on the 1st of May or soon after"—a crisis that would begin with the eight-hour-workday strike and inevitably pull into its vortex the masses of unemployed men followed by the police and militia sent to put it all down. "This will produce an outbreak . . . this is the occasion for which I think the Socialists are arming."[73]

Wilkinson's sensational story was picked up by the Associated Press and carried in papers across the nation. The editors of Chicago's other large daily scoffed at his scoop, calling it "silly," "idiotic," and "a cheap sensation." The *Chicago Tribune*, while not denying that there were radicals who were both extolling the virtues of bombs and preparing to use them, put this threat into perspective: "There are Socialists here and dynamiters here, as there are in New York and other cities, though the proportion of dynamiters to Socialists is too ridiculously small to be worth public notice." Likewise, the *New York Times*, while admitting, "It is not unlikely that some of the more crazy of these [socialists] spend their time in concocting secret plots and manufacturing dynamite bombs," thought a few such cranks could not amount to the dire threat that Wilkinson's blood-curdling report made them out to be. Rather, if they deigned to do more than bluff, "they would find the uprising that followed quite different from that which they profess to anticipate. There is no doubt that even in Chicago they would be promptly dealt with as criminals, with popular feeling all against them. Their wildfire would not spread, but would be summarily stamped out."[74]

As the year 1886 progressed, these "bluffs" began to take shape. In March policemen searching for a fugitive who had shot a pair of men broke into a workman's cottage in a Bohemian neighborhood on Chicago's West Twentieth Street. The cops did not find the man they were looking for, but they did stumble upon a steamer trunk, at the bottom of which, under a mound of rags, was a revolver, a pipe with a fuse capped at one end, and four curious round lead shells, each about the size of a baseball, with holes about a half an inch in diameter drilled through the top. Also in the trunk was a copy of Johann Most's handbook on the manufacture of explosives and bombs, *Revolutionaere Kriegswissenschaft*.[75]

Chicago's anarchists made no attempt to distance themselves from this discovery. The short-lived radical sheet *Anarchist*, published by the "Autonome Gruppen," which included Haymarket defendants Adolph Fischer and George Engel, reported that the police found dynamite shells and arrested a "comrade." The *Anarchist* praised the fugitive shooter for taking the law into his own hands and shooting men who had cheated him on a deal involving a mule, noting that there would be less swindling if only all workers would "act with the weapon in their hand and not with a lawyer."[76]

In New York, about an hour after midnight on the morning of March 9, 1886, a patrolman discovered a man climbing a fence behind a row house on Seventy-Second Street while another man stood watch. Carl Willmund and William Schlieman were arrested. Hidden in their clothes were a variety of weapons. Schlieman carried a .44 revolver and some small brass tubes filled with fulminate of mercury, a powerful explosive used in blasting caps. Willmund had a dirk hidden up his sleeve, a lead-filled club, and a pound bag of cayenne pepper. Inside Willmund's pocket was a letter written in German to Johann Most:

> My Dear Compatriot Most: Send the *Liberty* 545 Broome-street, where I have moved to. I am there in a small store, and cannot, therefore, for a while, get away, but I will try to come to the meeting on Sunday. If you have anything of importance you need only write me a few lines. I am at all times ready to act for our cause, even to the knife.[77]

Willmund's willingness to act violently for the cause may have been an idle boast but must be lent some credence, given the razor-sharp blade he hid in his sleeve and the truncheon he kept in his pocket.

The historical record indicates that some anarchist leaders did more than merely extol the transformative power of these weapons. Historians have generally refused to acknowledge what the anarchists on trial for the Haymarket bombing and their lawyers freely admitted during the proceedings: that at least three of the eight men on trial were actively engaged in collecting, manufacturing, or distributing explosives. The defense conceded that Louis Lingg, a member of the armed auxiliary of his anarchist-led carpenters union, manufactured and distributed bombs. August Spies boasted during his questioning that he ordered and experimented with dynamite. In addition to Spies's own unhelpful admissions, the prosecution revealed letters from Johann Most in which Most alluded to a shipment of explosives he had sent to Spies. The manager of the Aetna Powder Company denied that his firm knowingly sent any explosives to anarchists but said it would have been easy for them to have ordered them under false names.[78]

Between the time Spies admitted ordering dynamite from the Aetna Powder Company and his correspondence with Johann Most about dynamite shipments, Spies's *Arbeiter-Zeitung* reported that the Repoune Chemical Company had sold dynamite to the International Working People's Association. Clearly, running such a story is just the sort of boast that historians have described as useful bluster and publicity seeking. But Chicago's anarchist leaders did not stop there. When a German newspaper in Philadelphia, the *Tageblatt*, expressed its skepticism that Repoune would sell dynamite to the anarchists and published the chemical firm's denial of the story, Spies's newspaper took offense at being called liars and provided still more details to support their previous story:

> The catalog of the company with handwritten annotations on it can be viewed at the Arbeiter-Zeitung office. These annotations refer to dynamite for especially destructive purposes with notations of the prices. The accompanying writing is very typical and this can't be anything compromising for the company. The assumption that another person could have sent the catalog is either out of the question or at least very questionable since a business card was attached upon which was written in pencil in English: "Will move to Wilmington, Del." Equally so ridiculous is the speculation that this catalog came to us completely by accident because the envelope had the following address:
>
> Messrs. A. Spies and A. R. Parsons
> Secretaries of the Intern. W. P. Ass.
> 107 Fifth Ave., Chicago, Illinois
>
> So now may the crafty-devils from Philadelphia go back and ask the company if that is also true.[79]

After the Haymarket bombing, police searched Spies's and Parsons's editorial offices, and among their discoveries was what appeared to be a thinly veiled order for dynamite sent to Parsons: "Comrade Parsons, Providing we send you the following dispatch: 'Another bouncing boy, weight 11 pounds, all are well—signal Fred Smith,'—can you send us No. 1 for the amount we sent you by telegram. Please give us your lowest estimate. Also state by what express company you will send it to us."[80] The nomenclature "No. 1" corresponded to an invoice for "10 lbs. No. 1 ... $3.50; 100 TT caps,

$1.00; 100 feet double T fuse, 75 cts." discovered in Spies's desk from the Aetna Powder Company of Miller, Indiana.[81]

About the same time that Parsons was corresponding with Smith about shipping "No. 1," his American group had resolved to form a military company and "to establish a school on chemistry, where the manufacture and use of explosives would be taught."[82] While it could be that the plan to open a bomb-making school was not sincerely undertaken but was adopted for the purpose of adding force to their dynamite threats, there is at least one interesting piece of evidence from the pages of the *Alarm* that suggests they were real. A small correction appeared in the May 30, 1885, issue of a story that had run in the previous issue. The original story was a translation of a portion of Johann Most's book *Revolutionary Science* that provided a recipe for the manufacture of fulminate bombs. The editor of the *Alarm* pointed out that the word *mash* had been incorrectly used in place of *wash* and noted, "The difference is too great, for whoever shall try to mash fulminate of silver would never be able to wash it." This small item, again seemingly intended as information to those within the movement, suggests that someone close to the newspaper must have been familiar with the making of bombs, or such an error probably would not have been recognized. It also indicates that the editors believed that someone may attempt to follow their recipe, that their militant words had not only rhetorical power but persuasive power as well.[83] Similarly, in an editorial that mentioned the home manufacture of dynamite penned by "A. S.," presumably August Spies, mention is made of the problem of terrible headaches caused by the gases released in the heating of certain chemicals. Spies's knowledge of this headache issue points to some sort of personal experience.[84]

Around this time Albert Parsons was barnstorming the country, speaking on behalf of socialist and labor groups. Frequently he would extol the importance that workers arm themselves in order to resist the soldiers and police who would be sent to crush their movement. There is some evidence that Parsons may also have been engaged in spreading the gospel of dynamite in a more direct way as well.

Two years after the Haymarket trial had ended and nearly one year after the executions had been carried out, the Kansas legislature opened an investigation into a series of bombings, one that grievously injured the family of a railroad shipping clerk who made the mistake of bringing a suspicious package home, and another that destroyed a newspaper office. J. W. Whitley, who hosted Parsons during his visit to Topeka, Kansas, testified that after Parsons delivered his public street speech for the Knights of Labor, he returned to his house with some friends for a private conversation. Parsons, Whitley

remembered, shared with them specifics about how to manufacture dynamite. Another man present that night, C. S. Whitted, had a clearer memory,
ticking off who followed Parsons up to his rooms: fellow IWPA members
C. A. Henrie, Harry Vrooman, and possibly also Harry Blakesley. (Parsons
confirms this account himself with a report he published in the *Alarm* on
his stay in Topeka, writing, "In Topeka I found such stalwart champions of
revolutionary Socialism as Comrades, Henry [*sic*], Blakesley, Whiteley [*sic*],
Vrooman, Bradley, and others.") Whitted then provided a vivid description
of part of their late-night talk with Parsons:

> Q. State all that you do remember.
> A. I will say this much was very definite on my mind from the fact of my peculiar
> trade at the time. We talked on the use of dynamite.
> Q. Tell this committee what was said about the use of dynamite and if Mr.
> Henrie was present at the time of the conversation.
> A. Yes, he was present we were all there yet; Mr. Parsons gave us a formula for
> making dynamite. One of the boys spoke up and says, "There is Whitted
> who is a gas fitter and he can furnish us some gas pipe and we can make
> some gas pipe bombs"; I do not remember who it was that made the remark
> about my trade.
> Q. Are you able to give that formula that he gave that night.
> A. No, I cannot, He made quite a long statement in regard to the matter and
> among other things he said it was safe to manufacture it in a room well ven-
> tilated and of a low temperature; that the uniting of the acids with glycerine
> produced a stink like that of a dead person; that you had to use rubber gloves
> to protect your hands. I remember that part of it very distinctly. He said
> the acid would ruin your hands if it came in contact with them. Of course
> we talked quite a bit on the subject and upon other subjects until finally it
> became quite late and the meeting gradually broke up and we went home.
> I should judge it was after 1 o clock when we went home.[85]

There is a step in the process of mixing up homemade dynamite that involves
combining glycerin and nitric acid, an exothermic process that gives off
much heat and must be kept below a certain temperature to avoid exploding. This reaction does throw off brown fumes, though without knowing
the exact recipe it is difficult to know what they would have smelled like.
Though few would describe nitric acid fumes alone as smelling putrid like
a corpse, they are pungent. It is also true that contact with nitric acid will
discolor and irritate the skin to the point where it can begin to peel and
slough off.[86]

Overall, this description is generally accurate; it is essential to keep the
room cool and well ventilated, acids will damage the hands, and this stage

of the process is smelly. How would Parsons have known these details? Some of them are contained in Johann Most's handbook for revolutionaries, *Revolutionäre Kriegswissenschaft,* first published serially in *Freiheit* in early 1885 and translated and republished in Parsons's *Alarm* in the issue of April 4. However, that excerpt does not contain several of these specific details, such as which step in the process is smelly. Parsons presumably gathered this description from his own or one of his colleague's personal experience with the process.[87]

Whether or not Parsons conveyed this information from personal experience, from discussion with others, or from the study of Most's technical writings is less telling than the fact that he conveyed this information to an inner circle of fellow organizers in private rather than from the rostrum of a public meeting, where his advocacy of dynamite could have been merely rhetorical.

Fund-Raising by Any Means Necessary

It was an exciting and heady time to be an anarchist. All at once it seemed that the heretofore only imagined prospect of revolution was taking shape. A new age was advancing upon an alchemy of ingredients: the rising unity of the social revolutionaries built on a deeper understanding of the importance of force and deeds over slogans, ballots, and polite meetings; a working class awakening from its lethargy; and the invention of dynamite, the great leveler, as easy to concoct as ice cream.

At the inner core of every activist group are a few individuals more willing to take risks in the name of the cause. Within anarchist groups in both New York and Chicago were cadres willing to act on their principles. Such individuals are not always the most deeply dyed true believers. Sometimes such people are attracted to the deed and not the cause it serves. For this reason it is dangerous to infer something about the character of the movement as a whole from the covert and illegal activities that the most resolute or daring undertake in its name. Only when these actions are not well hidden and are implicitly condoned by the silence of those a degree or two removed from them do these extremes reveal much about the movement as a whole. Because of their secretive nature and their illegal activities, such cells leave only faint traces in the historical record. Usually their existence can only be inferred, and then without much confidence in the details. In the case of revolutionary anarchism in the 1880s, there are many intersecting lines of evidence that when overlaid reveal a consistent pattern—a pattern that exposes that a few in the movement not only talked of revolution but also took seriously the idea that the means justify the ends.

Edward Nathan-Ganz, the shadowy man also known as Alexander Rodenow, Bernhardt Wyprecht, or de Costa, seems to have been the apostle not only of revolutionary organization but also of new means of obtaining funds to support it. It appears that his message to those inside America's nascent revolutionary movement was initially shocking to them in the stark logic of its break with all social conventions and values. Nathan-Ganz urged the members of his newly created New York Social Revolutionary Club to resort to any means to acquire funds for their activities, particularly encouraging them to take up counterfeiting and burglary in support of their revolution. According to one member of the party, Nathan-Ganz spent hours one afternoon trying to convince saloon owner Justus Schwab to use theft and counterfeiting to build the revolution, nearly "talking to him to death." Whatever can be said of Nathan-Ganz, he does appear to have lived up to his own principles, funding his radical publishing efforts, transatlantic travels, and who knows what else by mail fraud and other schemes.[88]

While Justus Schwab was apparently reluctant to follow Nathan-Ganz's example and combine revolutionary and criminal activities, there were others in the club who were not so reticent. Soon after Nathan-Ganz left and headed to Boston, a new organization calling itself the Black Hand proclaimed its existence in the *Freiheit*. Its stated purpose was to act through "revolutionary skirmishes," "daring deeds," and "proofs of our power," as evident in its motto, "Be Up and Doing!" This was the Black Hand's only public communication, and nothing was heard of it until the next year, when a young German journalist, Paul Eberhard (who claimed to have attended college in Berlin with some of Bismarck's sons), sued a fellow journalist, Emil Klaessing, for ten thousand dollars for printing a libelous story that exposed Eberhard as a member of the Black Hand.[89]

Klaessing reported that the Black Hand was actually an international anarchist organization founded to support acts of terrorism on the Continent. Eberhard was supposedly a member of the Berlin Black Hand group and traveled to America to raise funds for its activities. On this shore Eberhard reportedly worked with New York's Black Hand to bomb a monument; send letter bombs to Cyrus Field, William Vanderbilt, and other industrialists; accumulate funds through arson and insurance fraud; and launder bonds stolen during a murderous robbery in Vienna. During the trial a number of witnesses swore to the existence of the Black Hand in New York City, including one of the witnesses for the plaintiff who testified that he knew of the group's existence but swore that Eberhard was not a member. After two days of hearings, a jury was persuaded that what Klaessing had reported was close enough to the truth not to have been libelous. New York investigators were well behind German spies who mentioned in their reports a year earlier that the social revolutionary clubs in America were employing criminal means to fund themselves.[90]

There were also reports of a Black Hand gang operating in Austria and Germany. Two years after the London Congress, one of its delegates, Herman Stellmacher, put force behind his words and shot dead a Viennese police informant while he took his morning stroll. Stellmacher later told a judge that he had shot the agent on behalf of Vienna's proletarians, apparently unaware of the irony that he had been chased down and subdued by a group of quarry workers who had witnessed the murder (one of whom Stellmacher shot). Stellmacher was a close friend of Johann Most and for a time was entrusted with editing Most's *Freiheit*.

Beyond his own revolutionary deed, Stellmacher was a conspirator with a group of two others (Anton Kammerer and Michael Kumics) who were implicated in the murders of seven other people. All were delegates to the anarchist meeting at St. Gallen, Switzerland, held in August 1883, and both Kammerer and Kumics had worked with Stellmacher and Most to smuggle copies of *Freiheit* into Germany and Austria after it was banned. In October they robbed a pharmacist's office in Strasbourg, beating a guard and the pharmacist to death. A month later the gang robbed a bank in Stuttgart after murdering a banker and cracking another man's skull. Ten days before Christmas, they shot and killed the police commissioner of Vienna on his way home in the evening. A fortnight later they raided the home of a Viennese banker, murdering him, his two sons, ages nine and eleven, and wounding their sixty-five-year-old nanny with an axe. The Stellmacher gang's robbery and murder spree finally came to an end when police arrested Kumics and later traced a number of the banker's bonds to an anarchist newspaper in Budapest, *Die Radikale*, which had received them from an anonymous donor who turned out to be Anton Kammerer.[91]

New York papers reported that Kammerer lived on Eldridge Street in New York City for several months in 1879 and 1880 "and was well known among Socialists and revolutionists in this city." Kammerer worked as a cigar maker and regularly attended the Socialist Labor Party meetings at the Germania Assembly Rooms on Saturday nights. Apparently dissatisfied with the moderate policies of the SLP, Kammerer was one of the founders of the Black Hand. Soon afterward Kammerer returned to Berne, Switzerland.

(Most's *Freiheit* reportedly announced the return of Kammerer to New York in November 1883, though at least one early chronicler of anarchism thought this was a ruse to throw Swiss detectives off his trail).[92]

From the moment of his arrest through his hanging, Stellmacher was a hero to those who preached propaganda by deed. New York's Social Revolutionary Club organized a mass meeting in Irving Hall to celebrate Stellmacher's courage. Johann Most addressed the crowd of more than a thousand, saying, "With shouts of joy does the proletariat learn of such deeds of vengeance. The propaganda of deed excites incalculable enthusiasm . . . As for America, the people of that land will learn one day that an end is to be made of the mockery of the ballot, and that the best thing one can do with such fellows as Jay Gould and Vanderbilt is to hang them on the nearest lamp-post." As was customary for such occasions, Most and the other organizers of the evening's program read out a series of resolutions, which were acclaimed by the applause of the crowd. The lengthiest of these concluded: "Brothers, we approve your actions; we approve your methods. Between you and your oppressors there can be no truce. Kill, destroy, annihilate, assassinate, even to the germ of your aristocracy. Have toward them no feeling of love. They are ignorant of such a noble emotion." Later that August, when news of Stellmacher's execution reached New York, a placard was posted on Canal Street between the Bowery and Hester Street, in the heart of Little Germany, that was addressed to the "proletariat of all countries" from the "New York group of the International Workingmen's Association" that read in part:

> In memory of the brave, self-denying, and faithful comrade, Hermann Stellmacher . . . But no tears flow. Mightier than our sorrows is our hatred. We think but of revenge for the annihilation of our best and bravest comrade . . . What he did he did unselfishly. He fought solely for the proletariat. Agitate! Organize! Foment a revolution . . . act and the universe is yours. This is the legacy of our martyred comrade . . . From the grave of Hermann Stellmacher come these words. Let them not be unheeded. Hermann Stellmacher is dead! Long live the propaganda of the act! Hurrah for the social revolution!

In spite of later evidence that prior to Stellmacher's crime spree he had offered to sell information to German authorities, he remained a hero to many anarchists, and his portrait graced the wall of the editorial offices of the New York *Freiheit* when a reporter visited years later.[93]

Soon after the Eisert axe murders, there were rumors that the stolen bonds had made their way to the United States. Austrian police reportedly cabled New York with information that some of the bonds had been sent to Johann Most. Another report claimed that some bonds had been received by anarchists in Chicago and sent to New York for cashing. One New York banker,

Charles Bischoff, did recall a boy who had attempted to cash a suspicious Kronprinz Rudolph Railway bond that he said he had received from a friend in Chicago. From there the trail ran cold, and neither New York nor Chicago police ever solidly connected Kammerer's activities with any Americans.[94]

However, one of the earliest chroniclers of the anarchist movement, August Sartorius von Waltershausen, did make such connections. Sartorius compiled his history of anarchism just a decade after these events, both from his own experiences and from correspondence and conversations with other participants in the movement. Unfortunately, his work is not diligently sourced, and many of his more interesting stories cannot be traced and rest on his word alone. Sartorius wrote that it was "proven" that money from American anarchists was sent to Europe, but he was not sure whether Stellmacher, Kammerer, Reinsdorf, or other famous terrorists ever received any.[95]

In the 1930s University of Michigan librarian Agnes Inglis carried on an extensive correspondence with all the survivors of the revolutionary 1880s she could locate. One of the "old-timers" she discovered and exchanged many letters with was Carl Nold, a former member of the New York group but better known as having been convicted of conspiring with Alexander Berkman to kill steel magnate Henry Frick. Nold remembered that there was a secret group known as the Groupe Schlüsselhein (Group Collarbone), "to which only the most desperate comrades of New York belonged." In another letter apparently responding to some detailed questions Inglis had sent him, Nold is cryptic but may have been referring to this time and place when he wrote, "As to details—There are many details not fit for publication as for instance: Robbery, arson, prostitution for purpose of getting money for propaganda."[96]

Firebugs

The much heralded day of May 1, 1886, the day the mass eight-hour-workday strikes were to commence, was but five weeks away when the individualist anarchist Benjamin Tucker published a devastating indictment of the revolutionary anarchists in his Boston *Liberty*. In a front-page article titled "The Beast of Communism," Tucker charged that a number of active members of Johann Most's New York group "have been persistently engaged in getting money by insuring their property for amounts far in excess of the real value thereof, secretly removing everything that they could, setting fire to the premises, swearing to heavy losses, and exacting corresponding sums from the insurance companies." Scant on details, Tucker's exposé did provide an overall estimate of the number of fires set by anarchists. He estimated that seven or eight fires were set in 1884, twenty in 1885, and at least six so far that year. This practice, Tucker believed, began as a means of raising money for the cause but soon devolved into a selfish racket. Herr Most, Tucker charged, "had nothing to do with originating the plots of these criminals and for a long time was unaware of what was going on; but it is none the less true that, after he was made aware of these acts, he not only refused to repudiate them, but persisted in retaining as his right-hand men some of the worst of the gang." The existence of arsonists within the anarchists of New York was "an open secret among the German-speaking Socialists of New York."[97]

Tucker did not present much evidence except for the curious, sudden, and unexplained resignation of New York's second most famous anarchist (after Most), Justus Schwab, from the management of Most's newspaper. Most and the *Freiheit* responded by warning their supporters to avoid Schwab and boycott his saloon. Schwab himself never directly explained his break with his former comrades, though he alluded to his qualms about their actions in a letter he wrote to Robert Reitzel, an individualist anarchist and editor of the literary magazine *Der Arme Teufel*, in Detroit:

> My dear Robert,
>
> Before these lines reach you, you have probably been enlightened through Liberty as to how I stand with Most. As for myself, I have so far amended the Jesuitical maxim: "The end justifies the means," as to say that the means must not desecrate the end.
>
> I regard myself as a member of the International Working People's Association . . . May I also be preserved in the exercise of an independent judgment over all deeds that come to my view! . . . Behind the scenes there are people from whom I am minded to turn away, on account of their peculiarities. However deeply I may be involved in the whirl and confusion of citizen life, I have not yet lost my conceptions of love, nobility, and decency. So be it well, if former "friends" choose to attack me: I can bear it, in the consciousness of never having proved recreant to the highest good and welfare of society.[98]

While Schwab made his criticisms of Most and his former comrades in private, Moritz A. Bachmann, one of the original anarchists in the city and a founding member of the New York Social Revolutionary Club back in 1881, published his misgivings. Like Schwab, Bachmann did not accuse New York's revolutionaries of any particular crime, but instead alluded to an immoral spirit that infected them: "Penetrated with the spirit of the 'Freiheit,' the members of the New York German Group of the International have become rude and devoid of all the better and more refined qualities of mankind. Day by day grows this spirit of rudeness and fanatical unreasonable desire for merciless cruelty."[99]

Chicagoan Dyer Lum, who took Parsons's place and edited the *Alarm* after Parsons was imprisoned, apparently received confirmation of Tucker's charges from others inside the anarchist movement. Lum wrote, "Unfortunately, men in whom I have the greatest confidence, and in whose word I have unbounded trust, have reason to believe that the charge is true."[100]

The rupture between Johann Most and Justus Schwab seems to have been precipitated by a particularly wanton arson that gutted two tenement buildings in late 1885 and resulted in the sentencing of Henry Kohout and his brother to prison for the rest of their lives. The facts, as testified to during Kohout's trial and later confirmed by him in a jailhouse confession, revealed a depraved disregard for life. Sometime in the fall of 1885, Henry Kohout arranged with a fellow Bohemian anarchist, John Kylian, to set fire to his apartment and split the proceeds of two insurance policies totaling nine hundred dollars. Kylian had unsuccessfully attempted to collect insurance money on a fire he set in his own rooms earlier that year.[101]

Kohout set his plan in motion after midnight on a Sunday night, a time when all was quiet and the other eighty people in his tenement were all asleep. Most of the dozen families in the building worked rolling cigars in their rooms for a boss who was also their landlord. One of Kohout's neighbors, looking across an airshaft, spotted blue flames erupting in Kohout's living room and raised the cry of "Fire!" The owner of a liquor store on the ground floor saw Kohout walk out of the building, fully dressed. Other residents had to clamber over disconnected fire escapes and in and out of windows to escape the spreading fire and ran into the street in their nightclothes. One man climbed from the fire escape through a window and into Kohout's room to try to put out the fire and saw some empty cans and a broken flask, all smelling of kerosene.

The fire swept through all five floors of Kohout's building and then leaped across a narrow alley and engulfed the upper stories of an adjoining tenement. On the top floor of that building, Mary Fialka, a forty-year-old single mother who supported her children, Mary, age seven, and Annie, age six, by cigar making, was overcome before she could get her girls to the fire escape, and all three were burned beyond recognition. Fialka was identified by her sister, who recognized her jewelry.

Firefighters who entered Kohout's charred rooms reported finding a stack of kindling and cigar molds mounded in his kitchen and an open trunk filled with the residue of some oily substance. They also noted that Kohout's apartment had been stripped bare of most belongings. Police at first detained Kohout for his own protection as a mob of burned-out residents roamed the neighborhood with vengeance on their minds, but after finding twenty watches and two fire insurance policies in his coat pockets, the officers decided to arrest him. Many of Kohout's belongings were later found in Kylian's apartment, where they had been taken before the fire was set.[102]

A police captain investigating Kohout's background interviewed "an old Bohemian" named Peter Skrbel who had been beaten up by his son-in-law, Frank Lamofsky, after the old man spoke out against anarchism to some of his friends. After his beating, old Skrbel seemed eager to tell the captain all he knew about his son-in-law's revolutionary activities. Skrbel told the police that Lamofsky had organized a revolutionary club, Anarchists' No. 3, for cigar makers, which included "a man named Schwab" and received the blessing of "Herr Most." Its constitution declared its purposes to be "the abolition of government, the extinction of capital, the annihilation of employers and the . . . manufacture of dynamite." Both Lamofsky and Kohout experimented with various recipes for explosives in their rooms and made such offensive odors that neighboring tenants complained to the landlord. Skrbel said he visited friends who lived in an apartment upstairs from Kohout two days before the deadly fire and smelled "a most abominable smell" rising from Kohout's flat.[103]

Apparently sensitive to Skrbel's charges, Johann Most immediately fired off a letter to Joseph Pulitzer, denying any connection to Kohout: "On behalf of the Anarchistic organization of New York, I am instructed and authorized to declare that no such club as 'Anarchists No. 3' has ever existed in this city. Henry Kohout, as well as his friend Lemofsky, are entirely unknown to our organization, and we totally disapprove of so reckless a procedure as experimenting with or manufacturing explosives in a house used for dwelling purposes." Most's primary biographer, Frederic Trautmann, however, wrote confidently that Most gave his encouragement to the arsonists' activities.[104] Details of this case dribbled out over the course of a trial that lasted from January 20 to February 4. This corresponds to the time that Schwab must have severed his ties to Most and was most likely the cause of the schism.

Tucker seemed to have an underlying reason for exposing the firebugs and those who harbored them. He apparently saw this as an issue that could clarify the factional lines in the anarchist movement between those who believed in the more extreme versions of propaganda by deed and those who were not willing to shed innocent blood. Tucker closed his exposé with a call for others in the movement to follow suit: "Every Anarchistic journal ought to copy this exposure and send it forth with the stamp of approval. The cause is entering upon a serious crisis. The malicious and the ignorant will do their utmost to damage it. Much will depend upon the promptness with which good men and true separate themselves from common criminals. *He who is not against their crimes is for them.*" By that standard the spokesmen for Chicago's anarchists stood by Most and the extremists. The *Alarm* reportedly refused to print Dyer Lum's column denouncing the arsonists in spite of Lum's being a longtime contributor to the paper. The *Arbeiter-Zeitung* dismissed Bachmann as a "Prussian spy."[105]

Supporting evidence for Tucker's exposé arrived on the eve of the Haymarket riot when the *New York Sun* published a lengthy report listing many of the names of the arsonists. Among the dozen named were Otto Nicolai, the Jersey City Heights agent for the *Freiheit*; Hermann Wabnitz, who was one of the thirty-four celebrated socialist exiles who arrived from Bismarck's Germany in 1880 aboard the *Silesia*; and W. Kubisch, who served as secretary of Group Astoria in the summer of 1883 and later that same year was a delegate to the Pittsburgh Congress of the IWPA. Joseph Kaiser, who was arrested in Chicago in 1890 on suspicion of being involved in a plot to blow up the Haymarket police monument and identified as a "New York anarchist," was noted as taking out a three-hundred-dollar insurance policy on May 7, 1883, and suffered a fire on May 14, which fire officials estimated damaged $25 worth of his goods but resulted in a settlement for $278.68. Wabnitz, Kaiser, and Nicolai were all slightly injured in a fire that burned a dry goods store in June 1885, which Tucker speculated was a case of the firebugs being bitten by their own pets.[106]

In 1887 a New Yorker by the name of George Mayer was sentenced to four years in Sing Sing for insurance fraud. The Greenwich Insurance Company grew suspicious when Mayer, a poor tenement dweller, submitted a claim for clothing lost in a fire totaling $418.75, which was close to what a man in his circumstances might earn in a year. Earlier that year Mayer had fallen in with a gang who helped him to take out the insurance policy and then to fill bladders with flammable liquids and lay long fuses in his Long Island apartment. Luckily for the other tenants, the fire was discovered before it got out of control.

Mayer's conviction would have fallen through the cracks of history except for the fact that he wanted revenge on the informer who had him sent up the river. One of his gang, Kleeman Schuetz (or Schultz), had turned informant and had not been prosecuted in return. Two other confederates skipped the city and could not be found. For Mayer, this was a great injustice, as he had only helped out on this one job, but, according to him, the others were experienced arsonists, having burned a dozen or more buildings in the greater New York area. Mayer swore out a lengthy prison affidavit with his lawyer in which he told everything he knew about the other members of his gang.

Besides Mayer, his gang consisted of Schuetz, a Mrs. Horst, and a man named William Scharf. The others, Mayer reported, were anarchists who constantly received letters from Johann Most and frequently visited the office of the *Freiheit*. One day Schuetz showed Mayer a number of different styles of bombs, some fashioned out of pipe, others round, and boasted that he had brought similar bombs to Chicago and thrown one at the police during the Haymarket meeting.[107] Police and several New York reporters investigated Mayer's account and satisfied themselves that Schuetz had exaggerated his role in Chicago and that, though living nearby in Pullman at the time of the bombing, he had a tight alibi for that night. Seven years later, however, a Chicago jury convicted six men and women on charges of arson and insurance fraud for setting ablaze at least seven buildings. The ringleader of the gang was William Scharf, who was said to have belonged to a Black Hand anarchist society in New York City.[108]

As the year 1886 approached, the number of those in anarchist ranks who earnestly prepared for armed action was growing. A militant spirit was spreading, one that combined a naïve faith in the power of new weapons with an overly rosy estimation of the willingness of the masses to rise and confront their oppressors, or at least the symbols of their oppression. The remaining step was to complete their philosophical break with Marxism's faith in the long-run importance of even corrupt or staunchly conservative trade unions.

CHAPTER FIVE

ANARCHISTS, TRADE UNIONS, AND THE EIGHT-HOUR WORKDAY

Toward the end of June 1885, the West Side Street Railway Company fired sixteen of its men. All happened to have been leaders of the drivers and conductors union at the firm, though the company insisted they were discharged for their poor work performance. This set off one of the most popular and disruptive strikes in the city since the Great Railroad Strike of 1877.

On the first day of the strike, police acted with restraint and largely chose not to respond when rocks rained down on the streetcars, except for police captain John Bonfield, who fired off a round that missed a youth who was cradling a big stone in his hand. One sheriff riding in a car was badly injured by a rock that burst through a window. The sympathies of the vast majority of the city's workers were with the strikers and against the company, and thousands crowded the sidewalks to jeer and yell "Rats!" as the streetcars and their police escorts passed by. Even those who were lukewarm on the union used the opportunity to vent their hatred for the company, a monopoly that scorned its captive customers with unreliable and uncomfortable cars, continually ratcheted up its fares, and ran as few cars as it could, forcing crowds of passengers to wedge themselves in or ride the running boards.[1]

The strike clamped Mayor Harrison into a political vise. On the one hand the vast majority of his constituents were against the company, but he could not entirely ignore either the law or the elites who expected him to protect property. Harrison's brilliance showed as he made sure reporters knew he personally had stopped a man from using an axe handle to pry up the tracks while also pressuring President J. R. Jones of the streetcar company to agree to arbitration. After the first day's violence, the mayor made a bid to give the city some breathing room and ordered the streetcar company to keep its cars in the barn the next day, claiming the police needed the time to prepare for a bigger show of force on July 3.[2]

If Harrison was hoping that the pause would bring the sides to the negotiating table, he was sadly mistaken, and following through with that big show of force became politically necessary. That morning as the streetcars clattered out of the barns driven by nervous scabs, Captain Bonfield adopted a new tactic to protect the cars. He deployed a line of officers at the front of the first car and ordered his men to clear the streets, sidewalks, and corners of all crowds and to club anyone who did not move aside quickly enough. Policemen who had been on duty for the previous eighteen hours, many having been abused and pelted with rocks, reveled in the free hand they were given and indiscriminately swung their hickories at anyone who seemed resistant, including a teenage girl, a grocer standing by his sidewalk vegetables, a newspaper hawker, a squad of diggers fixing a gas main, as well as a goodly number of actual strikers. Bonfield himself cracked a seventy-year-old man's skull. Some cops took advantage of the blanket order to settle some old scores: the worst criminal dens in the whole "Bloody Ninth" ward—Tom's Lodging-House and the West Side Tivoli—were invaded under the thin pretext of their having crowds milling about their doors. Lieutenant Shea shouted an order into the bar to "disperse," followed by another to his men, "Raid!" and "every policeman's club found a sensitive place in the person of some unfortunate." Hundreds of others were arrested and packed into the subterranean cells of the station houses, so many that desk sergeants gave up trying to book them all. They were a spirited bunch, cracking jokes at their jailers and singing "John Brown's Body" and "Stick to Your Mother," and other popular tunes at the top of their lungs.

As the morning wore on, the crowds grew bolder and the tide turned. A line of ten streetcars crawled down Western Avenue "at half the rate of a funeral," and when it passed Lake Street a group of strikers rushed from the shadows and seized the driver of the third car and dragged him into an alley. Police gave chase and retrieved the battered scab. A scattering of stones chased after the rescue party, and Bonfield loudly commanded his men to "shoot the first man who throws a stone." There were no more rocks at that stop. But as the train of cars approached Leavitt Street, it encountered a tall pile of curbstones, beer kegs, and even iron girders pulled from a construction site nearby laid across the tracks. Sporadic fighting around these barricades continued throughout the day.

In response to numerous complaints of the clubbing of innocent bystanders, Mayor Harrison called Captain Bonfield to his office. Bonfield defended himself brazenly, saying, "Mr. Mayor, I am doing it in mercy to the people. A club today to make them scatter may save the use of a pistol tomorrow."

Later that autumn, Bonfield's jaunty defense of the club prompted the city's Trades and Labor Assembly to protest to the mayor against his promotion to inspector, but during their discussions at Harrison's home, the labor leaders admitted that Bonfield had "performed his duty" though he "lost his head and clubbed innocent people unnecessarily."[3]

As the strike dragged on into its second week, the number of incidents had diminished, though the few clashes that flared up were just as severe. Streetcar 175 was rumbling down Van Buren Street and had just passed Robey Street when a small charge exploded on the tracks, stopping the horses. A crowd of several hundred surged forward, and when the four cops riding the streetcar hopped down to disperse them, one man, Thomas Gorman, unhitched the team before a policeman noticed and laid a blow across his forehead, exposing his skull. No sooner had Gorman dropped to the street than the crowd's fury was ignited and they overturned the streetcar and grabbed the scab driver, an unfortunate young man named Thomas Caruth, whose face was "pounded into a jelly." Having done all it could there, the mob moved south to Madison Street and overturned car 531, drove off the handful of officers protecting it, and then beat its driver and conductor.[4]

A week after the strike broke out, it unexpectedly ended with a promise by the president of the company to investigate the case of each of the sixteen men who had been fired allegedly for their union activities by the district superintendent. Each man was to be allowed to have a union representative present to help offer his case. The president pledged that if any man was found to have been fired for any insufficient or vindictive cause, he would be immediately rehired.[5] Though neither the president of the company nor union leaders would admit it, it seems that pressure from the mayor's office forced the company to concede.[6]

It was a qualified victory but a rare victory nonetheless in what was the largest and most popular strike in the city since the time of the Great Railroad Strikes of 1877. All the city's trade union leaders spoke out for the streetcar drivers and conductors, the Chicago Trades Assembly holding numerous meetings and coordinating mediations with both the city and the stubborn company. For the most part during the weeklong strike, one group remained quietly on the sidelines of the action. Partly this was due to the fact that Spies, Parsons, and their fellow revolutionaries of the International Working People's Association were excluded from most of Chicago's trade unions, as one observer put it, "like rags from cholera-infected Naples." But near the end of the strike, Chicago's social revolutionaries held a public meeting to discuss the meaning of the strike. To the surprise of anyone who had not been closely following the ideological and organizational twists and turns of Chicago's revolutionary movement, the speakers that night denounced the union and its members for ending their strike.

August Spies and his fellow speakers had nothing but contempt for the car drivers union, which urged peace and denied any participation in the violence. "If the strikers are what they claim to be—law and order citizens— they deserve to be shot down for preventing the street-car company from running its cars. Let them throw out this hypocrisy of being for law and order and the Internationals will be there like men." Sam Fielding followed, praising the beating the unionists received, calling it a "righteous clubbing . . . for pretending to be law and order citizens."[7] Albert Parsons also sneered at the workers' struggle in the *Alarm*, writing: "Altogether the strikers have no cause to shout themselves hoarse over their victory. The strike was led by democratic office-seekers, who had nothing truer or nobler to say than, 'we must win this strike,' 'Carter is your friend!' and 'Rats!'"[8]

The Chicago IWPA's deprecating attitude toward the streetcar workers' strike was no anomaly. Rather, it expressed their increasing alienation from the labor movement in the city along with a fundamental shift that had occurred in radical anarchist thinking and organizing over the previous half decade. While nearly uncritical support for the labor movement was a bedrock principle of American socialism from the time of the First International in 1863 to the formation of the Socialist Labor Party in 1879 (on the theory that even the struggle of a bad union served to develop class consciousness and in some small way to help build up the resources of the working class), it was a principle at first pushed aside at the London Congress of 1881 and then actively combated after the Pittsburgh Congress two years later. At these meetings anarchists hollowed out the old union ideals, preserving the shell of the idea while substituting a totally different rationale for labor activism. On the surface the Chicago anarchists claimed to still advocate on behalf of their local unions, but underneath this rhetoric the purposes of their support had fundamentally changed.

At the London Congress of 1881, where the revolutionary socialist movement first took some semblance of organizational form, the issue of support for labor unions was sidestepped. None of the resolutions or declarations that were agreed upon addressed the question of what the proper relationship between the revolutionary and trade union movements should be. One of the American delegates, most likely Marie Le Compte, touched upon this question in her report on conditions in America. Le Compte, formerly an assistant editor of the *Labor Standard* of New Jersey, who was well acquainted with the leaders and struggles of labor, observed: "The late strike of the brewers did not tell in our favor, the revolutionary workers not being able to penetrate their councils, which is the more regrettable because the opportunity for revolutionary propagandism was a very good one. It is our opinion that we should join all labor organizations."[9] Le Compte's purpose in urging all revolutionaries to join labor unions was to radicalize them, not to support the goals they already pursued. This strategy of "penetrating" unions for the purpose of "revolutionary propagandism" would later come to be known in socialist circles as "boring from within."

The question of what to do with trade unions also provoked some discussion at the Chicago conference later that year, with most delegates dismissing the existing labor movement and favoring a policy of "boring from within." A plank on the question of trade unions was reported by the resolutions committee. It read: "We declare it to be our duty as members of trades unions to strive for the amalgamation or federation of our hitherto isolated unions upon a national and international basis, to the end that wage-laborers everywhere may become more united in the great struggle for the overthrow of the domination of capitalism." August Spies opposed even this tepid endorsement of labor unions. Spies's future co-defendant in the Haymarket trial, Albert Parsons, tried to amend this proposal by adding a clause supporting shortening hours and raising wages until the wage system was destroyed, but his proposal was voted down by the others (including Spies) on the resolutions committee. After the congress as a whole worked over the platform, this union resolution was watered down to a point where the word *union* was entirely removed. Even this withered remainder of the resolution was about to be scrapped when someone suggested that it was "absolutely necessary to throw a little 'sop' to the trades-unions." A leader of the opposition to the resolution, who was not named, then caved in and said that though he was "bitterly" opposed to all trade unions, he was "just hypocrite enough to advocate the resolution, and hoped the hypocrisy of the congress would be unanimous." The hypocrite carried the day, and the Chicago revolutionaries went on record in favor of "the organization of workingmen and women (being the most interested in the solution of the social problem) into local, national, and international associations for the purpose of educating themselves as to the cause and circumstances which led to their enslavement, and to learn the remedies by which the evil may be abolished." Actually there was only one remedy envisioned by the participants to this meeting—a violent revolution—and the mission of the organization was to join unions so as to overcome their ignorance of this fact—in other words, to "bore from within."[10]

Thereafter those socialists who identified with the revolutionary wing of the movement became more openly dismissive of trade unions. By the spring of 1882, the Chicago organ of the Trades and Labor Assembly was compelled to complain of those "howlers" who disrupted the labor movement "because it is not revolutionary and radical enough." The editor complained of these "windy blatherskites": "When a feasible proposition is made for practical improvement of the actual conditions, these growlers will have nothing to do with it, because it does not go far enough, as they claim. The socialists or revolutionary socialists, as they call themselves in Chicago, have shown themselves in this role and made themselves obnoxious . . . What good have they accomplished with their opposition against trades unions?"[11]

Chicago's anarchist leaders never shied away from such accusations, even after they were convicted and in the process of legal appeals when they tried to burnish their image by distancing themselves from their most violent rhetoric. In the memoirs they drafted while awaiting their legal fate, many openly criticized not just particular unions but also the theory and practice of the trade union itself. Michael Schwab wrote, "Any thinking man must concede that strikes, boycotts, co-operation on a small scale and other means will not and can not better the condition of the working-classes, even not so-called factory laws can bring the sought-for result about." Oscar Neebe complained that he was frequently accused of working against the interests of trade unions, but defended himself saying, "We were not against them, only against the way these organizations were made and kept," which to his rival trade union leaders certainly read like a distinction without a difference. In his autobiography Louis Lingg was even more direct: "It had long since been my opinion that in the present state of society the working classes could make no gain in the direction of improving their condition by means and way of Trade Union, but, nevertheless, I participated in the organization of the latter, because I knew that the working men from their past and coming experiences and disappointments would soon become revolutionists."[12]

When the noted Chicago socialist fire-breather John McAuliffe committed suicide later that summer, one of the city's labor papers editorialized, "It is well known in Chicago that Mr. McAuliffe never favored trades-unionism. To him a trade-union was the embodiment of selfishness, in which the spirit of caste and aristocracy was fostered; besides he could not see *how* a trade-union, simply working to obtain an increase of pay, could ameliorate the condition of the working classes."[13]

Revolutionaries' disinterest in the mundane struggles of trade unions for better wages, hours, and working conditions was put on public display again when they assembled in Pittsburgh in 1883. The day before the congress opened, Johann Most's *Freiheit* featured an essay titled "Our Fundamentals" whose arguments set the tone for the rest of the gathering. Chief among these fundamentals was that "the struggle of the proletariat against the bourgeoisie must have a violent revolutionary character, and the wage struggle alone will not lead us to our goal." Most's own home club, New York Group 1, sent instructions with him to avoid "petty" demands such as those for shorter hours or better wages and instead to support trade unions only so as to radicalize them, to "bore from within."[14] Similar instructions accompanied Chicago's delegates to the convention, whose mandate urged them to "press at the Congress the recognition of the universal arming of the proletariat as indispensable, presupposition of the emancipation of the exploited, and, at the same time, to urge the workers to get in possession of arms."[15]

August Spies, who had opposed even a weak endorsement of trade unions at the earlier Chicago conference, was a member of the resolutions committee, which was put in the awkward position of having to respond to an elaborately detailed plan of action submitted to the convention on behalf of what appeared to be a bona fide labor union, the International Workingmen's Association, Pacific Coast Division (IAA in German abbreviation). Organized by the ambitious and bellicose San Francisco editor Burnette Haskell, the Pacific Coast Division of the IAA was actually a phantom—a secret organization that existed only in the pages of Haskell's *Truth* and that of his friend Joseph Buchanan's Denver *Labor Enquirer*. But neither Spies nor anyone else in Pittsburgh doubted that it was a real union of militant workers rising somewhere beyond the Rockies. In a confidential letter sent to Spies, Haskell depicted the IAA as a fully functioning revolutionary organization whose "socialist" leaders had previously "joined the Knights . . . with the aim of making the Knights of Labor take a front rank in the work of preparation for the coming revolution." When their plan of boring from within the Knights stalled due to their inability to influence "masses of working men" who were "densely ignorant, cowardly, and selfish" and misled by "designing politicians and 'would-be-politicians'" and "church people and masons," they concluded that "the Knights of Labor was perfectly useless save and except as the recruiting ground for some other organization." The organization they chose to affiliate with was the remnant of the organization founded at the London Congress of 1881 whose embers were kept alive by Englishman Henry Mayor Hyndman, who dutifully kept up its correspondence and answered Haskell's letters. Haskell and his socialist friends were attracted to the IAA because it stood upon the "doctrine of physical force and had foreseen and prophesied the coming Social Revolution, both of which we firmly believe."[16]

Haskell's elaborate plan of action, which involved establishing a network of independent cells whose members "will be prepared when the hour of revolt shall come, to assume leadership, rally and organize the people, inflame them with revolutionary fire and point out to them the road to success," was rejected by the delegates. But in a gesture of reconciliation, Spies crafted a resolution that pledged support for the IAA but made it clear that less militant labor organizations were not only undeserving of their help but also should be actively combated.

> In consideration, that we pay tribute to the progressive principles in labor unions—the abolition of the wage system, the cornerstone of a better and more just social system than that of the present and further,
>   In consideration, that the labor unions form an army of exploited and disinherited brothers and companions in distress which is called upon to knock down the economic building of the present for the purpose of general and free cooperation. With these words it is,
>   Decided: That we reach to the I.A.A. our brother hand and give to them our sympathy and help in their fight against the ever growing despotism of private capital, and,
>   Decided: That while we bring our fullest sympathy to such progressive labor unions and guarantee to them all the support possible we are determined on the other side to fight and when possible destroy all organizations which pay tribute to reactionary principles since they are enemies of the cause of worker emancipation or even humanity and progress.[17]

Two delegates, Victor Drury, of New York, and Albert Parsons, rose to object to Spies's resolution and urged its defeat, but their opposition was overwhelmed and Spies's resolution was adopted.

Unfortunately, Drury's and Parsons's reasons for objecting were not reported, and we can only speculate about them based on what is known of their general views. Drury and Parsons were both active members of the Knights of Labor, and both devoted their energies to radicalizing their unions. Drury was a high-ranking member of the Knights' powerful and contentious New York District Assembly 49 who actively pursued a "boring from within" strategy by organizing a secret association known as the Home Club, which tried to steer the Knights toward revolutionary policies. Parsons regularly blasted unions for thinking they could win any gains for their members through strikes. In his last public speech as a free man, the one he delivered from the wagon on Desplaines Street minutes before the bomb was thrown, he denounced the Knights for believing in strikes and for thinking they could "obtain redress within the present system, but that is impossible, in my belief." As both Drury and Parsons participated in existing unions with the hope of converting them to revolutionary purposes, they could hardly have objected to those portions of Spies's resolution praising such efforts. This leaves only the last "Decided" of the resolution, which calls on socialists to actively fight and "destroy" reformist labor unions. Such language went too far, not because such "reactionary" unions were worth defending on their own merits, but because to actively work against them precluded socialists from trying to bore in and capture them.[18]

Many revolutionaries' hostility to conventional trade unionism was reiterated a few hours later when delegate J. J. Reifgraber from St. Louis proposed a resolution that demanded that governments recognize the right of labor unions to incorporate. Reifgraber's modest resolution was voted down. After all, why defend the rights of labor organizations that have already been declared illegitimate and targeted for destruction?

Thus the Pittsburgh Congress broke down into two camps on the labor question: those who believed nonrevolutionary labor unions should be destroyed and those who thought they should be tolerated because they might be infiltrated and seized. With New York divided between Drury and Most, and Chicago divided between Spies and Parsons, the fault line between these two positions did not follow either a regional or an ethnic pattern. In the end the congress agreed on wording that split the difference: "The work of peaceful education and revolutionary conspiracy well can and ought to run in parallel lines." This compromise was also summed up in the congress's motto: "agitation for the purpose of organization; organization for the purpose of rebellion."[19]

Over the course of the year following the Pittsburgh Congress, Chicago's revolutionary clubs had little contact with the city's labor movement. Rather, in speech after public speech, revolutionary leaders freely denounced labor unions and pledged their resolve to penetrate and convert them to their own militant purposes. Adolph Fischer lectured before the South Side group on "The Unions and the International Workingmen's Association," in which his remarks were summarized as follows: "the I.A.A. does not oppose the unions as such, but that it fights against the reactionary tendencies" such as the principle of "a good day's wages for a good day's work." A week earlier Group Jefferson No. 1 listened to Comrade Fehling present a speech that examined why anarchists "would have nothing to do with unions." Comrade Fehling explained that "naturally the anarchists could not be persuaded to be enthusiastic about reform swindles and election humbugs." Anarchists "pointed to the uselessness of strikes" and instead "tried to prepare the people for the coming revolution."[20]

Subsequently, Chicago's social revolutionaries benefited from deep ethnic tensions that cleaved the city's labor movement into two. German tradesmen in several important unions whose numbers had been steadily growing, and who had long chaffed at their junior status in organizations directed by "English" leaders, finally broke away and formed unions of their own. Through this wrenching process a new cadre of bold and impassioned activists rose to leadership of these organizations. Many of these new leaders were social revolutionaries who lived up to the Pittsburgh Congress's declarations by steering their unions to prepare for revolution and fought tooth and nail against the "reformist" unions they left behind.

Just a month after the Pittsburgh Congress wrapped up, the Chicago cigar makers union split along ethnic lines with most of the German workers abandoning the Cigar Makers' International Local 14 for the newly formed revolutionary Cigarmakers' Progressive Union No. 15. (The Cigarmakers' Progressive Union arose in New York two years earlier, largely under the leadership of Victor Drury and his Home Club.) Local 14 responded by ordering its members to strike any shop where the Progressive Union members worked. The president of Local 14, William Brown, claimed the union had no other choice but to defend itself against the "kickers" of the Progressive Union, who tried "to disorganize us to further their Socialistic ideas." For a time it appeared as though Brown's tactics might backfire as the cigar manufacturers jumped on the union's quarrel as an excuse to lock out the much larger international union. But in the end the cigar companies caved and fired the members of the new Progressive Union.[21]

However, a handful of cigar makers stuck to their guns, and the Progressive Union carried on. Its meetings, however, more resembled the agitation meetings of the revolutionary socialists than those of practical unions. At its meeting in February 1884 the Progressive Union members circulated copies of the declarations of the Pittsburgh Congress and debated the merits of labor legislation, finally resolving that "the only means through which our aims, the emancipation of all mankind, can be accomplished is open rebellion of the despoiled of all nations against the existing social, economic, and political institutions."[22]

Similar tensions were felt in other unions across the city where the numbers of German members grew and outstripped the English who had grown accustomed to running them. At a meeting of the large carpenters union, a man interrupted the usual proceedings and demanded that the business be conducted in the German language. "Who are you talking for, anyhow?" asked one of the union officers. "For the Germans," he replied, whereupon someone shouted from the crowd, "D—n the Dutch," provoking a brawl that soon involved the union's president, who wielded a large club that was taken away and used on him before police arrived. Both the Germans and Bohemians left the union and formed locals of their own and affiliated with the soon-to-be-formed Central Labor Union. The national leader of the carpenters loudly attacked the splitters as "social anarchists" who "talk of petroleum, revolution and dynamite."[23]

Momentum for a radical and German union league built quickly. Cigarmakers' Progressive No. 15 persisted and in May issued a call to all the city's socialistic unions to establish their own city labor association, a rival to the long established Chicago Trades and Labor Assembly. Seven unions of cigar makers, carpenters, furniture workers, metal workers, typographers, tailors, and fresco painters, all German or Bohemian, responded and sent representatives. At this meeting the Central Labor Union (CLU) of Chicago was formed.[24]

Chicago's radical union movement had grown out of the deep ethnic tensions dividing the city's working class, just as the revolutionary socialists had grown out of the Socialist Labor Party, whose reins were held by a minority of Yankee and English leaders. For Chicago's revolutionary socialists, these developments could not have been more fortuitous, as they provided a receptive constituency for their proselytizing and allowed them to completely fulfill the doctrine agreed upon in Pittsburgh—"agitation for the purpose of organization; organization for the purpose of rebellion"—while fighting all the other "reactionary" unions in the city. Chicago's revolutionary leaders could claim to be advocates of labor and builders of labor unions while supporting only unions that were affiliated with the CLU and shared their revolutionary doctrines. But CLU unions shared few of the practical concerns of their "reactionary" enemies. Jacob Selig, a leader of the Cigarmakers' Progressive Union and the CLU, left little for his union to advocate beyond arming for the revolution when he criticized the Trades and Labor Assembly as being "men who have no higher aims than the abolition of prison labor, the enforcement of the eight hour day, prohibition of children under 14, fair days-wages for a fair-days work and political office from the Republican or Democratic party, [they] don't care which."[25]

Even after the formation of the CLU, Chicago's anarchists were quite open about their dismissive views of the trade union movement. In October 1885 the anarchist Central Labor Union devoted one of its public meetings to discussion of the topic "Trades Unions and Strikes." John A. Henry, a member of Parsons's American section, led off by railing against the proposed eight-hour-workday reform, a "half-hearted claim" at best and something of no benefit to the poor man in his battle with capital. Lucy Parsons followed, observing that trade unions could secure higher wages but ultimately had no power over capitalists. Even strikes were of little use, as employers frequently found them useful in eliminating excess inventory. Such reforms as the eight-hour workday would not bring about the "millennium," she argued, but it might "be the first step in revolution." Michael Schwab followed and expressed his view that trade unions once had been successful but had now become "old and useless."[26] The *Anarchist*, organ of the Autonome Gruppen, based on Chicago's north side, moaned in January 1886, "When will the workers be sick of this labor union swindle and organize politically in order to overthrow the system of today?"[27]

One element contributing to the anarchists' dim view of trade unions in general and even the possibility of radicalizing them under the best of circumstances, was their very low estimation of the intelligence, energy, and character of the working class. Lizzie Swank summed up these views well in the course of one of her many polemical letters to the *Labor Enquirer*:

> Now, if everybody was sensible, and open to conviction when the truth is placed before them, all we would have to do would be to set the philosophers to work to concoct a scientific plan of society, tell it to the people, and in a trice have it organized . . . But unfortunately we haven't that kind of people to deal with. People are not intelligent, are not meek and mild, and easily led into paths of wisdom and peace . . . The masses are apathetic, stupid and unwieldy.[28]

The only occasions on which the anarchists showed approval of trade unions was when they engaged in violent confrontations with their employers or the forces of the state. Anarchist newspapers largely ignored the 1884 strike of Ohio miners until they began blowing up mine heads. Then the American group passed a resolution that "this manly aggression meets with our full approval and that we call upon all other wage-workers to profit by their example."[29] As the struggle in the Hocking Valley intensified, the *Alarm* referred to the miners as "the advance guard in the grand army of labor."[30] Likewise, the McCormick workers became the favorites of the anarchists not because they dared to strike, which numerous other groups of workers did in the spring of 1885, but because they skirmished with Pinkerton guards and city police and even ambushed an omnibus en route to the barricaded factory and captured a crate of Remington rifles. Even after the striking machinists seemed to have won an unlikely and surprising victory, Albert Parsons took the stage at a meeting in the neighborhood of the factory and publicly discounted the workers' achievement as only a "temporary" victory "on a rather indifferent matter," adding that it was "purely a local affair and that so far from its having settled the labor question, it hadn't even decided it for that factory."[31]

According to a leader of the Chicago Trades and Labor Assembly, Mark Crawford, in early 1885 a delegation of TLA leaders met with Mayor Harrison to privately warn him about the violent plans of the city's anarchists. Crawford revealed to reporters after the Haymarket bombing that his union committee told the mayor that the anarchists were making bombs and advised the mayor to prevent them from holding their weekly agitation meetings on the lakefront. Crawford recalled, "We knew the bombs were being made, and we knew the action of the Anarchists would injure the labor cause."[32]

A full year before the Haymarket Riot, the Chicago Trades and Labor Assembly discussed plans for their coming Labor Day parade and voted to prohibit the "Anarchists and Socialists with their black and red flags" from participating. About a third of the labor delegates, led by George Schilling, opposed barring the anarchists from their parade but in the end could not derail the vote.[33]

In early 1885 when Joseph Buchanan was trying to organize western workers into branches of his reinvented International Workingmen's Association, he reported that he had heard it asserted by many in the labor movement that "Communist-Anarchists formed under the leadership of John Most into (Black) International, have decided upon a vigorous warfare against Trades unions as an important branch of their tactics." Buchanan noted that the national carpenters union charged that anarchists had intentionally ruined one of their locals, Union No. 21, and had designs upon another.[34]

The Eight-Hour-Workday Movement

In the same way that Chicago's anarchists rejected trade unionism, they sharply criticized most trade union reform proposals. In doing so they nearly missed their opportunity to participate in the largest labor movement of the century: the general strike wave for an eight-hour workday that roiled the nation in May 1886. As it was, Chicago's anarchists tacked from being opponents to becoming reluctant latecomers to the eight-hour-workday cause.[35] In speech after speech and article after article, Chicago's anarchists initially dismissed the eight-hour-workday demand as a meaningless concession that preserved the structures and relations of capitalism.

The national eight-hour-workday movement was launched in Chicago by the predecessor of the American Federation of Labor. In the fall of 1884, the Federation of Trades and Labor Unions (FOTLU), the national labor federation that would later evolve into the American Federation of Labor, held its convention in Chicago and first proposed a mass strike for an eight-hour workday. FOTLU's official position was that the eight-hour workday should be the movement's sole demand and that all questions of wages should be deferred. In the case of workers who had been paid by the day and worked a ten-hour day, reducing the number of work hours in the day to eight with no reduction in pay amounted to a 20 percent raise. For those workers who were paid by the hour, reducing the number of hours in the day meant their take-home pay would also go down by 20 percent, unless compensated by an hourly increase of the same percentage.

Most of the unions affiliated with the Chicago Eight-Hour League, a joint organization of representatives of Chicago's Trades and Labor Assembly and its Knights of Labor locals, seemed willing to make this sacrifice in the interest of social reform and worker solidarity. They stood firmly on the platform of "eight-hours' work for eight-hours' pay." To the leaders of the Chicago Eight-Hour League, winning the eight-hour workday, even without an increase in wages, was a great and worthwhile victory and one they believed would inevitably not only lead to higher wages and greater employment in the future but would also set in motion a dynamic that would initiate a rising spiral in workers' standard of living. When viewed within the frame of their own ideology, such trade union eight-hour advocates were not timid conservatives, but radicals who believed they were setting in motion the pebble that would become an avalanche.[36]

FOTLU's convention coincided with the launching of Chicago's first English-language anarchist paper, Albert Parsons's *Alarm*, and in its second issue Parsons had his first opportunity to comment on FOTLU's eight-hour-workday idea. In a front-page article summarizing the convention, the *Alarm* condemned the trade union conference as "a tame affair" without "any practical value to the down-trodden and starving workingmen of this country."[37] Over the course of its first year of publication, the *Alarm* chose not to mention this new eight-hour-workday initiative again.

This was surprising, for as late as 1879 Albert Parsons seemed to retain his faith that trade union action was a sure, if slow, path to socialism. After all, in 1878 Parsons was elected recording secretary of the Chicago Eight-Hour League and helped organize the Chicago appearance of Ira Steward, the "Father of the Eight Hour day."[38] At the time a leader in Chicago's Trade and Labor Assembly, which he praised for considering "all questions concerning work and wages in a deliberate, calm, and impartial manner," Parsons trumpeted the eight-hour workday, which he predicted would practically end unemployment and raise wages for all.[39]

In August 1885 Parsons and the *Alarm* received a circular from FOTLU encouraging all workers to demand the eight-hour workday or simultaneously strike on May 1, 1886. This provoked Parsons to write a lengthy critique of the proposal based on the idea that "it is the firm conviction of

Anarchists, based upon facts, that the hours of labor can not be reduced by working people so long as the machinery which displaces us and forces us into compulsory idleness and a destructive competition is held as private property." Reflecting the years he had spent as an eight-hour-workday activist, Parsons did not criticize the goal of the eight-hour movement. Rather, he seemed to suggest that the reason the eight-hour-workday reform was not achievable was because it was too challenging to the extant powers and structures of society: "to permit the wage-slave to control his hours of labor would be to tear up the foundation of [the capitalist] . . . system and to destroy it utterly." Here, then, was the Parsonian difference: an eight-hour workday was not wrong because, to use George Schilling's words, it was "soothing-syrup for babies"; rather, it was wrong because it was medicine that was far too powerful. Because the struggle over the number of hours in the workday shot to the heart of the capitalist alienation and exploitation of labor, it was intrinsically tantamount to revolution. "Will the possessors of property permit the propertyless to alter the system, or themselves manumit their slaves? We cannot believe it." Since the reform was itself revolutionary, if one was going to make war, it was better, Parsons argued, to fight in the name of the world one hoped to win. "Comrades, for pity's sake, do not longer waste your precious time in vain endeavors, but combine to remove the cause which makes labor the slave of capital. There is but one way and only one to control the hours of labor, to wit: The laborer must control the means of labor—capital!"[40]

A month later another eight-hour-workday circular from the FOTLU arrived on Parsons's desk, and he again seized upon the occasion to explain why the suggested reform was, by itself, of little interest to anarchists. In contrast to his earlier editorials, in which he had avoided criticizing the goal of a shorter workday and merely pointed out that its achievement required the violent overthrow of the capitalist system, in this column Parsons comes as close as he ever did to dismissing the eight-hour workday as "soothing syrup": "shortening the hours of labor is no real remedy. It still leaves people in the condition of masters and servants. The fact that the master and servant can more easily change places does not cure the matter."[41]

Like most other anarchists, Parsons saw no possibility that the demand for an eight-hour workday would be conceded by a significant number of employers or could be won without a fight. Having witnessed many strikes and street riots in Chicago, Parsons was confident how events would play out. "Will the manufacturing kings grant the modest request under such circumstances? No, Sir. The small ones cannot and the big ones will not. They will then draw from the army of unemployed; the strikers will attempt to stop them. Then come the police and militia ... Say, workingmen, are you prepared to meet the latter: are you armed?"[42]

The contrast between the anarchists and the trade unionists' attitudes toward the eight-hour workday was dramatized by their competing Labor Day parades in early September 1885. The CLU assembled at their usual spot, Market Square, and listened to speeches by future Haymarket martyrs Oscar Neebe, Albert Parsons, and August Spies, followed by the singing of a song, "The Red Banner," by the socialist Mannerchoir. Neebe railed against the trade unions, saying, "The Trades Assembly want [you] to reconcile yourself with capital, to live in an alley, to live between two piles of manure." Parsons followed the same theme, proclaiming, "We differ from the Trades Assembly, which advocates harmony and peace based upon the slavery of labor to capital." Neebe and several other parade marshals then mounted their horses and formed the crowd into files four abreast and led them off to Ogden's Grove, a picnic spot about five miles west of the city. Among the many banners held aloft by the marchers were those reading: "The fountain of right is might. Workingmen arm" and "Not to be a slave is to dare and do—Victor Hugo." The CLU's Labor Day parade seems to have passed without any references to the eight-hour workday.[43]

The following day the Chicago Trades and Labor Assembly devoted its Labor Day parade to kicking off the eight-hour-workday movement.[44] Just as the anarchist-led CLU had the day before, the TLA marched from the downtown out to Ogden's Grove. First in line was the stonecutters union, seven hundred strong, each decked out in floppy white hats and canes. Following were a number of floats carrying transparencies displaying many mottoes, a large number relating to the eight-hour-workday cause, including "Eight hours for work, Eight hours for rest, and Eight hours for recreation," as well as a picture of a reclining capitalist drinking wine with the caption "works two hours a day" next to one of a hardworking man with the words "works fourteen hours." Next came more than four hundred plasterers, sixty lathers, and four hundred sawyers with a dozen wagons loaded with lumber. Behind them were the four hundred members of Typographical Union No. 16, a division that included typographers, or "printers," from all the city's many newspapers save one—those who worked in the office of the anarchist *Arbeiter-Zeitung,* a local that belonged to the rival Central Labor Union, which was not invited to attend. The typographers marched with a working press shop that printed and distributed a newspaper called *Labor Holiday* along the route. Sixty broom makers marched with their namesakes on their shoulders, and three hundred cigar makers marched alongside a float bearing an immense cigar. They were followed by watchmakers, carpenters, coopers, barrel makers, horseshoers, iron molders, tanners, shoemakers, bricklayers, stonemasons, and others, most of whom had prepared wagons fully equipped to demonstrate their skills en route.[45]

Once at Ogden's Grove, the three thousand labor picnickers listened first to speeches by A. C. Cameron, former editor of the *Workingmen's Advocate* and local labor leader; "Labor's Congressman" Martin Foran of Ohio; and county judge Richard Prendergast, who orated, "If labor was united they would need no law to enable them to shorten the hours of labor. Eight-hour laws already passed were dead letters because the men who labored did not insist on stopping when they had worked for eight hours." The last speaker was Mayor Carter Harrison, who proclaimed himself a friend of labor but warned:

> Eat when you are hungry and drink when you are thirsty, but don't drink after your thirst is quenched. If you take the blue and the white from the flag and leave only the red it may lead to bloodshed, and that doesn't protect your property nor your lives. The Socialists have much that is good in them, but when they allow men who preach bloodshed, dynamite, and destruction to take the lead, socialism becomes an evil and not a blessing. [Applause.] I am a Socialist [laughter], but my Socialism teaches me as long as I can lift an arm or elevate my voice to sustain the Stars and Stripes—the Red White and Blue. [Cheers.][46]

Chicago's anarchists reflexively denounced the leaders of the Trades and Labor Assembly's Labor Day parade as "harmonizers, arbitrators and peace-makers who are vainly striving to inaugurate reform without disturbing anybody," or more colorfully as "Lickspittles and Flunkeys."[47]

Just two weeks after the TLA founded their eight-hour-workday committee and launched their campaign, the CLU held their first meeting on the issue. Somewhere between four hundred and six hundred people packed into Turner Hall on Twelfth Street to hear the anarchist position on the eight-hour workday. Future Haymarket prisoner Samuel Fielden spoke first, reviewing the "constant tendency to diminish rates of wages and extend the hours of labor," which led to strikes and confrontations. Fielden reviewed the ease with which capitalists ignored existing eight-hour-workday laws and how ineffective union efforts were to enforce them. The *Alarm* summarized Fielden's conclusion this way: "For these reasons the speaker was opposed to the eight hour law. It was not to relieve, but to make further profit out of their employes [sic] that employers here and there tried the experiment of reducing the hours of toil."[48]

Fielden was followed by typographer A. W. Simpson, who, like Fielden, denounced eight-hour-workday laws as useless, but went further and pointed out that even if unions won their demands, this would be no improvement, because capitalists would just raise the cost of goods, stealing back any gains the workers had made. Simpson criticized not just the demands for the eight-hour workday but also the union movement that wanted it. "Trade unionism is simply organized selfishness. It proposes to assist those laborers who are in the trades unions at the expense of those who are not." The only positive effect of an eight-hour workday, according to Simpson, was that it would "give trades unionists . . . more time to attend Socialist meetings and thus learn Socialism." Paul Grottkau, who spoke in German, was more sympathetic to the eight-hour cause, seeing it as an "advance" but only a "temporary" one, for once the working day was limited to eight hours, capitalists would introduce more machinery and rely more heavily on the labor of women and children, eventually creating even more exploitation than before. The only solution was systemic and revolutionary: "the whole social system must be changed" through armed and active resistance.[49]

When Grottkau was finished, future martyr August Spies rose and introduced a set of resolutions he had obviously prepared ahead of time. Composed of two "whereas" and two "resolved" statements, these resolutions are the clearest snapshot of anarchist thinking and belief about the eight-hour-workday movement in its infancy. They candidly stated the general anarchist opposition to the efficacy of the claims made for the eight-hour workday, claims that Albert Parsons, in an earlier day, once enthusiastically believed. More importantly, they plainly state the reasons for anarchist interest and involvement in promoting a reform they did not believe in.

Spies's resolution began with a few simple observations: that the movement for the eight-hour workday had been started by "organized wage workers" and that "it is to be expected" that this movement will be resisted by "the governing class" and their "Pinkertons, the police and state militia." With only these points in mind, and without any other discussion of the merits or promise of an eight-hour workday, Spies went directly to the resolutions:

> *Resolved,* That we urge upon all wage-workers the necessity of procuring arms before the inauguration of the proposed eight-hour strike in order to be in a position of meeting our foe with his own argument, force.

> *Resolved,* That while we are skeptical in regard to the benefits that will accrue to the wage-workers from the introduction of an eight-hour work day, we nevertheless pledge ourselves to aid and assist our brethren in this class struggle with all that lies in our power as long as they show an open and defiant front to our common enemy, the labor-devouring class of aristocratic vagabonds, the brutal murderers of our comrades in St. Louis, Lemont, Chicago, Philadelphia, and other places. Our war cry be: 'Death to the enemy of the human race, our despoilers.'"[50]

Just as the evening's chairman was about to put Spies's resolutions to a vote, a reformer by the name of James K. Magie stood and raised a point of order, noting that a discussion of the resolutions should be allowed. Magie then "denounced the revolutionary character of the resolutions" and advocated that workers "strike with the ballot, not the bullet," a suggestion that was met with hisses and howls and "shouts of 'rats' from all parts of the hall."

Magie's motion forced other anarchists to clarify how their purposes and goals were distinct from that of the eight-hour-workday movement. John Patrick Dusey, a member of Parsons's American group, vigorously defended the resolutions on the grounds that violent revolution was both right and necessary, concluding, "The bullet brought this nation into existence, and by the eternal God the bullet shall make us free men or dead men." Spies then weighed in, denouncing Magie as a "political vagabond" (Magie had once been an organizer of the Anti-Monopoly Party of Chicago), and elaborated on his resolution. His argument was paraphrased in the *Alarm* as follows: "To make the movement in which they were engaged a successful one it must be a revolutionary one. Don't let us, he exclaimed, forget the most forcible argument of all—the gun and dynamite."[51] The question was then put to a vote and passed with only a scattering of nays heard throughout the hall. The evening's proceedings suggest that in the minds of the anarchist leaders represented at the meeting, there was no contradiction between supporting the eight-hour-workday movement while at the same time trying to steer it into direct revolutionary confrontation with the authorities. While the anarchists' desire to radicalize the eight-hour-workday campaign by encouraging armed struggle may have seemed to those unfamiliar with anarchist ideology as an opportunist attempt to seize control of a popular movement that was not their own, in fact, from the anarchist point of view, the *only* way to truly win a shortened workday was to revolutionize society by violent means.[52]

By the fall of 1885 the differences between the Central Labor Union and the Trades and Labor Assembly on the eight-hour-workday issue were clear. In addition to the resolutions put forward by August Spies at the CLU's first eight-hour-workday meeting that urged workers to arm themselves, the CLU's distinctive approach to the issue of the hours of labor was clearly explained in the *Alarm*:

[The CLU] have valiantly taken up the task of organizing the vast army of employed and unemployed wage-workers, preparatory to an assault upon the strongholds of capitalism. The Central Labor Union is a revolutionary body which maintains that voluntary concessions by means of arbitration or legislation from the employing class is not to be expected. They therefore call upon all wage-laborers to organize and enforce their demands for the right to not only live, but live well, by every means in their power. They hold that labor can only acquire any rights whatever by the use of such force as may be necessary to overcome the opposition.[53]

Future Haymarket defendants August Spies and Samuel Fielden were unequivocal in their denunciation of the eight-hour-workday reform in the early fall of 1885, Spies arguing that it was a "lost battle" and Fielden noting that "whether a man works eight hours a day or ten hours a day, he is still a slave."[54] The *Anarchist*, the monthly launched on January 1, 1886, by future Haymarket martyrs George Engel and Adolph Fischer, exclaimed in its inaugural issue: "In opposition thereto we reject all reformatory endeavors as useless play which adds useless hope and miserable derision to the oppression . . . All endeavors of the working classes, as long as they do not aim at the overthrow of the existing conditions of ownership and do not put into practice the principle of complete self-government among themselves, are to us reactionary."[55]

At a meeting of the anarchists' North Side group in December 1885, a full room of revolutionaries approved a resolution that linked the eight-hour-workday demand and revolutionary action: "This assembly declares that the North Side Group I.A.A. pledged itself to work with all means for the introduction of the eight hour day, beginning on the 1st of May, 1886. At the same time the North Side Group cautions the working man not to meet the enemy unarmed on the first of May."[56] While this statement seemed to emphasize the use of arms as a defensive practice, Michael Schwab took the floor and emphasized that arms were for revolution: "If you think the anarchists are a sort of Pinkerton's guard for the working men's movement then you are mistaken. The anarchists arm themselves because they are working men. They preach arming in order that the working men should be able to liberate themselves."[57]

Right up to the great eight-hour strike deadline of May 1, 1886, Chicago's anarchist daily, the *Arbeiter-Zeitung*, carried letters and articles denouncing the eight-hour cause, "what good would the eight hour law do the idle working man . . . This demand would be of little benefit to the masses. An extortioner may treat once in a while his wageslaves, in order to make them work better, but he will never grant them the right of a larger share of the products of his labor. The only aim of the working men should be the liberation of mankind from the shackles of the existing damnable slavery." Chicago's anarchist leadership was one of the last elements of Chicago's labor movement to endorse the eight-hour-workday movement, committing itself in support only a few months before the first of May, by when all employers had to concede or face a general strike. By then Chicago's anarchists had swung around to a posture of support for the eight-hour-workday movement, primarily because they saw it as a Trojan horse from within which they might spring a workers' insurrection and hasten the "scarlet and sable lights of the JUDGMENT DAY."[58]

Months later one of the radicals close to August Spies, Joseph Gruenhut, whom the mayor had once appointed factory and tenement house inspector, was quizzed on the witness stand about August Spies's beliefs about the eight-hour workday. Gruenhut was asked when Spies had become "converted" to the eight-hour-workday reform. Gruenhut replied, "I don't suppose he was converted, he was compelled to it." An uncomprehending defense lawyer tried to straighten his answer and asked when Spies began expressing support for the idea. "I don't suppose he ever said that at all." The lawyer thought he'd take one more pass at this, still not grasping what Gruenhut was saying, and asked, "How do you know that he was enthusiastically in favor of the eight hour movement, if he never was in favor of it?" Gruenhut's answer summed up well the feelings of the revolutionary anarchists toward the eight-hour-workday movement and how their cynical engagement was so easily mistaken by later generations as sincere support: "I did not say that. I said that he was not in favor of the eight hour movement, it was of the eight hour mass meeting [he was in favor of]."[59]

CHAPTER SIX

FROM EIGHT HOURS TO REVOLUTION

Though the Chicago River was frozen and May Day was still four months away as the new year began, it was obvious to Chicago's anarchists that the eight-hour-workday movement was catching fire. The Trades and Labor Assembly and its Eight-Hour League, ably led by barrel maker George Schilling, were active in all corners of the city and winning ground by the day. TLA organizers held their organizing meetings among Chicago's Polish workers, the Eight-Hour League drafted lengthy manifestos to manufacturers, and the TLA held an eight-hour-workday benefit soiree at Cavalry Armory. Around the same time, the Eight-Hour League sent a circular to national labor newspapers requesting information about organizing efforts in other areas to better coordinate a general strike. It urged other unions to join the effort, saying, "There should be a general and simultaneous movement along the whole line of the labor army for the enforcement of eight hours per day."[1]

Chicago's TLA was emerging as a national leader in the eight-hour-workday effort. In January, Chicago's bricklayers union, one of the strongest components of the TLA, representing four thousand workers, used its clout at its union's national convention in St. Louis to push for a nationwide eight-hour limit to the workday but could only cajole their brothers to consider a compromise of nine hours. Seeing this issue as of paramount importance, Chicago's bricklayers bolted from their national union and established their own independent union and affiliated with the Knights of Labor. Before the month was out they had won an agreement from their employers in which the highest-paid workers would receive a cut in wages proportionate to their reduced hours, but the lower-paid hod carriers and mortar mixers and assorted unskilled laborers would receive a raise to maintain a daily wage close to what they earned before. That month the bricklayers voted the sum of five hundred dollars to aid fellow TLA members striking at a Chicago box factory.[2]

As the TLA's eight-hour-workday agitation gained adherents and even showed promise of victory, the rival CLU, not wanting to be left behind, rushed to adopt more moderate goals and rhetoric. Later that spring the CLU sent a letter to manufacturers and businessmen asking them for statistical information about their operations and for their opinion on the eight-hour workday. The CLU reported that of the seventy-five employers who responded, none of them expressed opposition to the eight-hour workday. When the TLA announced plans for a grand eight-hour-workday rally to be held in mid-April, the CLU expressed an interest in attending, humbly informing the press that it was "holding itself in readiness . . . but will not go unless invited." The TLA considered inviting their rivals in a debate that consumed an hour of their regular weekly meeting, at one point considering a motion to invite them on the condition they march into the meeting behind the Stars and Stripes rather than their red flag, but in the end the two groups were unable to agree on the terms of the invitation.[3]

The militant leaders of the CLU were forced to soften on the eight-hour-workday issue, because over the past year the rank and file of the CLU found the idea of an eight-hour workday increasingly appealing, and the anarchist leadership of the radical labor union was openly challenged. At a mass meeting of the Central Labor Union held above Zepf's Hall in late December 1885, Paul Grottkau was reported to have spoken "severely of the Anarchists, who by their actions, he said, were hurting the chances of the success of the eight-hour movement." This provoked hisses and shouts to have Grottkau tossed out of the room, but those protesting were outvoted. A resolution was then approved condemning "the hypocritical and unfriendly position taken by the Anarchists with regard to the eight-hour demand of the proletarians as that of reactionists, and in consequence hindering the accomplishment of the emancipation of the proletarians." (This may well have been the meeting George Schilling referred to years later when he was interviewed by historian Harry Barnard in which Schilling said he nearly came to blows with August Spies.) The following night the anarchist North Side group of the IWA branded the CLU's resolution as "slander" and urged "the working men of Chicago to eliminate from their meetings demagogues and slanderers who have sneaked into their meetings." Clearly, the pressure was building for the anarchist leadership to jump on the eight-hour-workday bandwagon or risk alienating its labor base.[4]

It was at this point that the solid wall of skepticism and scorn that the anarchists had long held against the eight-hour-workday reform cracked and the militants began proclaiming their devotion to the short-hours cause. On January 31 the IWPA held a mass meeting to champion the eight-hour workday, but try as they might the anarchists could still not speak unreservedly about the reform. Future Haymarket defendant Samuel Fielden was one of the keynote speakers, and the *Chicago Tribune* paraphrased him as saying that night that the socialists were "not very ardent in this movement because it was simply a readjustment of the wage system, which they wanted abolished altogether." Nor did the anarchist *Alarm* seize on this meeting with its usual gusto for reporting on such mass meetings. Unlike the lengthy reports in the *Alarm* covering other topics discussed at the other meetings, the only reference to this event reads: "The International Working People's association held a largely attended meeting on last Sunday in Zepf's Hall, about 500 persons being present, to agitate the eight hour question. Speeches were made by Sam Fielden and others."[5]

While Chicago's anarchists had taken their first small steps to publicly demonstrate their support for the eight-hour-workday movement, they could not quite restrain themselves from disputing its importance within the labor movement. At the very next meeting of the TLA's Eight-Hour League, anarchists verbally sparred with trade unionists over the reform's principles. That evening's program was a speech by manufacturer Thomas E. Hill, who had granted the eight-hour workday to his own employees. Hill repeated many of the standard Stewardian arguments: that an eight-hour workday would decrease unemployment, provide needed leisure to workers, and stimulate the demand for goods. As Hill finished, anarchist A. W. Simpson, a member of Parsons's American group and a typographer who carried dual membership in the TLA and the CLU, took the floor and "occupied ten minutes exposing what he termed the transparent fallacies of Mr. Hill's remarks." Simpson's objections were brave, one reporter present noting, "Mr. Simpson's remarks met with little sympathy from the audience."[6]

That same week, similar divisions between anarchists and unionists were evident just to the north in Milwaukee. On February 28 the distinguished Knights of Labor organizer Robert Schilling was the guest of honor at an eight-hour-workday rally in Milwaukee's Casino Hall. Upon the conclusion of Schilling's speech, an unidentified local leader of Milwaukee's anarchists attempted to step up to the platform to respond and was rebuffed. Anarchist supporters shouted for him to be allowed to speak while others cried "throw them out!" A few anarchists were picked up and carried from the hall, though worse fighting was averted when the presiding officer hastily gaveled the meeting to adjourn.[7]

As the month of March began, with six weeks to go before the May Day deadline, the TLA Eight-Hour League was in full swing. It had begun organizing the city's clergy to preach for the eight-hour workday, it had sent delegates to the shoemakers unions to plan eight-hour-workday strategy, and it was planning to open an eight-hour-workday headquarters office on the city's south side to begin coordinating efforts on a daily basis. It was receiving reports and coordinating efforts with other cities.[8]

Abundant proof of the TLA's effectiveness in organizing was displayed at a mass meeting held on March 15 to officially open the eight-hour-workday campaign. Described in the next morning's papers as a "monster demonstration" with an estimated four thousand people packed tightly into the west side's Turner Hall, and an overflow crowd unable to get in at least half again as large, this was easily the largest meeting seen in the city so far in the campaign. This crowd assembled from numerous columns of unionists who had gathered at their own halls around the city and marched behind brass bands and banners to the mass meeting. Once the formal preliminaries of introductions were dispensed, the evening's star speaker, Robert Schilling of Milwaukee, delivered his oration on the eight-hour workday. Some of Schilling's rhetoric rang with the same indignation heard in anarchist gatherings: "the laboring man died about twenty years earlier than others, and that all who had died were simply murdered by the outrageous system of labor in vogue." Unlike his anarchist adversaries, however, Schilling's proscription for this injustice was eight hours and patience—eight hours to employ one-fifth more workers and patience to wait for the rising wages that would follow. Schilling placed great faith in the power of consumerism, concluding that "the main thing the country needed was the elevation of the working classes, not only above necessity, but to a position where they would be able to enjoy some of the luxuries of life." Many of the speeches, both inside the hall and outside in the street, as well as the resolutions read out to great applause, emphasized that the eight-hour-workday movement was not a selfish effort but involved temporary sacrifice of wages in the interest of social uplift.[9]

Whether by moral suasion or threat, the TLA's demonstration of support for the eight-hour workday was soon followed by small but significant victories. Over the following two weeks it was announced that the Charles W. Allen and Company cigar factory, with its three hundred employees, would adopt an eight-hour workday. Allen's action was immediately followed by similar announcements at the Quincy Tobacco Company and at the firm of Gradie and Strotz. The Peter Fortune brewery quietly moved from two gangs laboring twelve hours to three gangs rotating eight-hour shifts. A meeting of seventy-five representatives of furniture manufacturers was reported to be leaning toward peremptorily adopting the eight-hour workday rather than later appearing to concede to union demands. Before an unusually crowded gallery, the city council considered an ordinance to establish an eight-hour limit for all city employees and for all contractors doing business with the city beginning May 1. Chicago's Baptist ministers, who had invited members of the Eight-Hour League to meet with them only to have George Schilling scold them for not paying attention to the poor in their midst and having "shoved the responsibility off onto the Almighty's shoulders," unanimously agreed to dedicate their sermons to the topic of the eight-hour workday in the coming weeks and even suggested holding a "grand eight-hour jubilee" at the cavernous Casino Rink with all the clergy of the city. The *Chicago Tribune*, on record as being opposed to the eight-hour-workday reform, seemed almost to praise its progress: "all the efforts of the leaders of the labor movement are being put forth in organization. Every branch of labor, from the drivers of beer-wagons to the fastidious barber, is being formed into local [Knights of Labor] assemblies. One thousand a week is probably not below the growth of the order in the city."[10]

The TLA's successes in the two weeks after its "monster demonstration" also seemed to have another, perhaps more significant effect; it appears to have persuaded the anarchist leadership to tone down their revolutionary rhetoric and to redouble their own organizing efforts. On a single day at the end of the month, Albert Parsons and Oscar Neebe led the organization of a founding meeting of a butcher's union at Greif's Hall. At another saloon on West Twelfth Street, August Spies urged a group of cloak makers, most of them teenage girls, to organize while Michael Schwab addressed a meeting of the fresco painters union on North Clark Street. According to a reporter's paraphrasing of his remarks, Parsons was a bit cagey, not fully explaining his revolutionary ideas but merely leaving the door open for them: "The object of the Central Labor Union was to see that men were not overworked or underpaid. No one would deny that the butchers were both. All over this country and other countries the workingmen were organizing so as to create an instrument by which they could regulate the work and the pay." Whether that instrument was the union, the eight-hour workday, or a socialist revolution, Parsons did not specify, though he did go on to endorse the eight-hour reform so that the men would not fall behind other unions.[11]

In the following weeks anarchist leaders dedicated themselves completely to the task of organizing workers into unions and urging these newly minted unions to demand nothing less than the eight-hour workday at ten-hour wages. Between March and May 1886, at least 32 trade unions with 4,453 charter members were organized, and nearly half of these unions and three-quarters of the workers in them demonstrated their sympathies by marching with the Central Labor Union at its eight-hour-workday parade on April 25. Keeping in mind that the 1,762 charter Knights of Labor, who generally had little sympathy for the anarchists, were organized during those same months in Chicago, slightly more than half of all the workers in the three months leading up to May Day were led into unions that were organized or influenced by anarchist leaders.[12]

Anarchists viewed these gains not simply as steps toward the success of the eight-hour-workday movement but also as signs that the revolutionary moment was closer than ever. Radicals had long hoped that the eight-hour-workday movement and its ultimate May Day deadline might conjure together the conditions for an insurrection. August Spies had boasted to a Knights of Labor leader in Michigan a year earlier that his organization was making plans to use the coming May Day strikes and tumults as the occasion to launch a takeover of Chicago.[13] Events that spring seemed to be playing out according to plan, prompting Spies's *Arbeiter-Zeitung* to crow on its front page: "The month of May may bring many a thing about which nobody dreams of to-day."[14]

Yet even though on the surface the CLU, the TLA, and the anarchist leadership were all pushing the same eight-hour-workday program, the rivalries and tensions continued. On Saturday, April 10, the Eight-Hour League held another "monster eight-hour rally," and this time in addition to the unions of the Trades Assembly, many assemblies of the Knights of Labor packed the cavernous armory building on the lakefront to its capacity of eight thousand and attracted a spillover crowd half again as large outside. Just as the meeting got under way, it was disrupted by a group of five hundred anarchist sympathizers who made a noisy exit from the building behind a red flag. Outside, Samuel Fielden jumped onto a pile of lumber and began competing against the Eight-Hour League's own speakers for the attention of the crowd. Fielden was followed by Parsons, who was described by one journalist as "violently assailing the Knights of Labor."[15]

Later in the pages of his *Alarm*, Parsons confirmed that he and other anarchists did give speeches outside the eight-hour-workday meeting but said they did not mean to disrupt or counter the efforts of the TLA. Rather, Parsons claimed, anarchists were present "in support of the object and purposes of the meeting."[16] As they had been arguing since the inception of the May Day movement, Parsons and other anarchist leaders undoubtedly believed that urging workers to arm and confront their oppressors was the only means whereby the eight-hour workday could be achieved, and thus, by definition, whatever incendiary language they may have used was, in their eyes, offered in support of the movement. However, this is clearly not how their actions were viewed by either the TLA or even their anarchist allies in the Central Labor Union. The following day the CLU rebuked the anarchist leaders by voting to not hold any demonstrations on May 1, "as the union would then come in conflict with the Knights of Labor and the Trades Assembly."[17]

The most visible anarchist expression of support for the eight-hour work-day was the parade and rally of the Central Labor Union held on the last Sunday, the workers' only day off, prior to May 1. Like the more famous and bloodier event that would follow a week later, it began at the widening of Randolph Street known as Haymarket Square. Alongside the pair of trolley tracks that ran down the center of the street, marshals in their best suits and official sashes organized the ranks and divisions of the parade. Eight divisions of marchers, each led by a brass band, eight thousand strong by one reporter's count, snaked eastward toward the tall buildings of the financial district behind a wide banner of the Central Labor Union. Upon reaching Lake Park, where the winds steadily blowing in from Lake Michigan made their red flags buck and snap, the throng crushed around the two wooden stands erected for the speakers. The crowd was raucous, yelling itself hoarse at every pronouncement from the two competing stages—Samuel Fielden, Albert Parsons, and John A. Henry on the English platform; August Spies and Michael Schwab on the German one. An engineer stopped his engine on the lakeside tracks nearby and pulled hard on his steam whistle, seconding the frequent exclamations of the crowd. After an hour of speech making, when the last speakers drew the event to a close, few in the crowd had drifted away.

The organizers of the parade and the rally must have been pleased; they could not have wished for a better turnout or finer weather for their demonstration. But to some observers the event was odd, strangely devoid of discussion of the eight-hour-workday issue that was the purported reason for their gathering. According to one reporter on the scene, "Very little was said about eight hours except to use it as a lever to urge still greater demands on the employers of labor." This observation may have been an unfair one, as Michael Schwab had yelled, "Arm yourselves. After the first of May eight hours and not a minute more." August Spies followed and framed the eight-hour workday as just a stepping-stone to revolution: "Be not beggars any longer . . . Be men now; break down the doors of your extortioners instead of timidly knocking on them. Conquer the lost manhood. After you have introduced the eight-hour day now then let there be no halt. Onward is the motto in the march of triumph. Until the last stone of the robber bastile is removed and enslaved humanity is free."[18]

Louis Lingg, the young anarchist firebrand who was organizing the lumberyards and mills in southwest Chicago (and who would later be convicted of the Haymarket bombing and take his own life in jail), distributed a letter to his workers that depicted the coming May Day as the time of their revolutionary liberation:

> Now, workingmen of the Southwest Side, I beg of you to make use of this opportunity. Do not let this go by like a dream. Remember, we are all one. It does not matter whether you are on the South, North, or West Side; we must all fight for a purpose. Do not stay at home and let your brothers be killed when you can help them and make your cause a victory. Come in large masses, come often, come promptly. If you do this, everything will be an easy matter for us to undertake. Our labor will be rewarded . . . The first of May is coming near. We will have to kill the monster. We must be ready to meet him. This is our only chance now. Probably we will not have this opportunity to meet the monster so that we can fight him with our weapons. You must kill the pirates. You must kill the bloodsuckers; and for the first time in ages the poor workingmen will be made happy. Our work is short; we do not want a thirty years war. Be determined. Do not let your near relation, if he is an enemy, stand in your way. Doing all this, then, the victory is ours.[19]

Lingg's military rhetoric was not unusual. As the May Day deadline drew closer, anarchist calls for workers to arm themselves became both more frequent but also more specific. On April 30 the *Arbeiter-Zeitung* advised workers "to conceal their arms so that they will not be stolen by the minions of law." The following day the paper instructed readers to burn membership and minute books, to check ammunition, and to "clean your guns."[20]

Anarchist newspapers intensified their violent rhetoric at the same moment that a number of prominent manufacturers caved to workers' demands. The Wolffe Company was the first foundry to agree to the eight-hour workday. The day before the deadline, the association representing all the picture frame manufacturers in the city agreed to set the eight-hour workday as its standard. Some of the smaller packinghouses—International Packing, Sliberhorn Packing, and the Chicago Packing and Provision Company—acted without consulting with their packingmen's association and offered their men the "eight hour system." The P. Lichtenstadt brick-making company broke ranks with other brick-making firms and granted an eight-hour workday with ten hours' pay three days before the strike deadline. The Western Boot and Shoe Manufacturers Association met at the swanky Palmer House and, after receiving a delegation from the boot cutters' union, agreed to set the eight-hour workday as the standard in its trade, issues of wages to be postponed for a subsequent meeting in two weeks. The South Chicago Planing Mill, Brand and Hummel Brewery, and the Southside Railway Company all announced they would run on eight-hour shifts. The Rand McNally Company offered its printers ten hours' pay for a nine-hour workday. Hess Stove Works and Hercules Iron Works both agreed to run eight-hour shifts.[21]

Just as the number of firms conceding the eight-hour-workday demand seemed to be reaching a tipping point, anarchists seemed intent on avoiding agreements at all costs. A strike of 250 workers at Rothschild's Son's Saloon Fixtures and Furniture factory, many of whom had probably marched in the third division of the CLU parade that Sunday, was seemingly victorious on Tuesday when the owner, Julius Rothschild, conceded an eight-hour work-day for ten hours' pay. However, the union's CLU walking delegate arrived, "waved his umbrella over his head, and ordered the men to throw down their tools." The union representative then reportedly demanded, in addition to the eight-hour workday with full pay, the closing of a sister furniture plant in Cincinnati and the movement of all of its production to Chicago.[22] One Rothschild worker explained to a reporter how he felt used: "You have no idea of how ashamed I am of our action in this hasty strike. Why, if we had been left alone by the union agitators we wouldn't have struck at all. We are being used as a cat's paw for a lot of crazy Dutch socialists."[23]

Another big shop organized by the CLU furniture-makers union, that of the billiard table maker Brunswick, Balke and Collender, became the site of a strike and lockout after the company's management had agreed to both the eight-hour workday and a substantial wage increase, but the union then demanded that the firm fire the one employee who had refused to become a member of the union. The holdout worker, George Roeder, a devout Roman Catholic, stated that his conscience would not allow him to march behind the union's red flag. Once he was made an issue, Roeder chose what he considered the honorable course and quit rather than become the cause of a major strike. This, too, was not enough, and the union then objected to Brunswick's refusal to accept Roeder's resignation and declared a strike anyway. Brunswick's plant manager decided he had had enough of this disagreement and locked out the entire workforce.[24]

Chicago's labor leaders concluded that the anarchist leadership aimed to wreak the eight-hour-workday movement in order to keep the revolutionary pot boiling. George Schilling, chairman of the Eight-Hour League, condemned these strikes in the movement newspaper, the *Eight Hour Day*: "Some of the unions, we regret to say, have gone off half-cocked and are complicating this eight hour question too much with that of wages, and herein lies the greatest threat to this movement in the city . . . Men who have more passion than brains and are full of braggadocio must be put aside." Schilling and Chicago's non-anarchist labor union majority called for workers to negotiate and settle those strikes in progress and to avoid provoking more in the future, a course diametrically opposed to that of the city's revolutionary-minded anarchist leadership.[25] Fed up with the machinations of the CLU, the official mouthpiece of the Chicago Knights denounced them as a "body of outlawed anarchists who falsly [sic] claimed to be representatives of labor and leaders in the eight-hour movement."[26]

Mainstream newspapers amplified the trade unions' complaints against the anarchists. The *Chicago Mail* warned that Parsons and Spies were planning to exploit the expected strike wave for their own violent ends. "Parsons and Spies have been engaged during the past six months in perfecting arrangements for precipitating a riot today . . . They have no love for the eight-hour movement and are doing all they can to hamper it and prevent its success . . . Mark them today. Keep them in view. Hold them personally responsible for any trouble that occurs. Make an example of them if trouble does occur."[27]

These philosophical differences also divided the rank and file, leading several of the city's unions to split between "pure" eight-hour-workday advocates and militant factions. The Carpenters and Joiners Union split along ethnic lines; the English-speaking sections bolted after accusing their German-speaking colleagues of pushing "exorbitant" demands.[28] Disagreements between anarchist and non-anarchist clothing makers and pressers disrupted a union meeting and led to a split, with those opposed to the anarchists walking out.[29]

In spite of the rising tensions between the anarchists and the trade union leadership, the first May Day began surprisingly quietly. The great west-side manufacturing district, with its thousand factories and quarter million workers, was "was still and noiseless as a tomb." On the southwest side, one reporter observed: "all the machinery was idle and the only business that was 'rushing' was that of the saloons, in every one of these were congregated crowds of men, in many cases being harangued by a wild-eyed Bohemian in a polygot tongue." The boys employed at the J. S. Kirk Soap Company found themselves locked out but made good use of their holiday by playing ball in the street in front of the factory.[30]

A crowd of several hundred striking freight handlers gathered under the Harrison Street viaduct and marched to the Michigan Southern freight houses, where two strikers pushed through the window of a weigh house and opened the doors to the crowd. A wagonload of police was on the scene in a flash, and the officers pushed the strikers out of the building, tossing one particularly vocal protester bodily into the street, whereupon the strikers, who had been advised by their trade union leaders to refrain from violence, melted away. In the tense southwestern part of the city, another outdoor meeting called by Lumber Workers No. 1 turned into an impromptu march of, by one estimate, eight thousand marchers.

From the north side, a line of more than a thousand furniture workers with wooden shavings tucked in their hatbands paraded over the State Street bridge into the downtown to stand before the tall office building of Meyers, Sons and Company and sang songs to celebrate the firm's conceding of the eight-hour workday. Reporters noted that no red flags were displayed by the woodworkers.[31]

Worse, from the perspective of those who wished for a spiral of sharpening conflict, the momentum of employer concessions seemed to build. Gates Iron Works, McGregor Engine Works, Simonds Manufacturing, Chicago Die and Machine Works, and Wolff Copper and Brass all accepted the eight-hour-workday demands of their men. A half-dozen sash and door manufacturers—Blintze and Baker; E. L. Roberts Company; Gass and Phillips; Ganger, Oliver and Company; Campton and Brothers; and the Herman Kirchoff Company—all caved in to the demand for an eight-hour workday. Some of the largest employers in the city, the rolling mills, Union Steel, though not giving any ground, reported no problems with their operations.[32]

For George Schilling and his fellow leaders of the TLA's eight-hour-workday effort in the city, the strikes were succeeding about as well as could have been expected. Many employers had conceded without a struggle, and the thousands of workers who had been forced to strike or were locked out were conducting themselves peacefully. The greatest danger, it seemed to these trade union leaders, was the question of what the anarchists would do. Now that the great May Day deadline had arrived, would the anarchists settle for the eight-hour workday, or would they push for more? Schilling aired these concerns in the TLA's *Eight Hour Day*, warning workers against the radicals whom he feared were bent on wrecking the eight-hour-workday movement:

> Some of the unions, we regret to say, have gone off half-cocked, and are complicating this eight hour question too much with that of wages, and herein lies the greatest danger to the movement in this city . . . THE EIGHT HOUR DAY deprecates the action of these unions who have thereby complicated the situation, and are likely to endanger the success of the movement . . . The coming week is the most responsible in the history of the labor movement of Chicago. Strikes must be averted if possible. Those under way should be settled, through the art of diplomacy, instead of continued hostilities.[33]

That same day the anarchists replied and confirmed Schilling's fears. Their rallying cry, emblazoned across the top of their daily newspaper, was "No Compromise!" The *Arbeiter-Zeitung* urged workers not to settle with their "extortioners"; not to trust "the rascally trimmers, who by the smoothness of their treacherous tongues have succeeded in placing themselves by fraud at the head of the labor unions"; and urged "if George Schilling and confederates declare that they are the ones to fix your wages, then sit down on those scallawags."[34]

In the months building up to the May Day deadline, the CLU and the Eight-Hour League had respected a chilly silence about each other's activities. But as the deadline passed, the underlying differences broke into the open. On Sunday, May 2, at a meeting of the Trades and Labor Assembly, a resolution was introduced to create a joint working committee that would include all labor organizations in the city, including the Central Labor Union. The fact that this obvious step had not been taken months before was a telling indication of the great distance between the two organizations, but the reception given the motion exposed a much deeper well of anger toward anarchist involvement in the eight-hour-workday movement. Andrew Cameron, a prominent leader of the labor movement in Chicago and editor of the influential *Workingmen's Advocate*, denounced the idea, saying that the Eight-Hour League and the CLU had no interests in common and that the CLU had discredited the eight-hour-workday movement. Other speakers figuratively wrapped themselves in the American flag and vowed to never march behind the red one. George Schilling and others who sponsored the motion were then forced to explain that they hoped that by working with the CLU they would be able persuade its unions to withdraw their unreasonable demands for the good of the movement. Apparently, few thought there was much chance of this happening, and the idea of creating a joint committee did not carry.[35]

Later that evening several hundred tailors and seamstresses filled Zepf's Hall and listened to a Knights of Labor organizer who was attempting to form them into a Knights chapter. When someone in the crowd called for a German speaker, anarchist leader August Spies pressed to the front and began speaking. The Knights organizer "got mad when Spies began talking and pounded the table with his fist and gavel," but was unable to prevent Spies from persuading the group to form an independent union affiliated with the CLU.[36]

Similar clashes took place all over the city. The employees of furniture maker A. H. Andrews and Company, who were meeting to consider the firm's offer of a 10 percent raise, grew "weary of the impertinence of the agitators and cries of 'Put 'em out!' rang throughout the hall." The union president, "a diminutive, insignificant, red-headed socialist named Stauschgieischgt, or thereabouts," was thrown out the door.[37]

When the city's two Brewers and Maltsters Unions arranged to meet at Zepf's Hall to hear from their negotiating committee what the brewers' employers association was prepared to offer, political and ethnic tensions combined to ruin their solidarity. Brewers and Maltsters No. 1 was nearly all German while Local 2 was nearly all English, one union meeting in an upstairs room while the other convened downstairs. The English union leadership recommended adoption of their employers' offer, calling it "fair enough." Upstairs the German brewers were swayed by the arguments raised by August Spies and his "conclave of red flag apostles" and voted to demand a "full increase of wages" along with the right to drink an unlimited amount of beer on the job (the bosses had offered the union just four beer breaks and proposed limiting the guzzling to three mugs in a sitting). In the end the two locals were unable to agree on a unified position, the president of the English local complaining that "the crowd up-stairs want to run everything. They have got us into a fight and it seems as though they want to dictate to us." The English union leaders told their members that "they didn't want any socialists skulking about their meeting places in the future." Across the city in a different meeting hall that same night, August Spies moved a meeting of curriers to accept no compromises and to hold fast to their demand for an eight-hour workday at nine hours' pay.[38]

TLA leader George Schilling, who had been organizing the stockyards for months, found his efforts undermined by radicals who pushed the pack-inghouse workers to reject any compromise with the packers. Schilling struggled to keep workers' demands limited to the eight-hour workday and their heads cool. He addressed a mass meeting of stockyard workers and urged them to not insist on higher wages but to settle for shorter hours and then watch as wages naturally rose over time. The men had to wait only about a day before one small company, the Fairbanks Canning Company, broke employer ranks and offered its workers the eight-hour workday with nine hours' pay. Schilling was not pleased: "Mr. Schilling questioned the propriety and policy of asking too much, but upon being assured by the representative that the men could do their work in eight hours, concluded to withdraw his advice."[39]

Other smaller packers buckled under the pressure, the Chicago Packing and Provision Company, previously mentioned, and Hutchinson's Packing House offering their packinghouse workers the choice of an eight-hour workday for nine hours' pay or a nine-hour workday for ten hours' pay. Just as it seemed that the leading meatpacking firms, Armour and Swift, might follow suit, a break that would undoubtedly lead to the capitulation of the rest of the industry, radicals from an allegedly "secret Bohemian society" rushed in to spoil the compromise. At Swift, what a reporter described as the "socialistic, communistic, anarchistic element" led a walkout of more than a thousand laborers and then refused management's offer of nine hours' pay for an eight-hour workday. Later that day at a mass meeting of packers at Frederick Hall, the radicals and the trade unionists fought for control:

> Those who went to the hall were accompanied by the anarchistic element, which seemed ready to do anything to make trouble. One of these earnest advocates of devastation and destruction concluded he had struck the right time to make a grand demonstration. In this he was ably seconded by more of the same sort, and suddenly the air was made blue with profane shouts, while these hoodlum anarchists yelled and raised a red flag. But their effort was a weak one and did not receive that hearty approval which the bloodthirsty anarchists expected. The better element seemed to assert itself among the men at once. Some of them became so incensed at the open insult that they made grave threats of violence upon the leaders in the red-flag movement. The rag was hooted down, and those who had a hand in its elevation were warned to not again attempt such a movement.[40]

On Monday morning, May 3, twelve hundred workers arrived at the Nelson Morris Packing Company but refused to enter the factory until their demands for an eight-hour shift for ten hours' pay were granted. Mr. Morris met with a delegation and agreed to eight for nine. When the delegation announced the agreement to the strikers, radicals demanded rejection of the terms but could not prevail, and the men went to their benches. Later that night a "monster meeting" of packinghouse laborers drew more people than the large hall could accommodate. The crowd spilling out the doors strained to listen as the chairman announced that the biggest firms, including Swift and Armour, had agreed to work on an eight-hour day on a ten-hour pay basis. Schilling told reporters that he now had confidence that the packing workers would win "a final victory."[41]

Given the deep divisions within the labor movement over the tactics and goals of the struggle for an eight-hour workday, it is not surprising that the violent conflict first broke out not between workers and employers or workers and police but between workers themselves. On the Wednesday before May Day, two soap workers were surrounded and beaten by other employees of Kirk's soap factory on the north bank of the Chicago River on Water Street.[42] In an editorial in the May 2 edition of the *Arbeiter-Zietung*,

August Spies seemed to encourage such actions when he wrote, "The only danger lies in the inclinations of the conservative elements to compromise with the bosses. Any man who advocates a compromise should be sat down on at once."[43] That same day, Saturday, a group of more than one hundred union carpenters marched to a building site on Congress and Halsted Streets and told the workers there that they had one minute to put down their tools and go on strike. Before the confused workers could discuss what to do, the mob attacked, and the workers ran for their lives, two of them ducking into Rosenbeck's store on Congress Street, where they barred the door until the jeering crowd gave up and marched on to other parts of the city.[44]

The day the anarchists had long awaited, a day they had dared to dream was destined to explode in class warfare and social revolution, was disappointingly peaceful. Sunday passed without any significant clashes and a mounting number of employer concessions. Most of the city's foundries had conceded to an eight-hour schedule, and TLA leader George Schilling reported that eight hundred tobacco workers, seven hundred streetcar employees, three hundred barrel makers (Schilling's own trade), three hundred retail employees, and more than three thousand packinghouse workers had won the eight-hour workday. To anarchists who had long envisioned that this change would bring a more militant outburst from workers, these rapid concessions of employers, the discipline of the trade unions, the peaceful demonstrations of strikers, and the calculated restraint of the police all must have been very disappointing and deepened radicals' dread that the revolutionary moment was slipping away.

Clearly, from the perspective of the revolutionaries, who had prepared for months, possibly years, for this moment, the working classes of Chicago were failing to act out their historic role. Events were not following the anarchist script. When the weekend began, the anarchist mouthpiece instructed the rank and file to act quickly and not miss the opportunity presented by the weekend strikes. In an article published on Sunday morning titled "Now or Never," *Die Fackel* observed: "Everything depends upon quick and immediate action. The tactics of the bosses are to gain time; the tactics of the strikers must be to grant them no time. By Monday or Tuesday the conflict must have reached its highest intensity, else the success will be doubtful. Within a week the fire, the enthusiasm, will be gone, and then the bosses will celebrate victories."[45]

This sense of urgency helps explain one of the greatest unanswered puzzles underlying the sequence of events that led to the Haymarket bombing. Why, at every milestone along the path to the bombing, did anarchists seem to be anticipating events rather than reacting to them? Several critical actions were made by the men who would later be tried for the conspiracy prior to the bombing: on Sunday morning, May 2, George Engel unveiled his plan to ambush police stations; the next morning, Monday, May 3, the coded signal calling the armed groups to meet appeared in the *Arbeiter-Zeitung*; the next afternoon, another code word, *Ruhe*, was inserted in the *Arbeiter-Zeitung* calling the anarchist militias to muster at their prearranged spots. Each of these actions actually took place before the events to which the anarchists appeared to respond. Engel's Bohemian Hall meeting that formulated military tactics to support the workers' uprising happened before there had been any significant violent incidents in the city. The coded message that called the armed men to the basement of Greif's Hall was inserted in the paper hours before the McCormick riot that was the subject of their meeting broke out. The issue of the *Arbeiter-Zeitung* that contained the trigger word *Ruhe* hit the streets around two o'clock, six hours before the riot that the revolutionary militias were supposedly responding to.[46]

None of these actions make sense if the anarchist leaders of the city were simply responding to the evolving strike situation on the ground. Fischer, Engel, and the North Side group in Bohemian Hall agreed to Engel's plan to attack outlying police stations but were not prepared to act on it the next day when an actual riot did break out. Rather, it took another meeting the next evening to flesh out a more proactive plan, one that involved not only preparing to react to a riot but also to bring together all the combustible material needed to start one.

Even late the next morning when the typesetters at the *Arbeiter-Zeitung* set into their frames the code summoning all the armed groups to meet that night, "Y.—Komme Montag Abend," the city was calm. Montag began with large crowds assembling and parading, but all of these protests fizzled short of violence. At 8:00 AM fifty lumber shovers gathered in front of their yard and told their manager they were striking. They then marched through the district, gaining adherents from other yards as they went, many willingly but others not so much. Reporters observed that the marchers carried wooden sticks and clubs, and some of the reluctant workers they encountered "thought discretion the better part of valor" and put down their tools. By midmorning their numbers had swelled to the hundreds. Though the crowd was "riotous and noisy," it dispersed without challenging the wagonload of police who made their stand outside Loomis Martin and Company.[47]

While lumber workers marched through the southwest side, another group of marchers wound their way through the needle district on the near north side. Led by a brass band and men carrying aloft banners, a mallet, and at least one axe, a mixed parade of tailors and seamstresses moved from shop to shop, calling out the workers, which, in most cases, seemed easy to do: "As soon as they heard the music of the band their heads popped out of windows. The sight of their parading sisters was enough. Down on the floor went overalls, cheap hand-me-down clothes, etc.; on went hats, bonnets, and shawls, and in a moment a patter of footfalls upon the staircases, and shouts shrill and merry were the farewells which fell into the ears of the astonished employers. Frantic cries, mingled with the choicest expletives known to the Scandavian [*sic*] tongue, and earnest appeals to return, all alike were unavailing."[48]

Of greater concern to the authorities were the three thousand freight handlers who snaked through the heart of Chicago, following the great railroad trunk lines south, moving from warehouse to warehouse. Railroads were better prepared than the protesters; the brass band the organizers had invited never arrived, while the massive freight houses were circled by hundreds of special police. Unlike the parades in the other districts, the freight men failed to shut down railroad operations for more than the time it took their parade to pass by, and, most disappointing to those who were hoping for a revolutionary spark, no scuffles broke out.[49]

There were that day several places where the anarchist leadership could have lent their support to workers protesting for the eight-hour workday, but they chose to focus their efforts in the lumber district. It was an area where casual labor, low wages, an insular Bohemian ethnic enclave, corrupt aldermen, and abusive policing combined into a particularly combustible brew. All observers recognized that this district was as volatile as the dry lumber stacked in the yards. Days earlier a Knights of Labor organizer had predicted that if trouble came, it would come first in the lumber district, where socialists had made great inroads.[50]

When the largest lumber-shovers union announced an outdoor meeting for Monday, May 3, at 3:00 PM to hear their union leaders' report on their ongoing negotiations with the companies (two of whom had offered the eight-hour workday at nine-hour rates), the radicals trumped them by showing up earlier and gathering a crowd. August Spies and fellow radicals muscled the president of the lumber-shovers union, Frank Haraster, aside and turned the gathering into their own mass rally. Though Spies and his defenders later argued that they were there merely at the invitation of the German Lumber Workers Union, an affiliate of the CLU, this union was little more than a paper organization, having been organized just a few weeks before by the militant firebrand Louis Lingg.[51]

The thousands of angry and anxious lumber workers had unfortunately arranged to meet in a patch of open prairie along Blue Island Avenue a few hundred yards from the McCormick Reaper Works, which had long been the anarchists' favored target in the area. For more than a year the massive and modern factory had been the anarchists' leading example of capitalism's industrial oppression while its owner, Cyrus McCormick II, had been the very symbol of the heartless tycoon. Anarchist papers ran feature stories "touring" McCormick's opulent Rush Street mansion, pointing out his art collection, his Persian carpets, and his failure to pay his "wretches" a living wage. During a strike at the factory a few months earlier, hawkers sold little books titled *McCormick's Lockout Songs* for a nickel a piece. Anarchist John Dusey, who was known in the movement as "Dynamite" Dusey, flung a challenge at a meeting of Parsons's American group: "I'll give a man $100 who will take the life of McCormick tomorrow. One nice little, round lead ball will do the work." (Parsons publicly scolded Dusey for his outburst.) Louis Lingg, one of the anarchists in the city who seemed to be more interested in actions than making speeches, had been arrested for fighting during a strike at McCormick Reaper Works back in March.[52]

According to one reporter on the scene, the radical speakers that afternoon preached schism and violence, quoting one as railing: "Quit the Knights of Labor; they will never do you any good: join the Central Labor union, which will help you to your rights and freedom . . . With revolver in one hand and your knife in the other and bombs in your pockets, march on to revolution and freedom."[53] When the bell in the cupola of the McCormick factory tolled six times, marking the end of the workday, Spies was speaking to the crowd and someone stepped forward, gestured to the factory, and yelled out, "On to McCormick's. Let us drive off the scabs," or "Now, boys, let us go for them damned scabs at McCormick's," or "Go up and kill . . . the damned scabs," depending on which witness is to be believed. A mob immediately ran off across the prairie to attack the "scabs" leaving work. These so-called scabs were all long-term employees of the McCormick factory who had learned during their lunch break that their boss had granted their demand for the eight-hour workday. As the mob neared the factory, they threw stones and beat those who were unlucky enough to be caught outside the factory gates. Two police officers held back the mob until reinforcements galloped in, scattering the crowd by shooting freely.[54]

One reporter on the scene observed that as soon as the police opened fire, "the rioters were prepared to retaliate. They fired at the officers from ambush, with weapons of all patterns and calibre. Bullets whistled right and left and off to the southward a half-dozen men on a shed kept up a plunging fire." Likewise the *Arbeiter-Zeitung* account of the riot, written by August Spies himself, praised those "few of the strikers [who] had little snappers [*knippsdinger*] of revolvers, and with these returned the fire." Spies then described how he tried to get those who had arms and were leaving the riot to go back and continue the battle: "The writer ran back, he implored the people to come along—those who had revolvers in their pockets, but it was in vain . . . The battle was lost."[55]

The riot that began at the gates of the McCormick factory spilled out through the surrounding neighborhood wherever police confronted knots of idle men. William Casey, a large, brawny cop known as "the horse detective," and three fellow officers trundled into a wagon one of the young rioters who had been shot and drove him to his home, which was not far away on Seventeenth Street. Casey carried him into his house, and while he was taking a report with the man's family, a crowd had gathered outside and quickly grew to such an alarming size that the cops in the wagon beat a hasty retreat, abandoning their fellow officer. When Casey emerged from the house, he was set upon by the mob. The horse detective sent his first assailants to the ground but was overwhelmed. Vaclev (or Hynek) Dejnek yelled out for someone to get a rope, and someone looped a clothesline around Casey's neck and he was dragged toward a nearby lamppost. At this moment police reinforcements dashed through the crowd, leveling their revolvers while helping the horse detective climb into their wagon.[56]

Several men were later arrested and convicted for various crimes related to this incident, including rioting, assault, and attempted murder. Two of them had close ties to the anarchists. The man who prosecutors later claimed first called for Casey's rope was Dejnek, who was reported to have been employed by the *Arbeiter-Zeitung* as the paper's carrier in the district. Another man charged with assault was Jacob Mikolanda, one of the founders of the socialist movement in Czechoslovakia, editor of Chicago's Bohemian anarchist newspaper, *Budoucnost*, and one of the five Chicago delegates to the Pittsburgh Congress of 1883, which formed the anarchist International Working People's Association.[57]

During the McCormick riot, August Spies took a streetcar back to his newspaper office and composed the most inflammatory broadside he had ever written. Reporting that the police, the "bloodhounds," had killed six workers who "had the courage to disobey the supreme will of your bosses," the sheet screamed for action: "If you are men, if you are the sons of your grand sires who shed their blood to free you, then you will rise in your might . . . To arms we call you, to arms!" Rushed to the printer, the sheets were sped around the city by fast riders. Oscar Neebe handed them around Franz Hein's saloon on Division Street and told Hein, "It is a shame that the police act that way, but maybe the time comes that it goes the other way."[58]

Adolph Fischer brought a stack of the revenge circulars to the secret meeting of the armed men who had been summoned to Greif's Hall by the coded message placed in the anarchist newspaper before the McCormick riot had broken out. George Engel repeated the militant plans he had proposed the day before, and the group agreed to arm and assemble when the signal *Ruhe* appeared in the newspaper. Fatefully, the basement conspirators made their plans to call a protest meeting at the Haymarket Square. The next morning Fischer printed the famous Haymarket broadside that contained the instruction, "Workingmen Arm Yourselves and Appear in Full Force!" The paper's editor, August Spies, later claimed that he ordered Fischer to remove this line because it was "foolish," but his concern that morning seems hard to fathom given that just the night before he was authoring another broadside that began with the line "Workingmen, to Arms!!!" and ended with "To arms we call you, to arms!" About the same time that Spies was placing the *Ruhe* message in his newspaper, Albert Parsons took an advertisement to the offices of the *Chicago Daily News* that on behalf of the "Agitation Committee" called "every member" of his American group to meet at seven-thirty that evening at the *Arbeiter-Zeitung*'s headquarters for "important business." Parsons's American group had never called a general meeting at the editorial offices of the paper before, having for months held its meetings at 106 E. Randolph Street, a block away from city hall. Parsons and others later claimed the "important business" that was to be conducted involved planning for support of striking sewing girls, though no sewing girls appeared to have attended this meeting. In fact, striking sewing girls held at least three meetings of their own the day before the Haymarket riot, one female striker telling a reporter that "we are not red-flag or socialistic people and we have no use for Spies or the Arbeiter-Zeitung."[59]

That morning when eight-hour-workday leader George Schilling saw a copy of Spies's revenge circular, he was "red-hot" and "unbosomed himself" to a reporter, speculating that "these leading anarchists . . . sneakingly issue inflammatory documents" and that they "hope by them to inflame some hair-brained crank to acts of violence." Schilling ended by calling them "cowards, all of them." The actions of the anarchists over the previous two days provided plenty of reasons for Schilling to believe that their purpose was to provoke violence. However, in just a few hours his name-calling would prove unjustified when a few anarchists proved their mettle by throwing a bomb and engaging police in an exchange of gunfire.[60]

The revolutionary anarchist movement that had been coalescing and developing for a decade reached its great divide that chilly Tuesday night. A labor reform movement that the anarchists ridiculed and denounced but adopted as it gained popularity provided the stimulus and focus for action that their movement had long lacked. Though anarchists embraced the eight-hour-workday movement because they saw in it a vehicle for their more sweeping aims, in doing so they committed themselves to a specific point of action—that fateful May Day weekend—and thereby forced the issue of their theories of action and revolution. Had they not married their ideas of the propaganda by deed to the eight-hour workday, they may well have gone on happily marching in their halls, airing incendiary speeches at the lakefront, and brandishing their homemade bombs for the benefit of reporters and newcomers to the movement without incident. But the heady combination of transatlantic anarchist ideology and American labor organizing drew them toward a revolutionary commitment that many ran from at the critical moment when the exploding bomb itself posed the ultimate question of commitment or flight. The men who conspired to carry bombs throughout the city that night, and the man who stepped across that divide and tossed his hissing bomb at the police, operated under a unique set of beliefs that had been slowly shaped by the experiences and aspirations of a generation of radicals scattered from Russia to America's Pacific Coast. Haymarket's blast was not the work of one disgruntled worker, one fanatic, or even one small group of miscalculating radicals. It was the culmination of an ideological movement.

EPILOGUE

The Haymarket bomb failed to ignite the popular insurrection that anarchists had dared to hope for, but its blast also snuffed out the very movement that had created it. The swift arrest and trial of eight anarchist activists for the murder of patrolman Mathias Degan shifted the priorities of Chicago's anarchist movement from ratcheting up class tensions to defending their imperiled leaders. Through the course of a lengthy trial, appeals, and a campaign for clemency, the anarchist movement was not only crushed by the nation's first red scare, but it also consciously assisted in its own destruction by denying its own ideals and rewriting its own history. Men's lives were at stake, and the needs of the moment required that anarchists downplay their interest in violence as propaganda, in the transformative powers of dynamite, and in the moral necessity of bloody revolution.

As soon as Chicago's police dragnet began scooping up every anarchist they could lay their hands on, the anarchists' rhetoric changed. Not only was the labor leadership of the anarchist union movement jailed, but the ideological leadership represented by the editors of the most influential anarchist newspapers were put behind bars as well. Both the replacements for August Spies and Albert Parsons, while committed socialists, did not share their predecessors' beliefs in revolutionary action and pulled these publications back to the mainstream of socialism.

Very close to the time of the bombing, Joseph Dietzgen moved from New York City to Chicago. Dietzgen was one of the national leaders of the Socialist Labor Party; editor of the party's organ, *Der Sozialist*; and an internationally renowned Marxist theorist (Marx himself had introduced him to the International Congress at the Hague as "our philosopher"). Soon after practically the entire staff of the anarchist *Arbeiter-Zeitung* had been swept up in the police dragnet and both its editor (Spies) and its assistant editor

(Schwab) were tried, Dietzgen offered his services to the Socialistic Publishing Company's directors and was entrusted with the editor's chair.[1]

At any other time, Dietzgen's courageous offer would have been rejected by the radicals who had hewn the *Arbeiter-Zeitung* and its sister publications into the vanguard of revolutionary anarchism in America. For years before 1886, these publications had denounced Dietzgen, his newspapers, and the SLP generally as dreamers, backsliders, and traitors to the working class. Dietzgen himself privately admitted in a letter to his friend Friedrich Sorge that he had serious ideological differences from his colleagues. He was not bothered by anarchism, he noted, meaning anarchism as a philosophical position, but he was disturbed by "Mostism," which he understood "makes a system of violence." Over the next two years Dietzgen pushed these publications toward the center of the socialist movement and toward his own ideal that "the terms anarchist, socialist, communist, should be mixed together so that no muddle head could tell which is which."[2]

Parsons's successor as the editor of the *Alarm* was Dyer D. Lum, a Yankee reformer from the evangelically "burned-over" region of New York who had graduated from the abolitionist movement to fighting in the Civil War. A bookbinder by trade, Lum was both prone to intellectual enthusiasms of the moment and fiercely independent in his opinions. He dabbled in spiritualism until he turned skeptic and published an exposé titled *The "Spiritualist" Delusion*. He embraced the Greenback Party when its prospects brightened briefly in the 1870s, but then attacked it as he swung decisively against electoral politics. Like other Yankee radicals, his résumé of interests encompassed an encyclopedia of nineteenth-century movements, as he variously embraced Fenianism, suffragism, land reform, monetary reform, cooperation, pro-Mormonism, and the eight-hour workday.

Having been influenced most recently by Benjamin Tucker's group of individualist anarchists, Lum remodeled the *Alarm* on the pattern of Tucker's journal, *Liberty*, expanding its scope to include the opinions and ideas of the pacifistic and evolutionary socialists of Tucker's stripe and aligning it more closely with the Knights of Labor.[3]

In addition to dampening the revolutionary rhetoric of Chicago's anarchist movement, Lum also contributed to denying such thinking ever characterized anarchists in the Windy City. Lum was the author of the earliest history of the Haymarket event, *A Concise History of the Great Trial of Chicago Anarchists in 1886*. In this book, written in the heat of the campaign to save the Chicago Seven from the gallows, Dyer Lum selectively quoted from the writings of the leading Chicago anarchists in an effort to soften their statements. While knowing that it would be absurd to deny some of the anarchists' most widely reported violent statements, Lum portrayed the anarchists' calls to use guns and bombs as purely defensive measures and their plans for revolution as simply abstract notions.

For example, Lum distorted the Pittsburgh Manifesto of 1883, a document that plainly embodied the ideas of propaganda by deed and immediate revolution, by presenting what he termed an "extract [that] will more clearly define their position." Lum then proceeded to quote only those portions of the preamble to the Pittsburgh Manifesto that were theoretical rather than exhortative. He quotes up to a segment of the manifesto that argued that class conflict was inevitable and that history shows "that all attempts in the past to reform this monstrous system by peaceful means, such as the ballot, have been futile." At this point Lum breaks off his quotation, hiding from the reader what follows, the peroration where the manifesto declares: "there remains but one recourse—FORCE! . . . It is, therefore, your right, it is your duty, says Jefferson—'to arms!'" While Lum notes that the Pittsburgh Manifesto presented "in vivid colors the inequalities of the present social system [and] the necessity for revolutionary action," he does not mention that the first and foremost principle adopted by the gathering was "Destruction of the existing class rule, by all means, i.e., by energetic, relentless, revolutionary and international action."[4]

Throughout his polemic, Lum selectively edits and even changes direct quotations to defang the anarchists' pronouncements. Only in his opening paragraph are the anarchists associated with the idea of planning or preparing for offensive revolutionary action, of wishing to "precipitate a revolution," an accusation that he claims was "the theory of the press" and that the rest of his book was dedicated to refuting.[5] Lum's book had far-reaching influence, especially as its pacified anarchists and their equally distorted legal circumstances fired the interest of literary impresario William Dean Howells, who recommended it to his wide circle of influential friends.[6]

The idea that Chicago's anarchists were misunderstood intensified with their martyrdom. Captain William Perkins Black, the anarchists' lead attorney, eulogized over the graves of Parsons, Fischer, Engel, and Spies: "They were called Anarchists . . . They were painted and presented to the world as men loving violence, riot and bloodshed for their own sake; as men full of an unextinguishable and causeless hatred against the existing order. Nothing could be further from the truth. They were men who loved peace, men of gentle instincts." The anarchism they were tarred with was not the anarchism of the bomb thrower, but the philosophical anarchism of the dreamer: "the Anarchy of which they spoke and taught—what was it, but an attempt to answer the question, 'After the revolution, what?' . . . their creed had to do with the to-morrow of the possible revolution, and the whole of their thought and their philosophy, as Anarchists, was the establishment of an order of society that should be symbolized in the words, 'order without force.'"[7]

Dyer Lum's earlier attempt to simply suppress the fact that Chicago's anarchists publicly and loudly argued for violent action was eventually abandoned by the next generation of radicals, who adopted a more nuanced approach to defending their memory. In 1912 Floyd Dell, a Chicago novelist and critic best known as a managing editor of the *Masses* magazine, contributed a chapter on the history of anarchism in Chicago to the authoritative multivolume history of Chicago edited by J. Seymour Currey. Unlike earlier historians of Chicago's anarchist movement, Dell did not hide the fact that the anarchists employed, in his words, a "real luridness and violence of language," but instead devoted a significant portion of his essay to explaining why the anarchists really did not mean any of the things they said.

Dell argued that the anarchists used their violent language as a means of compensating for their failure to attract recruits. As their numbers dwindled, "their obscurity perhaps increased their irresponsibility," and the anarchist leaders began to ratchet up their advocacy of violent action as a means "to frighten the bourgeoisie." Ultimately, Dell concluded, "violence was a matter of talk and never a matter of action."

The culmination of this tendency was the anarchists' advocacy of bomb making and enthusiastic praise of dynamite. Dynamite, a recent and seemingly fantastically powerful invention, was more a symbol than a tactic for Chicago's anarchists. As Dell observed, it was "a sign to the oppressors of the earth that their reign was not forever to endure." The dramatic rhetoric of bombing became popular with the anarchists, not because they planned a bombing spree, but, Dell says, "to attract attention to their real beliefs—it was a way of shocking the public into attention." Alongside its shock value, the dreaded specter of a working class armed with bombs was calculated to leverage political gains, or as Dell puts it, "if lawmakers and employers could be persuaded of the existence of a party ready to use violence to secure its ends, they might make concessions."[8]

In support of his thesis, Dell offered little beyond a tautology: the words of the anarchist leaders were not violent, because the anarchists were "peaceable" individuals. The anarchist leaders could not have been serious when they repeatedly called upon their followers to arm themselves and prepare for violent revolution, because they were themselves "personally gentle" "idealists after the manner of Thoreau and Tolstoi." The anarchists were not, he claimed, even "accustomed to the use of firearms." Those pipes and shells that August Spies liked to brandish in front of reporters, claimed Dell, were "made largely in the American spirit of 'bluff.'"

For a century the Dell thesis became enshrined in the left as a leading interpretation of the Chicago anarchists' ideology. The Dell thesis has been exceptionally durable because its premises are extremely difficult to refute. It begins with the presumption that the anarchists' own statements are insincere, and if this is so, then the largest documentary record available to us—namely, the anarchists' own statements and writings—are of no use in determining the validity of this premise. By rendering the bulk of the documentary record irrelevant by definition, the Dell thesis is sustained by both the romanticism of historians who wish to preserve the memory of the "martyrs" and the difficulty of finding evidence outside of the statements of the anarchists themselves that can bear upon the essential question, Did they mean what they said?

When the left adopted May 1 as its international worker's holiday, the Haymarket event grew even larger in the lore of American socialism. As it did, the details of the beliefs of Chicago's anarchists were dulled further so that these folk heroes could serve a wide array of ideological tendencies. As the American Communist Party rose in the late 1920s, it adopted Chicago's executed anarchists as its own movement's martyrs, in spite of the ideological differences between them. Lucy Parsons became a regular speaker at Communist rallies and a May Day parade dignitary into her late eighties until her death in 1942.[9]

Just as the Communist Party downplayed the *anarchism* of the Haymarket martyrs and celebrated their martyrdom to labor and free speech, a scholarly basis for this shift was laid. Henry David was a red diaper baby (named for Henry David Thoreau) who later boasted that his career showed that in those days a "left person and a Jew might make it in the academic world." David wrote his Columbia University dissertation on the Chicago anarchists from their origins in earlier socialist movements through to Altgeld's pardon of the last three Haymarket prisoners and then published it in 1936 as *The History of the Haymarket Affair*. Over the course of his career, he earned a reputation as a scholar who "approached history as part of his political commitments."[10]

While David charted some of the violent rhetoric, the "physical force tendency" and outburst of "propaganda by deed" rhetoric, he simply discounted its importance or its centrality to Chicago's militants. Summarizing the resolutions hammered out at the London conference that launched the IWPA on the grounds of force propaganda, David concludes, "The vagueness of doctrine which is so typical of the movement of 1881 remains a notable characteristic for some years to come, and further indicates the lack of orientation." Even after the supposed fuzziness of London was clarified by the even more strident pronouncements made at the Pittsburgh Congress of 1883, David finds the means to partition these ideas away from the radicals in Chicago: "When the Pittsburgh Congress declared for force, it was thinking essentially in terms of the European revolutionary movement. It thus sanctioned a policy and a method which had not been accepted in this country to any appreciable extent even in radical circles."[11]

David's domestication of Chicago's radicals was partly in reaction against the tendency among establishment historians to depict American anarchists as alien, wild-eyed, bomb-throwing maniacs. Even after David's book was published, Chester McArthur Destler, president of the American Historical Association, described Chicago's anarchists as devotees of an "alien ideology" who "went on to exploit the McCormick Reaper strike and the Eight-Hour movement in such a manner as to invite police intervention and furnish an opportunity for 'propaganda of the deed' at Haymarket."[12]

David's powerful challenge to historical orthodoxy was written at the wrong time to succeed in winning public acceptance of labor's martyrs. As the Cold War heated up, the labor movement purged its left wing, and the Communist Party went underground, even the labor movement's embrace of the anarchists loosened. By the 1950s the Haymarket story was no longer memorialized with marches through Chicago on May Day or used as a reminder of past sacrifices at labor rallies as it once was. For a generation afterward, the Haymarket story went untold and unsung until the New Left stirred in the 1960s.

In the spring of 1969 there was a sudden renewal of interest in the Haymarket Riot. Reviving the tradition that had lapsed since the 1930s, a group of labor activists organized a commemoration of Haymarket "martyrs" on May 4. Unlike the solemn wreath-laying at the anarchists' tomb in Waldheim Cemetery that characterized observances earlier in the century, Les Orear, William Adelman, and William Garvey organized a public event that featured author and historian Studs Terkel delivering a speech from a wagon on the very site where the bomb had been thrown eighty-three years before. Over the previous summer, Orear, Adelman, and Garvey had founded the Illinois Labor History Society (ILHS) to preserve the memory of Haymarket and other labor landmarks. The May 4 commemoration and the founding of the ILHS coincided with the publication of the first new book about the event since Henry David's: *The Autobiographies of the Haymarket Martyrs*, a collection of memoirs penned by the condemned anarchists from their death row cells compiled by Philip S. Foner. Also, in 1969 Dyer Lum's contemporary vindication of the anarchists charged with the bombing, *The Great Trial of the Chicago Anarchists*, a book originally published in 1887, was reprinted.[13]

By the 1970s a scholarly consensus formed around the idea that Chicago's anarchists were not unlike the New Left radicals of that time—prone to speaking in extremes and reveling in scaring the public by boasting of their vast underground organization and militant plans, but in their hearts quite moral, reasonable, and dedicated to incremental progress. While the Thomas Nast cartoon of the dagger- and bomb-wielding anarchist was sorely in need of correction, the revisionist project undertaken by these historians eventually hardened into a new caricature of its own as the weapons the anarchists extolled as the road to the future were erased from the picture. Haymarket was rediscovered and recharged with ideological power after 1969 not because of its inherent historical importance, but because it served well as the symbol of state repression and indigenous radical dissent that the former activists of the New Left sought to find.

Anarchists were pacified and disarmed by New Left historians in a number of ways. Many simply denied that there is any historical evidence of American anarchists stockpiling, constructing, distributing, or employing weapons in pursuit of their aims. They discounted the anarchists' violent calls to action as calculated attention-seeking behavior and shifted attention away from the anarchists' unique tactical ideology by instead focusing their studies on the anarchists' more abstract principles and ultimate goals. Finally, social historians detailed the rich cultural and associative life of the anarchists—a "movement culture" filled with picnics, singing societies, plays, poetry, festive street parades, and lakeshore rallies—casting the anarchists in a sympathetic light that illuminated their humanity. How could a group of men and women who played with their children, loved their spouses, and enjoyed singing and dancing plot a bloodbath?[14]

Paul Avrich retread much of the same ground but with a slightly different tactic for insulating the Chicago martyrs from their own words. Avrich observed how Johann Most was a towering figure without equal in the United States in his advocacy of the use of revolutionary force. So great was his shadow that he "established his preeminence over the revolutionary left." Avrich argues, "From 1883 to 1886 virtually the whole social revolutionary movement was the expression of the ideas and vision of this one man." It was Most and his East Coast disciples, not the Chicago revolutionaries, who pushed through the blood-curdling language of the Pittsburgh Congress. "Most and his followers disdained any temporizing with the existing order, which had to be destroyed root and branch," but "the delegates from

Chicago and the Midwest adopted a different position . . . [and] remained devoted to the cause of trade unionism." However, in Avrich's account, Most steamrolled the milder Chicago faction, and the declaration "was framed entirely in the spirit of Mostian intransigence and contained no mention of [the Chicago faction's] trade-union action."[15]

When forced by his sources to acknowledge that Chicago anarchists actively encouraged arming and building bombs, Avrich relies on the militants' post-Haymarket exculpatory insistence that all such proposals were defensive in nature. He claims that it was inevitable that the police or the militia would eventually unleash their terror upon the workers movement and for that day they must be prepared: "The revolution was on the horizon. Of that they were certain. Nor was it they who would bring it. They were merely preparing the workers for the inevitable; and every new repression, every drubbing by the police, brought the day of reckoning a step closer. It was this belief that accounts for their call to arms, which while taken by the authorities as exhortations to violence, were more in the way of warnings to the workers to be ready for the impending upheaval."[16]

Even after tracing the actual collection of arms on the part of Chicago's anarchist leaders, their drilling and military preparations, even their hoarding of explosives, Avrich finds them, much like Floyd Dell decades before, just gasbags and blowhards.

> Of the eight Haymarket defendants . . . it is true, all had spoken out in favor of dynamite. All, moreover, believed in retaliatory violence and rejected docile submission to the forces of capital and government. For most, however, their humanitarian outlook shrank from the methods that in theory they justified and professed . . . they were men of ideals who, especially in times of economic distress, made rash and provocative statements, but themselves did nothing more violent than to assist in the arming of workers in preparation for what they regarded as the inevitable confrontation with capital.[17]

Likewise, James Green, in his popular account of Chicago in the Gilded Age and the dramatic events of Haymarket, scarcely mentions the rise of revolutionary force ideas or the romance of dynamite among the anarchists. But even when this fact does peek out from behind his curtain, Green denies that these ideas had anything to do with Chicago's anarchists. Taking a cue from Avrich, Green blames Johann Most for exciting his audiences with his "talk of manning the barricades and dynamiting police stations." Most's inflammatory rhetoric may have "galvanized young German socialists like August Spies and Michael Schwab, who felt mired in the tedium of their own propaganda." But their interest in Most's extremism ended there. With nary a shred of documentary evidence to stand on, Green concludes, "Though they were thrilled by Most's speeches, Chicago's social revolutionaries did not form conspiracies or launch violent assaults on authorities . . . [They] remained convinced by Marx and Engels that the road to socialism was a long one and that there were no shortcuts through individual acts of terror."[18]

In order to complete his makeover of Chicago's revolutionaries into patient and peace-loving socialists, Green revived the Dell thesis, explaining that when anarchists like Spies or Parsons advocated throwing bombs, they were only trying to "frighten authorities" and attract attention with their "bomb-talking."[19] Even though these radicals urged the use of violence, Green refuses to believe this advocacy was anything but rhetorical or, at worst, simply prudent self-defense: "In any case, the Chicago anarchists advocated the use of force as a defensive strategy for workers involved in life-or-death struggles with armed forces, not as a means of inspiring terror through indiscriminate killing."[20]

Over the past quarter century, as scholars and left activists have tamed Chicago's anarchists into martyrs to free speech, the eight-hour workday, and labor's rights, they have been rendered safe and accordingly expanded in popularity. As the most troublesome and disturbing aspects of the Chicago anarchists' revolutionary beliefs were submerged beneath their celebration as labor heroes, the martyrs were even bestowed with official recognition.

On May 1, 1998, a group of labor activists, trade union officials, and a representative of the National Park Service, stood solemnly in Forest Home Cemetery in Chicago. They had gathered on labor's most sacred day, May 1, International Workers Day, a holiday memorializing the execution of five Chicago labor leaders in 1886. At their feet a squat brass plaque read:

> Haymarket Martyrs' Monument has been designated a National Historic Land-mark. This monument represents the labor movement's struggle for workers' rights and possesses national significance in commemorating the history of the United States of America. 1997. National Park Service. United States Department of the Interior.[21]

The rebels who had once plotted to topple the state now enjoyed its protection and seal of approval. They were no longer remembered for the radical tactics of force and confrontation they pioneered. Rather, they had become official victims, symbols of the excesses of a distant corrupt age. Their memory now served an important purpose. In their wrongful deaths, they marked the progress of the state that recognized them. In mourning these five dead men, the state celebrated itself.

While no one can speak for the dead, few who have read their writings and noted their deeds could imagine that Lingg, Fischer, or Engel would have tolerated the uses to which their memory had been put. Had they defiantly proclaimed their part in the bombing, had they regretted as some of their supporters had only the number of bombs thrown that night, they may have escaped the ironic twist of their legacy. Had they been buried as soldiers and not victims, their names would not have been written in schoolbooks or official markers. But their stories may have lived on in song, in graffiti, in rebel lore. They may still.

NOTES

Introduction

1. For example, the *Encyclopedia of the American Left* is befuddled. It can only say, "Chicago 'social-revolutionaries,' as they styled themselves, drew upon various sources including Marxism, Bakuninism, and Natural Rights theory as they promulgated doctrine." *Encyclopedia of the American Left*, 2nd ed., ed. Mari Jo Buhle, Paul Buhle, and Dan Georgakas (Oxford University Press, 1990), 45. This is not much of a definition, because the entry fails to explain just what this "doctrine" actually comprised or what distinguished these "social revolutionaries" from other radicals. Bruce Nelson, in his often-cited social history of Chicago's anarchists, devotes a chapter to considering their beliefs but also remains baffled. If, Nelson writes, "Mikhail Bakunin and Peter Kropotkin epitomized nineteenth-century anarchism, then Chicago's IWPA [International Working People's Association] was not anarchist . . . [their] ideological evolution . . . [is] best understood as a transcendence of nineteenth-century republicanism . . . not an evolution from socialism to anarchism but from republicanism, through electoral socialism, to revolutionary socialism." Bruce Nelson, *Beyond the Martyrs: A Social History of Chicago's Anarchists, 1870–1900* (New Brunswick, N.J.: Rutgers University Press, 1988), 171.

2. Robert Hunter, *Violence and the Labor Movement* (New York: MacMillan, 1914), 68.

3. Richard Ely, "Recent Phases of Socialism in the United States," *Christian Union*, May 1, 1884, 414.

4. John Rae, *Contemporary Socialism* (London: Wm. Isbister, Ltd., 1884), v, 5.

5. "Socialistic Movements in England and the United States," in *Frank Leslie's Popular Monthly* (New York: Frank Leslie Publishing House, 1886), 21:519. While this author's analysis was spot-on, his crystal ball was a bit cloudy, as he predicted, "There is no risk of Anarchical Socialism ever becoming a serious danger among us. [In America] even with recruits from our foreign element, [they] are not numerous enough to indulge in perilous law-breaking, and the temptations to law-breaking

by any but offenders who well deserve and will obtain ready punishment for their offenses, are too few and slight."

6. Lucy Parsons, *Famous Speeches of the Eight Chicago Anarchists* (1910; repr., New York: Arno Press, 1969), 39.

7. Intellectual historians have long overused *anarchism* as a descriptive term, having to qualify it so thoroughly as to leave it without much meaning of its own. Peter Kropotkin causes most historian writers trouble, because his career, which spanned the "actionist" era of the 1880s, seems particularly inconsistent. James Billington, for example, cannot quite pin him down, noting that he both urged "insurrectionary deeds" and declared that "a structure based on centuries of history cannot be destroyed with a few kilos of explosives." Billington thus can only define Kropotkin by what he was not: Kropotkin "left the term populism behind in Russia and rejected Bakunin's term collectivism for anarchist-communist or simply anarchist . . . The philosophical perspective of Kropotkin's anarchism fell somewhat in between the violent atheism of Bakunin, and the nonviolent religiosity of Tolstoy." James H. Billington, *Fire in the Minds of Men: Origins of the Revolutionary Faith* (New York: Basic Books, 1980), 416–17.

Chapter 1. The Conspiracy

1. Testimony of William Seliger, Haymarket Affair Digital Collection (hereafter, HADC), Chicago History Museum, Vol. I, 508. (The HADC is available online at http://www.chicagohistory.org/hadc/hadctoc.htm.) For more on the question of Lingg's alleged attendance at the Greif's Hall meeting, see note 17 below.

2. *Chicago Tribune*, Apr. 19, 1884, 15.

3. Ibid., Aug. 29, 1878, 8; on the Socialistic Publishing Company, see Michael J. Schaack, *Anarchy and Anarchists: A History of the Red Terror and the Social Revolution in America and Europe: Communism, Socialism, and Nihilism in Doctrine and in Deed: The Chicago Haymarket Conspiracy and the Detection and Trial of the Conspirators* (Chicago: F. J. Schulte and Company, 1889), 66; *Chicago Tribune*, Nov. 28, 1878, 8; Feb. 6, 1880, 8; on the National Liberal League, see *Chicago Tribune*, Oct. 31, 1881, 7.

4. HADC, Vol. I, 146–48.

5. Ibid., 148–50.

6. Ibid., 105.

7. Record #1554, *Cook County Coroner's Inquest Reports*, May 1886, Illinois Regional Archives Depository, Northeastern State University, Chicago, Illinois; *Chicago Tribune*, May 4, 1886, 1.

8. HADC, Vol. I, 108.

9. Waller testified as to the meaning of "Y" (HADC, Vol. I, 55, 66). Spies testified about the daily deadlines and publishing schedules of the *Arbeiter-Zeitung* (HADC, Vol. N, 30).

10. HADC, Vol. I, 59–60.

11. See Huber's testimony in Schaack, *Anarchy and Anarchists,* 328, 347, for example. Haymarket historians have chosen not to speculate upon the meaning of these codes. Paul Avrich avoids analyzing it by saying, "Why it was inserted, however, remains a mystery." Paul Avrich, *The Haymarket Tragedy* (Princeton, N.J.: Princeton University Press, 1984), 192. Henry David asks, "Who sent the request for its insertion to Spies? And what was the motive? These questions are no more answerable today than they were in the dingy courtroom where Judge [Joseph E.] Gary presided in 1886." Henry David, *The History of the Haymarket Affair: A Study in the American Social-Revolutionary and Labor Movements* (New York: Farrar and Rinehart, 1936; reissued New York: Russell and Russell, 1958), 262. But this is no great mystery. Clearly, the motive for putting such a code in the newspaper was to assemble the troops and either to prepare for the revolution should it come or to whip one up. Either way, the timing of this code and the one on the day before suggests that there were those in the movement and probably in the editorial offices of the Socialistic Publishing Company who expected trouble because they were themselves orchestrating it. In fact, the only source distancing August Spies from these codes is his own testimony. James Green avoids the whole issue by not mentioning the coded signals at all. James Green, *Death in the Haymarket: A Story of Chicago, the First Labor Movement and the Bombing that Divided Gilded Age America* (New York: Pantheon Books, 2006).

12. *Chicago Tribune,* July 24, 1877, 5; Apr. 21, 1878, 5; Sept. 20, 1884, 2; Nov. 28, 1884, 1; Apr. 29, 1885, 2.

13. HADC, Vol. I, 62; Schaack, *Anarchy and Anarchists,* 328, 333.

14. Schaack, *Anarchy and Anarchists,* 254.

15. Ibid., 358. Gruenberg's statement begins directly quoting Engel, but the final enclosing parenthesis is missing in Schaack's version, and I have ended the quote where the context seems to dictate it should end.

16. Schaack, *Anarchy and Anarchists,* 333.

17. Ibid., 302. John Thielen also told Schaack that Lingg offered to furnish bombs at this meeting. Haymarket historians have accepted defense assertions that Louis Lingg, the admitted bomb maker, did not attend the secret Greif's Hall meeting (see Avrich, *Haymarket Tragedy,* 273), but John Thielen told police investigators that he did see Lingg in Greif's basement (Schaack, *Anarchy and Anarchists,* 252). William Seliger, Lingg's landlord and co-conspirator, testified that he attended the carpenters' union meeting that Lingg supposedly attended but did not see Lingg there (HADC, Vol. I, 551). Gustav Lehman, who stood guard at the door of Greif's basement room during the meeting, remembered seeing Seliger arrive but did not recall Lingg, confirming that some of the men from the carpenters meeting did indeed walk the block down Lake Street to Greif's. Lehman also testified that after the basement meeting, he walked home from Greif's saloon with both Seliger and Lingg (HADC, Vol. J, 205). According to Schaack, Lingg gave his own statement that included his admission that he had indeed attended the Greif's basement meeting: "I . . . attended a meeting the same night, at No. 54 West Lake Street, which was held by the armed sections" (Schaack, *Anarchy and Anarchists,* 276). Schaack made the same report

from the witness stand at the trial (HADC, Vol. K, 589). Several men who testified
for the defense provided alibis for Lingg. Ernst Neindorf, who chaired the carpenters
meeting, claimed that Lingg was "there throughout the meeting," but when asked
directly if he saw Lingg at the end of the meeting, he could not remember if he had
(HADC, Vol. M, 373–74). Another carpenter, Jacob Sherman, heard Lingg give a
fifteen-minute report at the beginning of the meeting at nine o'clock and said he
thought Lingg was there until the end (HADC, Vol. M, 376–79).

18. *Chicago Tribune*, Aug. 25, 1879, 8; Sept. 8, 1879, 8; Apr. 26, 1886, 3; Aug.
30, 1867, 2.

19. HADC, Vol. I, 102. William Tuttle, a reporter for the *Chicago Times*, swore
that he saw a number of men wave their pistols in the air after Parsons asked rhetori-
cally, "What will you do?" Tuttle remembered the moment clearly: "I think I could
describe the man, and would know him if I saw him: he stuck up his hand like that
(illustrating) with a revolver in it and said, 'We will shoot the devils' or some such
expression. And I saw 2 others sticking up there [*sic*] hands near to him who made
similar expressions, and had what I took to be at that time revolvers: but this one
man I speak of I took particular notice of him, and remember his appearance, and
saw his revolver very plainly in his right hand" (HADC, Vol. K, 173).

20. *Chicago Tribune*, Oct. 17, 1866, 4.

21. Ibid., Apr. 12, 1882, 6; May 4, 1882, 8.

22. HADC, Vol. L, 28.

23. HADC, Vol. M, 44, 101.

24. HADC, Vol. I, 112.

25. Ibid., 527–28.

26. HADC, Vol. N, 65–66.

27. Schaack, *Anarchy and Anarchists,* 176.

28. "Account of the Haymarket Riot," *Chicago Herald*, May 5, 1886, 1.

29. Ibid., 2.

30. *Chicago News*, May 4, 1886, 1. Johann Most was the most famous proponent
of revolutionary violence at this time, especially of workers flinging dynamite bombs
at the police.

31. Ibid.

32. Schaack, *Anarchy and Anarchists,* 253.

33. HADC, Vol. I, 522–26.

34. Schaack, *Anarchy and Anarchists,* 281.

35. Ibid., 254.

36. Max Nettlau, *Anarchisten und Sozialrevolutionäe: die Historische Entwicklung
des Anarchismus in den Jahren, 1880–1886* (Berlin: Asy-Verlang, 1931), 387.

37. *Commonweal* (London), May 29, 1886, 71; *New York World*, Nov. 9, 1887, 1.

38. Former Communist Party member turned FBI informant Louis Budenz was
distantly related to Lizius. According to Budenz, his father's cousin married Lizius's
brother. Louis Francis Budenz, *This Is My Story* (New York: Whittlesy House, 1947),
26. For the arrival with Parsons, see *Chicago Tribune*, June 22, 1886.

39. *New York Times*, May 6, 1879, 1.

40. *Chicago Tribune*, May 22, 1886, 3.

CHAPTER 2. FROM RED TO BLACK

1. *Chicago Tribune*, July 22, 1877, 8.

2. *Chicago Tribune*, July 24, 1877, 5; *Annual Report, Chicago Police Department for 1877* (Chicago: Chicago Printers, 1878), 5; John J. Flinn and John E. Wilkie, *History of the Chicago Police* (Chicago: Police Book Fund, 1887), 162–63.

3. Lucy Parsons, ed., *Life of Albert Parsons* (1889; repr., Chicago: Lucy Parsons publisher, 1903), 12–13. Parsons's own account is corroborated in the main by a report in the *Chicago Tribune*: "prior to their departure Supt. Hickey warned them that the citizens would not tolerate Commune leaders in such dangerous times as the present and in the event of a mob of laborers obtaining control of the city, capitalists would offer any sum to see the leaders of such a mob strung up to a telephone pole" (*Chicago Tribune*, July 25, 1877, 7).

4. Robert V. Bruce, *1877: Year of Violence* (1959; repr. Chicago: Quadrangle Books, 1970), 245–47.

5. *Chicago Tribune*, July 26, 1877, 8.

6. Ibid.

7. *Chicago Tribune*, Aug. 10, 1877, 8; Bruce, *1877: Year of Violence*, 243.

8. Karl Marx and Friedrich Engels, *The Marx-Engels Reader*, 2nd ed., ed. Robert C. Tucker (New York: Norton 1978), 62–63, 218–19, 165.

9. Karl Marx, *Capital: A Critique of Political Economy* (New York: Vintage Books, 1977), 1:929.

10. Richard B. Saltman, *The Social and Political Thought of Michael Bakunin* (Westport, Conn.: Greenwood Press, 1983), 99–100; Sam Dolgoff, ed., *Bakunin on Anarchism* (Montreal: Black Rose Books, 1980), 166.

11. Michael Bakunin, "The Program of the International Brotherhood" (1869), in Dolgoff, *Bakunin on Anarchism*, 155.

12. Paul Thomas, *Karl Marx and the Anarchists* (London: Routledge and Kegan Paul, 1980), 284–86.

13. Scholars have long misunderstood the origins of the break between Marx and Bakunin by seeing it backward: their philosophical differences did not lead them to different organizing strategies; rather, their organizing strategies, which in turn were based on their theories of how a revolution would occur, determined their more abstract systems and theories.

14. Qtd. in James Joll, *The Anarchists* (Cambridge, Mass.: Harvard University Press, 1979), 90–91.

15. Marx's machinations are well chronicled in Thomas, *Karl Marx and the Anarchists*, 314–26.

16. Michael Bakunin, "The Paris Commune and the Idea of the State" (1871), in Dolgoff, *Bakunin on Anarchism*, 268.

17. Qtd. in Nunzio Pernicone, *Italian Anarchism, 1864–1892* (Princeton, N.J.: Princeton University Press, 1993), 13.

18. *Le Révolté*, Dec. 25, 1881, 1.

19. Billington, *Fire in the Minds of Men,* 356 (see intro., n. 7); Michael Bakunin, "Letters to a Frenchman" (1870), in Dolgoff, *Bakunin on Anarchism,* 195–96.

20. Andrew R. Carlson, *Anarchism in Germany* (Metuchen, N.J.: Scarecrow Press, 1972), 1:80. The bulletin's full title was *Bulletin de la Fédération jurassienne de l'Association internationale des travailleurs* (Pernicone, *Italian Anarchism,* 115). See also Ulrich Linse, "'Propaganda by Deed' and 'Direct Action': Two Concepts of Anarchist Violence," in *Social Protest, Violence, and Terror in Nineteenth and Twentieth-century Europe,* ed. Wolfgang J. Mommsen and Gerhard Hirschfeld (New York: St. Martin's Press, 1982), 201–29.

21. Qtd. in Caroline Cahm, *Kropotkin and the Rise of Revolutionary Anarchism, 1872–1886* (Cambridge: Cambridge University Press, 1989), 79.

22. Carlson, *Anarchism in Germany,* 83–84, appendix 1.

23. In believing the revolution was close, not a distant historic goal that might take generations of alienating capitalist development and the gradual construction of class consciousness through a steady and theoretically sound socialist strategy, the revolutionaries could afford to take a uniquely ecumenical point of view: "The Association as such . . . should not express itself on the political division of votes. It leaves, however, to its members complete freedom of action in this area" (Carlson, *Anarchism in Germany,* appendix 1).

24. Paul Avrich, *Anarchist Portraits* (Princeton, N.J.: Princeton University Press, 1988), 242–43. On Brousse, see David Stafford, *From Anarchism to Reformism: A Study of the Political Activities of Paul Brousse with the First International and the French Socialist Movement, 1870–1890* (Toronto: University of Toronto Press, 1971), 70–71 (*Arbeiter-Zeitung* quote on p. 79); Andrew R. Carlson, "Anarchism and Terror in the German Empire, 1870–1890," in Mommsen and Hirschfield, *Social Protest,* 175–200.

25. Or as Stafford notes, such doctrine was "a perfect intellectual safety net; if one tried the tactic and succeeded—then all well and good; if one tried and failed—then it was propaganda by the deed" (*From Anarchism to Reformism,* 87).

26. Cahm, *Kropotkin,* 77–78.

27. Ibid., 77.

28. "Notre action doit être la révolte permanente, par la parole, par le'écrit, par le poignard, le fusil, la dynamite" (*Le Révolté,* Dec. 25, 1880, 1); Linse, "'Propaganda by Deed,'" 202.

29. *Kropotkin's Revolutionary Pamphlets; A Collection of Writings, by Peter Kropotkin,* ed. Roger N. Baldwin (1927; repr. New York: Dover Publications, 1970). *L'Esprit de Révolte* appeared serially in *Le Révolté* (Paris) May 14, 28, June 25, July 9, 1881. Carolyn Cahm persuasively argues that at the time Kropotkin penned *L'Esprit de Révolte,* he was already moving away from the idea of propaganda by deed. *L'Esprit de Révolte,* however, was ambiguous in its advocacy of violence and

could be read as either supporting violence meant only as a spark to insurrection or violence as a means of education. See Cahm, *Kropotkin*, 159–60.

30. Patricia R. Turner, "Hostile Participants? Working-Class Militancy, Associational Life, and the "Distinctiveness" of the Prewar French Labor Movement," *Journal of Modern History* 71 (Mar. 1999): 28–55; Ernst Victor Zenker, *Anarchism: A Criticism and History of the Anarchist Theory* (1895; repr. New York: Putnam's, 1897), 285–86; quotes in Marie Fleming, *The Geography of Freedom: The Odyssey of Elisée Reclus* (Montreal: Black Rose Books, 1996), 133–34.

31. *The First International: Minutes of The Hague Congress of 1872*, ed. Hans Gerth (Madison: University of Wisconsin Press, 1958), 189–90 (Hepner quote on p. 218).

32. Ibid., 242.

33. Raymond H. Dominick III, *Wilhelm Liebknecht and the Founding of the German Social Democratic Party* (Chapel Hill: University of North Carolina Press, 1982), 134–54, 217–25; Gary P. Steenson, *"Not One Man! Not One Penny!" German Social Democracy, 1863–1914* (Pittsburgh: University of Pittsburgh Press, 1981), 30–31; Christine Heiss, "German Radicals in Industrial America: The Lehr und Wehr Verein in Gilded Age Chicago," in *German Workers in Industrial Chicago: 1850–1910: A Comparative Perspective*, ed. Hartmut Keil and John B. Jentz (Dekalb: Northern Illinois University Press, 1983), 211; Richard Schneirov, *Labor and Urban Politics: Class Conflict and the Origins of Modern Liberalism in Chicago, 1864–1897* (Urbana: University of Illinois Press, 1998), 54–55.

34. Paul Avrich, a historian who is well acquainted with the history of anarchism in Europe, writes as if American anarchists were unmoved by European anarchist ideas until Johann Most arrived in America, concluding absurdly, "From 1883 to 1886 virtually the whole social revolutionary movement was the expression of the ideas and vision of this one man" (*Haymarket Tragedy*, 67).

35. Cf., Stanley Nadel, *Little Germany: Ethnicity, Religion, and Class in New York City, 1845–1880* (Urbana: University of Illinois Press, 1990); Richard Jules Oestreicher, *Solidarity and Fragmentation: Working People and Class Consciousness in Detroit, 1875–1900* (Urbana: University of Illinois Press, 1989), 51; Rudolf A. Hofmeister, *The Germans of Chicago* (Champaign, Ill.: Stipes Publishing, 1976), 10–11.

36. Bruce Nelson, *"Arbeiterpresse und Arbeiterbewegung*: Chicago's Socialist and Anarchist Press, 1870–1900," in *The German-American Radical Press: The Shaping of a Left Political Culture, 1850–1940*, ed. Elliot Shore, Ken Fones-Wolf, James P. Danky (Urbana: University of Illinois Press, 1992), 81–83.

37. Soon after the *Vorbote* appeared, it provoked the founding of a competing labor paper, the *Arbeiter Freund*, which was hailed by the *Tribune* as advising workingmen to be "law-abiding citizens of the United States, and that there is no need of a social revolution" (*Chicago Tribune*, Feb. 22, 1874, 13). On Klings in the IWA, see *Woodhull & Claflin's Weekly*, Apr. 6, 1872, 4; Renate Kiesewetter, "German-American Labor Press: The *Vorbote* and the *Chicagoer Arbeiter-Zeitung*,"

in *German Workers' Culture in the United States, 1850 to 1920*, ed. Hartmut Keil (Washington, D.C.: Smithsonian Institution Press, 1988), 140. On Kling's saloon, see *Chicago Tribune*, June 30, 1875, 8; Feb. 24, 1875, 7; Feb. 27, 1875, 11. Schneirov, *Labor and Urban Politics*, 54–55; *Chicago Tribune*, Dec. 23, 25, 1873, 1. Historians have insisted for so long on interpreting every schism and action through the prism of Lassalleans versus Marxists that they missed nearly every ideological change and nuance of the period. (Cf. John R. Commons et al., *History of Labour in the United States* [New York: Macmillan, 1918], 2, ch. 2 passim; Philip S. Foner, *History of the Labor Movement in the United States* [1955; repr. New York: International Publishers, 1975], ch. 2 passim; and Howard H. Quint, *The Forging of American Socialism: Origins of the Modern Movement* [Indianapolis: Bobbs-Merrill Co., 1953], 13.) The Workingmen's Party of Illinois was supposedly Lassallean as was its Chicago leader, Carl Klings. Sometimes this confusion is evident in even a single essay: Renate Kiesewetter notes on page 147 of her article "German-American Labor Press" that Klings was once a leader of the Lassalean General German Workers' Association and then broke with Lassalle before emigrating to America. Earlier, on page 140, Klings appears as a leader of the "Lassallean political wing of the party in Chicago." Yet Klings is known in the literature on the German SAPD as "Marx's most devoted follower in Germany." Richard W. Reichard, *Crippled from Birth: German Social Democracy, 1844–1970* (Ames: Iowa State University Press, 1969), 134. In the view of the Republican *Chicago Tribune*, Klings was the leader of the "incendiary, blatant *Vorbote* clique" that drove out of the movement "all the sensible and conservative leaders" (Feb. 24, 1875, 7); *Chicago Tribune*, June 14, 1875, 8. On Klings's saloon, see *Chicago Tribune*, Feb. 24, 1875, 7; Feb. 27, 1875, 11; June 30, 1875, 8. On Klings and the founding of *Vorbote,* see *Chicago Tribune*, May 25, 1874, 3; June 21, 1875, 8. The *Chicago Tribune* noted around the time of the SLP's first election in the spring of 1878 that Klings had been "bounced" by socialist leaders because "if he could have had his way he would have led the Socialists into a revolution and turned things upside down" (May 2, 1878, 8).

38. Lyser also served as the editor of *Der Sozialdemokrat,* the national organ of the Social Democratic Party of the United States, a short-lived offshoot of the First International that followed its German namesake in expelling him from his post and from the party within a year. From there it was to Milwaukee, where he took the helm of the *Sozialist.* In 1878 he moved south to Chicago, where he served as editor of a succession of radical papers, first the Saturday *Vorbote,* then the Sunday *Fackel,* and finally the daily *Arbeiter-Zeitung.* Lyser boasted of having attended hundreds of socialist demonstrations in Germany in *Vorbote,* June 29, 1878, 2; "German Socialism in America," n.a., *North American Review* (Feb. 1879): 377. Lyser is noted as speaking publicly in Chicago in *Chicago Tribune,* Oct. 29, 1876, 8; Heinz Ickstadt and Hartmut Keil, "A Forgotten Piece of Working-Class Literature: Gustav Lyser's Satire of the Hewitt Hearing of 1878," *Labor History* 20, no. 1 (1979): 127–44. On Gelaff, see Marion Tuttle Marzolf, *The Danish-Language Press in America* (New York: Arno Press, 1979), 41; William Dwight Porter Bliss,

A Handbook of Socialism (New York: C. Scribner's, 1895), 162; Camille Martinet, *Le Socialisme en Danemark* (Paris: Société d'Éditions Scientifiques, 1893), 55–59; *Chicago Tribune*, Apr. 28, 1878, 3. Biographical sketches of Conzett, Grottkau, and Lyser are found in *German Workers in Chicago: A Documentary History of Working-Class Culture from 1850 to World War One*, ed. Hartmut Keil and John B. Jentz (Urbana: University of Illinois Press, 1988), 406–407.

39. Hartmut Keil, "A Profile of Editors of the German-American Radical Press, 1850–1910," in *The German-American Radical Press: The Shaping of a Left Political Culture, 1850–1940*, ed. Elliot Shore, Ken Fones-Wolf, James P. Danky (Urbana: University of Illinois Press, 1992), 20, 25. Herman Schlüter, *Die Internationale in Amerika* (Chicago: Deutsche Sprachgruppe der Sozialist. Partei der Ver. Staaten, 1918), 321. *Chicago Tribune*, May 9, 1887, 1; *Karl Marx and Frederick Engels Letters to Americans, 1848–1895*, ed. Alexander Trachtenberg (New York: International Publishers, 1953), 290.

40. Timothy Messer-Kruse, *The Yankee International: Marxism and the American Reform Tradition, 1848–1876* (Chapel Hill: University of North Carolina Press, 1998).

41. "The Formation of the Workingmen's Party of the United States: Proceedings of the Union Congress Held at Philadelphia, July 19–22, 1876," ed. Philip S. Foner, AIMS Occasional Series No. 18 (New York: American Institute for Marxist Studies, 1976), 5, 13.

42. On German railroad history, see Colleen A. Dunlavy, *Politics and Industrialization: Early Railroads in the United States and Prussia* (Princeton, N.J.: Princeton University Press, 1994).

43. *Vorbote*, Jan. 5, 1878, 1; Jan. 26, 1878, 4.

44. Stanley Nadel, "The German Immigrant Left in the United States," in *The Immigrant Left in the United States*, ed. Paul Buhle and Dan Georgakas (New York: State University of New York Press, 1996), 51.

45. Judson Grenell, unpublished autobiography (1930), 29–30, Joseph Labadie Papers, University of Michigan Library, Ann Arbor, Michigan.

46. It should be noted that the Workingmen's Party Convention of 1876 did entrust a committee to publish the proceedings in both German and English (authorizing three thousand copies in German and two thousand in English), but the committee published only in German (Foner, "Formation of the Workingmen's Party," 22, 38). See also, *Socialist Labor Party Platform, Constitution, and Resolutions Adopted at the National Congress of the Workingmen's Party of the United States Held at Newark, New Jersey, Dec. 26–31, 1877* (Cincinnati, 1878). Not everything the Newark Congress did was a break with its doctrinaire past. The congress refused to seat two Yankee radicals, George Madox and Leander Thompson, who were once members of notorious Section 12 of the IWA, the home section of Victoria Woodhull. It also clung to an anti–women's-suffrage plank (Messer-Kruse, *Yankee International*, 249).

47. Oestreicher, *Solidarity and Fragmentation*, 80–81; William Frederic Kamman, "Socialism in German American Literature," PhD diss., University of Pennsylvania,

1917, 30; *Chicago Tribune*, June 16, 1878, 5; Records of the New York Section, Socialist Labor Party Papers, Minutes of the Section for May 10, 1878.

48. Commons et al., *History of Labour*, 2:281. See local section reports in the *National Socialist* throughout 1878; *An-Archist* (Boston) 1, no. 1 (Jan. 1881): 20.

49. *Chicago Tribune*, Mar. 11, 1878, 5; Mar. 18, 1878, 8; Apr. 3, 1878; Nov. 9, 1878, 3.

50. Ibid., Apr. 3, 1878, 1.

51. Ibid., Apr. 28, 1878, 3; Keil and Jentz, *German Workers in Chicago*, 105.

52. *Chicago Tribune*, Apr. 3, 1879, 4; Schneirov, *Labor and Urban Politics*, 87–89; *Chicago Tribune*, Apr. 29, 1879, 6.

53. Alfred Theodore Andreas, *History of Chicago from its Earliest Time . . .* (Chicago: A. T. Andreas Co., 1886), 3:143. Estimates of party strength are given in Nelson, *Beyond the Martyrs*, 65 (see intro., n. 1). Nelson overlooks Stauber's important committee appointment, writing instead, "The socialists were relegated to minor committees (wharfing privileges, harbors and bridges, and farmers' markets)" (66).

54. The socialist vote in ward 14 was 1,718 in 1879. Stauber's vote there in 1880 was 1,410 (Andreas, *History of Chicago*, 3:865, 867). Josiah Seymour Currey, *Chicago: Its History and Its Builders* (Chicago: S. J. Clarke Publishing Co., 1912), 379. Stauber's opponent, James J. McGrath was considered a reform Republican, principally known for successfully sponsoring bills while in the Illinois Assembly that made it a criminal offense for any employer to blacklist its employees and forbidding any city in the state from licensing "houses of ill-fame." Fremont O. Bennett, *Politics and Politicians of Chicago, Cook County, and Illinois* (Chicago: Blakely Printing Co., 1886), 256.

55. The common misinterpretation of the role of election fraud in molding socialist ideology at this time is rooted in a willful misrepresentation of the recollections of Chicago labor leader George Schilling, a figure who had one foot in the anarchist camp and the other in the mainstream labor movement and from this position enjoyed a unique vantage point on the radical movement of the 1870s and 1880s. Historians of the Haymarket era frequently repeat Schilling's assertion that Stauber's corrupt election loss in 1880 "did more, perhaps, than all other things combined to destroy the faith of the Socialists in Chicago in the efficiency of the ballot." Lucy Parsons, ed., *Life of Albert R. Parsons with a Brief History of the Labor Movement in America* (Chicago: 1903), xxviii. But neither of the two most influential Haymarket historians, Henry David or Paul Avrich, quotes Schilling's very next line: "From that time on the advocates of physical force *as the only means* of industrial emancipation found a wide field of action for the dissemination and acceptance of their ideas" (emphasis added). Had they done so, it would have been clear that Schilling was not arguing that the stealing of Stauber's council seat changed the minds of any of the anarchist leaders; it simply helped illustrate the case they had long wished to make about the uselessness of voting. Schilling indicated that those socialist editors, leaders, and thinkers who had long debated the question of electoral participation from within the framework of a Marxist position of great skepticism,

among whom could be counted all of those radicals who would later play leading roles in the Haymarket drama, were not themselves moved by what happened to Stauber's votes, but exploited the issue to build their own power in the socialist and labor movements. Avrich quotes Schilling on page 48 (*Haymarket Tragedy*); David on page 60 (*History of the Haymarket Affair*). Green also mistakes his citation; this quote is found in Parsons's "Autobiography" on page 17, not page 36 (Green, *Death in the Haymarket*, 331n14). Schilling, "History of the Labor Movement" (xx) and Albert Parsons, "Autobiography," in L. Parsons, *Life of Albert Parsons*.

Of all the individuals who would eventually emerge as leading anarchists in Chicago, Albert Parsons is generally characterized as the best example of an anarchist whose hard experiences in the corrupt world of Chicago politics propelled him from liberal labor reformer to militant revolutionary. James Green describes Parsons's disillusionment with democratic methods as being a gradual process that culminated with socialist candidate Stauber losing his aldermanic seat as a result of ballot-box stuffing: "For many socialists like Albert Parsons, already dejected by the fickle habits of Chicago voters, this blatant case of fraud crushed what little faith they retained in the efficacy of the ballot. 'It was then,' Parsons remembered, 'that I began to realize the hopeless task of political reformation.'" Green leaves out Parsons's previous line, which indicates that he was not referring directly to the Stauber case at all: "In the fall and spring elections of 1878-'79-'80 the politicians began to practice ballot-box stuffing and other outrages upon the Workingmen's party. It was then that I began to realize the hopeless task" (L. Parsons, *Life of Albert Parsons*, 17). James Green, *Death in the Haymarket*, 90. Green incorrectly cites Parsons's quote, saying it is found on page 36. See Green, *Death in the Haymarket*, 331n14.

This may be, but there is also significant evidence that Parsons's and other Chicago militants' disillusionment must have been nearly complete toward the earliest of these dates. Prior to the spring election of 1878, Parsons gave an interview in which he expressed himself in favor of arming protesters as the surest means to gaining workers' rights. Parsons boasted that "the workingmen of this city are arming themselves . . . we intend to carry our arms with us and if the armed assassins and paid murderers employed by the capitalist class undertake to disperse and break up our meetings, as they did in such an outrageous manner last summer, they will meet with force worthy of their steel . . . We hope these things may cause people everywhere to stop and think. We know the social revolution began last July. The issue is made, and sooner or later, it must be settled one way or the other." Though Parsons prefaced his remarks by saying "the ballot-box is our first remedy," his electoral-minded colleagues did not appreciate his militant tone and pointedly snubbed him when they drew up their list of speakers for the SLP's big mass meeting later that summer, telling one reporter that Parsons was "at variance with [the] political action of the Socialistic Party." *Chicago Tribune*, Apr. 26, 1878, 7; Aug. 18, 1878, 8.

56. Robert W. Goodrich, "On the Road to Wyden: The Expulsion of Johann Most from the German Social Democratic Party, 1878–1880," master's thesis, University

of Wisconsin, 1994, 26; Johann Most, *August Reinsdorf und die Propaganda der That* (New York, 1885), 16–17.

57. Cahm, *Kropotkin,* 86–90; Carlson, *Anarchism in Germany,* 115–18.

58. Felice Orsini threw a bomb at Napolean III in 1858, and Giuseppe Fieschi attempted to kill King Louis-Philippe in 1835. Translated quotes by Cahm, *Kropotkin,* 86, 90. Goodrich, "On the Road to Wyden," 35.

59. Carlson, "Anarchism and Terror," 178–81; Dominick, *Wilhelm Liebknecht,* 267–74; Goodrich, "On the Road to Wyden,"42.

60. Figures on SAPD-banned organizations are from "Bismarck and the Socialists," *New Englander and Yale Review* 9, no. 5 (1885): 723; Linse, "'Propaganda by Deed,'" 210.

61. Frederic Trautmann, *The Voice of Terror: A Biography of Johann Most* (Westwood, Conn.: Greenwood Press, 1980), passim; Max Nomad, *Apostles of Revolution* (Boston: Little, Brown, 1939), 256–78. See also "Bachmann and the International," *Liberty,* May 1, 1886, 8.

62. Vernon L. Lidtke, *The Outlawed Party Social Democracy in Germany, 1878–1890* (Princeton, N.J.: Princeton University Press, 1966), 77. Quote from *The Annual Register: A Record of Public Events . . . for the Year 1878* (London: 1879), 302; Carlson, *Anarchism in Germany,* 191; Tom Goyens, *Beer and Revolution: The German Anarchist Movement in New York City, 1880–1914* (Urbana: University of Illinois Press, 2007), 66–67; Günter Bers, *Wilhelm Hasselmann, 1844–1916: Sozialrevolutionärer Agitator und Abgeordneter des Deutschen Reichstages* (Köln: Einhorn-Presse, 1973), 52–55. Read more on Hasselmann below in this chapter.

63. Goodrich, "On the Road to Wyden,"53–99.

64. Trautmann, *Voice of Terror,* 99. Tom Goyens incorrectly describes the work of Bakunin's that Most published in that September 1880 issue as "*Revolutionary Principles.*" None of Bakunin's works go by that title. Goyens, *Beer and Revolution,* 60. *Freiheit* (London), Dec. 11, 1880; "Die Taktik der revolutionaaeren Arbeiter-Partei," July 10, 1881. The best translation of the *Catechism* can be found in Philip Pomper, *Sergei Nechaev* (New Brunswick, N.J.: Rutgers University Press, 1979), 90–94. For more on Nechaev and Bakunin's *Catechism of the Revolutionist,* see ch. 3.

65. *Freiheit* (London), July 10, Sept. 18, 25, Oct. 9, 1880; Carlson, *Anarchism in Germany,* 283–302 (quote on p. 199).

66. Reports of exiles arriving can be found in *National Socialist* (J. Franz), June 22, 1878, 2; (Fritz Glogauer) July 6, 1878, 8; *Vorbote,* Dec. 11, 1880, 2.

67. *National Socialist,* July 6, 1878, 4. Incoming correspondence, Dec. 16, 1879, Records of the National Executive Committee; New York City American Section Minutes, July 5, Aug. 7, 1878, May 22, 1879, Records of State Committees and Local Sections, Records of the Socialist Labor Party of America, State Historical Society of Wisconsin.

68. Letter from "Procursor" (William West) in New York dated Jan. 9, 1879, *Socialist,* Jan. 25, 1879, 2; letter from "Procursor" in New York dated Jan. 16, 1879,

Socialist, Feb. 1, 1879, 2; support for the plan and the full text of the proposal are printed in a letter from C. E. Collenburg, *Socialist*, Feb. 22, 1879, 3.

69. *Socialist*, June 21, 1879, 2.

70. New York City American Section Minutes, Mar. 3, 1879, Records of State Committees and Local Sections, Records of the Socialist Labor Party of America, State Historical Society of Wisconsin.

71. On Hasselman, see Marcel Van Der Linden and Gregory Zieren, "August Sartorius von Waltershausen (1852–1938), German Political Economy, and American Labor," in *August Sartorius von Waltershausen: The Worker's Movement in the United States, 1879–1885*, ed. David Montgomery and Marcel van der Linden (Cambridge: Cambridge University Press, 1998), 28–64; Bers, *Wilhelm Hasselmann.*

72. Bers, *Wilhelm Hasselmann,* 3–39, 45–46; quote from Israel S. Clare, *The Unrivaled History of the World* (Chicago: Werner Co., 1893), 5:1787. Trautmann, *Voice of Terror,* 107.

73. Trautmann, *Voice of Terror,* 107. Bers, *Wilhelm Hasselmann,* 52. Hasselmann's article appeared in the July 31, 1880, issue of *Freiheit.*

74. Goyens, *Beer and Revolution,* 71–72; A. Sartorious von Waltershausen, *Der Moderne Socialismus in den Vereinigten Staaten von Amerika* (Berlin: Hermann Bahr, 1890), 175.

75. *Vorbote,* Feb. 12, 1881, 1. *New York Times,* Feb. 2, 1881, 3.

76. *Vorbote,* Mar. 12, 1881, 4.

77. Ibid., June 22, 1878, 8; The National Executive Committee's resolution actually read: "We therefore *request* all party members to withdraw from said military connections, and particularly *urge* all sections to avoid any official connections with such bodies; and to require that no arms be carried in their processions" (emphasis added; *National Socialist* [Cincinnati], June 22, 1878, 5). See also June 29, 1878, 5 and July 6, 1878, 5.

78. *Chicago Tribune,* June 17, 1878, 5. *Vorbote,* June 22, 1878, 8. Examples of Grottkau's language are in *Chicago Tribune,* Feb. 17, 1879; Jan. 20, 1879, 8. Interestingly, at the Gotha Congress, Grottkau sided with those attacking Wilhelm Hasselmann's paper *The Red Flag,* saying it was not sufficiently grounded in scientific socialism but appealed to workers only on a "knife and fork" basis (Bers, *Wilhelm Hasselmann,* 45).

79. *National Socialist* (Cincinnati), July 13, 1878, 5.

80. *Vorbote,* July 20, 1878, 4; SLP Board of Control Papers, Aug. 8, 1878.

81. *Socialist* (Chicago), Nov. 2, 1878, 1.

82. Letter from "Procursor" in New York dated Jan. 9, 23, 1879, *Socialist* (Chicago), Jan. 25, 1879, 2; Feb. 8, 1879, 2; Swinton's speech reprinted Feb. 15, 1879, 3; Mar. 22, 1879, 1.

83. *Socialist* (Chicago), Dec. 21, 1878, 5; Jan. 4, 1879, 1.

84. *Vorbote* noted that it was being officially suspended as a party organ, although the section that published it was not. It also noted that it shared editorial offices with the *Socialist,* which remained in good standing (*Socialist,* Jan. 4, 1879, 1). Frank

Hirth was editor of the *Socialist* until he resigned in early June 1879 (*Socialist*, June 28, 1879, 1); *Chicago Tribune*, Oct. 30, 1879, 7; Oct. 31, 1879, 6.

85. *Chicago Tribune*, Oct. 7, 1879, 9; Nov. 1, 1879, 8; Nov. 3, 1879, 8; Nov. 6, 1879, 4. Curiously, Bruce C. Nelson characterizes Sibley's criticisms of Grottkau as praise. Citing the same issue of the *Tribune*, Nelson writes, "Sibley pointed to the prestige of the Germans and the debility of the American socialists" (*Beyond the Martyrs*, 67).

86. *Chicago Tribune*, Apr. 7, 1878, 5.

87. Ibid., Jan. 19, 1880, 8; July 5, 1880, 6. Schilling reference in Nelson, *Beyond the Martyrs*, 68. See also Ehmann to Van Patten, Nov. 30, 1880, Incoming Correspondence, Socialist Labor Party Papers. Mark A. Lause, *The Civil War's Last Campaign: James B. Weaver, the Greenback-Labor Party, and the Politics of Race and Section* (Lanham, Md.: University Press of America, 2001).

88. Morgan to NEC, July 19, 1880, Morgan to Van Patten, July 20, 1880, M. Schalck to NEC, Aug. 4, 1880, Incoming Correspondence, Records of the Socialist Labor Party of America, State Historical Society of Wisconsin.

89. *Chicago Tribune*, July 5, 1880, 6.

CHAPTER 3. THE BLACK INTERNATIONAL

1. Vera Cohn, *Apostles into Terrorists: Women and the Revolutionary Movement in Russia of Alexander II* (London: Maurice Temple Smith, 1977), 78–79, 198–99; *New York Times*, Mar. 14, 15, 1881, both p. 1; Francis Johnson, *Famous Assassinations of History* (Chicago: A. C. McClurg and Co., 1903), 372–78.

2. *Chicago Tribune*, Mar. 21, 1881, 3.

3. *New York Times*, Mar. 15, 1881, 2; Mar. 16, 1881, 2; *Chicago Tribune*, Mar. 15, 1881, 3.

4. *New York Times*, Mar. 16, 1881, 2. Note how the Chicago SLP's resolution was worded in such a way that simultaneously praised the nihilists' actions while categorically walling off such actions from America. By this construction, those nations like the United States that enjoyed freer speech, press, and ballot already possessed a path to progress. Strikingly different was the response of the social revolutionaries, who drew no such distinctions.

5. H. Oliver, *The International Anarchist Movement in Late Victorian London* (London: Croom Helm, 1983), 13; Trautmann, *Voice of Terror*, 45 (see ch. 2, n. 61); Nomad, *Apostles of Revolution*, 273–74 (see ch. 2, n. 61).

6. Isaiah Berlin, "Herzen and Bakunin on Individual Liberty," in *Russian Thinkers*, ed. Henry Hardy and Aileen Kelly (New York: Penguin, 1978); Ernst Viktor Zenker, *Anarchism* (New York: G. P. Putnam's Sons, 1897), 148.

7. Karl Heinzen, "Murder," in *Voices of Terror: Manifestos, Writings, and Manuals of Al-Qada, Hamas, and Other Terrorists from around the World and Throughout the Ages*, ed. William Laqueur (New York: Reed Press, 2004), 57–67; Karl Marx

and Friedrich Engels, *The Communist Manifesto,* ed. Ellen Meiksins Wood (New York: Monthly Review Press, 1998).

8. Carlson, "Anarchism and Terror," 19–20 (see ch. 2, n. 24); Trautmann, *Voice of Terror,* 213.

9. Qtd. in James H. Billington, *Fire in the Minds of Men: Origins of the Revolutionary Faith* (1980; repr. New Brunswick, N.J.: Transaction, 2009), 395.

10. Ludwig Büchner, *Force and Matter: Empirico-philosophical Studies, Intelligibly Rendered,* trans. J. Frederick Collingwood (London: Trübner and Co., 1864), 258.

11. Nikolay Gavrilovich Chernyshevsky, *A Vital Question; or, What Is to Be Done?* trans. Nathan Haskell Dole, Simon S. Skidelsky (New York: T. Y. Crowell, 1886), 288. Benjamin Tucker brought out one of the first English translations of this book: Nikolay Gavrilovich Tchernychewsky, *What's to Be Done? A Romance,* trans. Benjamin R. Tucker (Boston: Tucker, 1886).

12. Ana Siljak, *Angel of Vengeance: The "Girl Assassin," the Governor of St. Petersburg, and Russia's Revolutionary World* (New York: Macmillan, 2008), 105–6.

13. James Joll, *The Anarchists,* 2nd ed. (Cambridge: Harvard University Press, 1980), 78. See also "Bakunin and Nechaev," ch. 3 of Avrich, *Anarchist Portraits,* 32–52 (see ch. 2, n. 24); Richard B. Saltman, *The Social and Political Thought of Michael Bakunin* (Westport, Conn.: Greenwood Press, 1983), 131–35. The best translation of the *Catechism* can be found in Pomper, *Sergei Nechaev,* 90–94 (see ch. 2, n. 64).

14. Pomper, *Sergei Nechaev,* 90–94.

15. *Freiheit* (London), Sept. 18, 1880; *Freiheit* (New York), March 18, 1883; "Bakunin's Groundwork for the Social Revolution," *Alarm,* Dec. 26, 1885, 2. Parsons inaccurately attributes the *Catechism* exclusively to Bakunin (Jan. 23, 1886, 4).

16. *Labor Enquirer* (Denver), Aug. 25, 1883, 4.

17. Sartorious, *Der Moderne Socialismus,* 171.Sartorius claims Nathan-Ganz was arrested for fraud in Paris in 1888, where he was living under the name "daCosta." Paul Avrich claims Nathan-Ganz arrived in the United States in the 1870s and settled in Boston. However, steamship lists show that Nathan-Ganz (as Alexander Rodenow) arrived from Liverpool in 1880 (*New York Times,* July 26, 1880, 8). See also "The Queen v. Ganz," *Law Journal Reports for the Year 1882* (London: F. E. Streeten, 1882), 422; *New York Times,* Mar. 30, 1881; *Handwörterbuch der Staatswissenschaften,* ed. J. Conrad, L. Elster, W. Lexis, and Edg. Loening (Jena: Verlag von Gustav Fischer, 1898), 313–14; Frans Bernard Enthoven, *Studie Over Het Anarchisme Van de Daad* (Amsterdam: Scheltema en Holkema's Boekhandel, 1901), 35. Paul Avrich dismisses Nathan-Ganz as "a shadowy figure" who, quoting Josef Peukert, was "the model of an arrogant, insolent fop" and, quoting Benjamin Tucker, was a "refined and rather fascinating crook" (qtd. in Avrich, *Haymarket Tragedy,* 57).

18. Trautmann, *Voice of Terror,* 99, 249. Tom Goyens incorrectly describes the work of Bakunin's that Most published in the Sept. 1880 issue as "Revolutionary

Principles." None of Bakunin's works go by that title (*Beer and Revolution*, 60). *Freiheit* (London), Dec. 11, 1880; "Die Taktik der revolutionaaeren Arbeiter-Partei," July 10, 1881.

19. *Evening Standard* (London), Aug. 20, 1881, 2.

20. Undated clippings, "Edward Nathan-Ganz," in Nettlau Papers, International Instituut voor Sociale Geschiedenis, Amsterdam; Carl Wittke, *Against the Current: The Life of Karl Heinzen* (Chicago: University of Chicago Press, 1945), 73–75; *Vorbote*, Dec. 4, 1880, 2. See also Benjamin Grob-Fitzgibbon, "From the Dagger to the Bomb: Karl Heinzen and the Evolution of Political Terror," *Terrorism and Political Violence* 16, no. 1 (2004): 97–115.

21. Letter of Dr. Nathan-Ganz dated Dec. 1, 1880, Nettlau Papers, International Instituut voor Sociale Geschiedenis, Amsterdam.

22. *An-Archist* (Boston), vol. 1, no. 1, Jan. 1881 ("Advance Sheet"), Labadie Collection, Hatcher Graduate Library, University of Michigan; emphasis in original.

23. Ibid. For a fledgling journal, *An-Archist* received unusual notice from all quarters, mostly attracted by its uncompromising militancy. The parody magazine *Puck* noted its arrival, observing of Nathan-Ganz's article on barricade warfare, "Everybody ought to know what to do when a coup d'etat takes place in New York. We think we should be inclined to make barricades of all the Broadway stages, and should then feel that we were benefactors of our species." *Puck* (New York), Dec. 29, 1880, 280.

24. Haymarket historians have mistakenly represented this as an early sign of tragedies to come: a case of the suppression of anarchist free speech. According to Paul Avrich, Nathan-Ganz's *An-Archist* was quickly "suppressed by the police because of the violent nature of its contents" and for which Nathan-Ganz then "spent two months in a Boston jail" (*Haymarket Tragedy*, 57). News reports at the time, however, indicate that anarchist ideas were not the reason the *An-Archist* ran into trouble with the law. See *New York Times*, Mar. 30, 1881, 2; Jan. 26, 1881, 2; *New York Herald*, qtd. in *Liberty*, May 17, 1884, 1. Even his friend and fellow anarchist publisher Benjamin Tucker admitted that it was "his arrest on a charge of swindling that killed the paper after the first number." Tucker reportedly contributed an essay to the second and last issue of *An-Archist* titled "Herbert Spencer and Anarchism" (*An-Archist* [Boston], vol. 1, no. 1, Jan. 1881), and he inherited Nathan-Ganz's lists of subscribers and correspondents, which allowed him to start his more famous and long-lived anarchist journal, *Liberty: Not the Daughter but the Mother of Order* (Dr. Charles L. Hartmann to Max Nettlau, Mar. 12, 1931, Nettlau Papers, International Instituut voor Sociale Geschiedenis, Amsterdam; also collected by Princeton University Press and published online at Google Books). When *Liberty* first appeared, Kropotkin's famous anarchist journal *Le Révolté* predicted it would "continue to spread the principles of anarchism" that were in the *An-Archist* (*Le Révolté* [Geneva], Sept. 3, 1881, 4). *Boston Globe*, Mar. 28, 1881, 2; Apr. 5, 1881, 1. On Tucker, see Wendy McElroy, *The Debates of Liberty: An Overview of Individualist Anarchism, 1881–1908* (Lanham, Md.: Lexington Books, 2003),

ch. 1.; William O. Reichert, *Partisans of Freedom: A Study in American Anarchism* (Bowling Green, Ohio: Bowling Green University Popular Press, 1976), 141–200. See also Heiner Becker, "The Mystery of Dr. Nathan-Ganz," *Raven* 2, no. 2 (1988): 118–45.

25. "The Revolutionary Congress," *Liberty*, Aug. 20, 1881, 4; Oliver, *International Anarchist Movement*, 14–17. Avrich claimed that "none of the newly formed social revolutionary groups in the United States sent its own delegates to the London Congress," thereby neatly separating the proceedings in England from radicals in America. However, one paragraph later Avrich confusingly admits that at least two Americans were in attendance. After admitting that Nathan-Ganz and Le Compte were present in London, Avrich hastens to downplay their significance by saying they "did not, strictly speaking, represent social revolutionary groups." By what criteria Avrich makes this conclusion is not clear, the only indication being his explanation that the Confederación de los Trabajadores Mexicanos "contained both anarchist and non-anarchist members" (*Haymarket Tragedy*, 56–57). If Avrich defines social revolutionary groups as those having only "anarchists" for members, then most of the participating organizations at the London Congress were not social revolutionary (*Haymarket Tragedy*, 56–57). See *Le Révolté* (Geneva), July 23, 1881, for a roster of delegates.

26. Goyens, *Beer and Revolution*, 78; Nettlau, *Anarchisten und Sozialrevolutionäe*, 187–99.

27. See letter of Le Compte to Tucker, published in *Liberty*, Aug. 25, 1883, 3. Paul Avrich described her unflatteringly as "an exotic and somewhat mysterious figure" who "styled herself 'Miss Le Compte, Prolétaire'" and had "a special sympathy for outlaws and tramps" that led her to give romantic speeches about vagabonds and pirates. Despite listing an impressive radical résumé, Avrich faults her for being "in her middle years" and implies that she merely dabbled in radicalism and dropped out of the movement sometime after 1883 "for reasons which remain obscure" (*Haymarket Tragedy*, 56–57). Were Marie Le Compte not evidence of the strong affinities between American and European anarchistic ideas, Avrich would probably have celebrated her revolutionary spirit. Max Nettlau, whom Avrich chose to quote, faulting her for not being young (*nicht ganz junge*), also observed that she was someone who always took the most revolutionary stance on a position (*Anarchisten und Sozialrevolutionäe*, 197). As for the organization of "Boston Revolutionaries" whom Marie Le Compte represented, nothing is known other than that her credentials were signed by John W. Wilkinson and Walter Elliot. Elliot remains a mystery, but this Wilkinson may have been the same Wilkinson who was a piano maker in Cambridge, had served as a lieutenant and captain in the Forty-third New York Regiment during the Civil War, and in 1883 was elected to the Massachusetts House of Representatives on the Republican ticket and appointed to its Committee on Labor (Nettlau, *Anarchisten und Sozialrevolutionäe*, 197). Official Gazette, Commonwealth of Massachusetts, Biographical Sketches of the Members of the Executive and Legislative Departments . . . (Boston: Wright and Potter Printing Co., 1885), 11.

28. Nettlau, *Anarchisten und Sozialrevolutionäe*, 217–19. One of the three members of the resolutions committee, Nathan-Ganz (known in the records only as "delegate No. 22") reportedly authored those sections of the congress's declaration having to do with the necessity of studying chemistry: "Whereas the technical and chemical sciences have rendered services to the revolutionary cause and are bound to render still greater services in the future, the Congress suggests that organizations and individuals affiliated with the International Workingmen's Association devote themselves to the study of these sciences" (Dr. Charles L. Hartmann to Max Nettlau, Mar. 12, 1931, Nettlau Papers, International Instituut voor Sociale Geschiedenis, Amsterdam). Nathan-Ganz reveals his coded number in an interview published in the *Evening Standard* (London), Aug. 20, 1881, 2.

29. Carlson, *Anarchism in Germany*, 252–53 (see ch. 2, n. 20).

30. "Revolutionary Congress," 4.

31. Avrich, *Haymarket Tragedy,* 58. See also Carlson, *Anarchism in Germany*, passim.

32. *Liberty: Not the Daughter*, Aug. 20, 1881, 2.

33. Avrich writes of the London Congress, "The new organization became a fearful spectre in the eyes of governments throughout the Western Hemisphere, which suspected it of being the directing power behind various acts of assassination and terror committed in the ensuing decades. Such suspicions were utterly without foundation" (*Haymarket Tragedy*, 58). While I would agree that there is little evidence that the IWPA directed or ordered any attacks, the fact remains that IWPA perpetrators were closely connected to prominent participants in the London Congress, such as Josef Peukert and Johann Most. See Carlson, *Anarchism in Germany,* passim.

34. "Revolutionary Congress," 4; emphasis in original. Though this report was signed anonymously by "Delegate 22," Nettlau identifies delegate 22 as Nathan-Ganz (*Anarchisten und Sozialrevolutionäe*, 197). George Woodcock, in *Anarchism: A History of Libertarian Ideas and Movements* (1962; repr. Peterborough, Ont.: Broadview Press, 2004), finds Nathan-Ganz to be one of the most fervent advocates of violence and bombing at the congress (215–16). More on Nathan-Ganz in chapter 2.

35. *Liberty* (Boston), Oct. 15, 1881, 1.

36. *Liberty: Not the Daughter*, Oct. 15, 1881, 1.

37. The account of Joseph Swain can be found in *Liberty: Not the Daughter*, Nov. 12, 1881, 4.

38. *Vorbote*, Oct. 29, 1881, 8; *Chicago Tribune*, Oct. 22, 1881, 8.

39. *Vorbote*, Oct. 29, 1881, 8; *Chicago Tribune*, Oct. 21, 1881, 12.

40. Henry David accurately characterized August Spies's views of the ballot question in the following way: "Spies suggested that election activities offered an excellent field for agitation. He argued that though the election of their own men and labor representatives to office might not result in much immediate gain, at least it enhanced the chances of favorable legislation, and when such laws—as always—were ignored, there would be additional reason for agitation to make them effective" (*History of the Haymarket Affair,* 70–71).

41. David mistakenly describes the committee on resolutions as the "committee on platform" and also confuses its membership, writing that the vote on the electoral plank was four to two, with Schwab, Peterson, Blum, and Swain opposed (*History of the Haymarket Affair*, 71). Blum, however, was never elected to the committee of five (*Vorbote*, Oct. 29, 1881, 8; *Chicago Tribune*, Oct. 22, 1881, 8; Oct. 23, 1881, 11). Avrich inaccurately claims that the political plank was put to a general vote of the congress and voted down (*Haymarket Tragedy*, 60). Rather, as the *Tribune* reporter explained, "All the [committee] reports were received, and then debated by sections. This process occupied a long time, but the debate was on questions of wording only" (*Chicago Tribune*, Oct. 23, 1881, 11). Selig Perlman's seminal interpretation of this congress is: "In the discussion of the platform of the proposed national organization, New York showed itself more radical than Chicago. Schwab condemned in unqualified terms all participation in political campaigns, while Spies, Winnen, and Parsons were still in favor of the use of the ballot for agitational purposes. Schwab's attitude prevailed at the convention and the political plank was rejected." John R. Commons et al., *History of Labour in the United States* (New York: Macmillan, 1918), 2:291–92.

42. *Liberty: Not the Daughter*, Nov. 12, 1881, 4; *Chicago Tribune*, Oct. 24, 1881, 6.

43. *Vorbote*, Nov. 12, 1881, 8.

44. Ibid. Spies was in favor of participating in the fall elections but was outvoted.

45. *Chicago Tribune*, June 7, 1882, 12.

46. Trautmann, *Voice of Terror*, 78–79.

47. *Chicago Tribune*, Dec. 29, 1882, 3; Trautmann, *Voice of Terror*, 119.

48. *Christian Index*, Jan. 11, 1883, 11.

49. *Truth*, Jan. 10, 1883, 1.

50. Ibid., Apr. 14, 1883, 1.

51. Ibid., Apr. 21, 1883, 1.

52. Ibid., May 19, 1883, 1.

53. Ibid., June 23, 1883, 1. This prophet of violent revolution and bomb throwing was a typical Yankee radical of his age. William N. Slocum was a veteran newspaper man, having run a Republican newspaper, the *Santa Cruz News*, on the eve of the Civil War and later taking over as editor of the *San Jose Telegraph and Mercury*, which he renamed simply the *San Jose Mercury*. By the 1870s Slocum had left the regular newspaper business and instead edited a spiritualist reform newspaper in San Francisco with his wife, Amanda, called *Common Sense*. During this period, the Slocums took into their home Flora London, who while she was their guest happened to gave birth to a son, Jack, who would go on to a radical and literary career of his own. "Early Republican Newspaper of California," *Overland Monthly and Out West Magazine* 13, no. 5 (Nov. 1874): 483–85; J. P. Munro-Fraser, *History of Santa Clara County California* (San Francisco: Alley, Bowen and Co., 1881), 537; *Common Sense* (San Francisco), see Aug. 1, 1874, 140, 146; Richard O'Connor, *Jack London: A Biography* (New York: Little, Brown and Co., 1964), 25. Slocum is also the author of a somewhat tamer 1878 pamphlet titled "Revolution: The Reorganization of Our Social System Inevitable." *Socialism and American Life*, ed.

Donald Drew Egbert, Stow Persons, Thomas D. Seymour Bassett (Princeton, N.J.: Princeton University Press, 1952), 2:317.

54. *Truth*, June 30, 1883, 1.

55. Ibid., Aug. 4, 1883, 1.

56. Ibid., May 19, 1883, 1.

57. Ibid., May 26, 1883, 3.

58. *Arbeiter-Zeitung*, Mar. 16, 1883; David, *History of the Haymarket Affair*, 89.

59. David, *History of the Haymarket Affair*, 90. On Drury, see Robert Weir, "Here's to the Men Who Lose!": The Hidden Career of Victory Drury," *Labor History* 36, no. 4 (1995): 530–56.

60. *Truth*, Dec. 1, 1883, 1; Trautmann, *Voice of Terror*, 253–57.

61. *Arbeiter-Zeitung*, Aug. 20, 1883. The general meeting then elected Parsons, Spies, George Meng, and Balthasar Rau as their delegates.

62. *Truth* (San Francisco), Nov. 17, 1883, 1.

63. Ibid., Oct. 20, 1883, 3.

64. Ibid., Oct. 27, 1883, 2.

65. Trautmann, *Voice of Terror*, 121–22.

66. Dyer Lum, *A Concise History of the Great Trial of the Chicago Anarchists in 1886* (Chicago: Socialistic Publishing Co., 1887; repr., New York: Arno Press, 1969), 15–16.

67. *Truth* (San Francisco), Nov. 17, 1883, 1; Dec. 1, 1883, 1.

68. Schneirov, *Labor and Urban Politics*, 93 (see ch. 2, n. 33); *Chicago Tribune*, Mar. 26, 1883, 3. See also Feb. 5, 1883, 8; Jan. 21, 1884, 8.

69. *Offizielles Protokoll der National-Konvention der Sozial Arbeiter Partei von Nord-Amerika* (New York, 1886); Howard H. Quint, *The Forging of American Socialism* (Indianapolis: Bobbs-Merrill, 1953), 24–25.

70. *Chicago Tribune*, Oct. 30, 1886, 2.

71. *Labor Enquirer*, Sept. 4, 1886, 2.

72. Edward B. Mittelman, "Chicago Labor in Politics, 1877–1896," *Journal of Political Economy* 28, no. 5 (1920): 418–23.

CHAPTER 4. DYNAMITE

1. *New York Times*, Apr. 1, 1882, 8.

2. Benson J. Lossing, *The Two Spies: Nathan Hale and John André* (New York: D. Appleton and Co., 1907), 108–21; *American Architect and Building News*, Oct. 18, 1879, 127.

3. *New York Times*, Apr. 1, 1882, 8.

4. Ibid., Feb. 24, 1882, 5. The full text read:

> Too long hath stood the traitor's shaft,
>   A monument to shame,
> Built up to praise a traitor's craft,
>   To sanctify ill fame.

Are freemen bound to still forebear
  And meekly still implore,
When conquered foes their altars rear
  Within our very door?

This vulgar and insulting stone
  Would honor for all time,
Not sneaking André's death alone
  But black Ben Arnold's crime.
And they who thus can glorify
  The traitor and his deeds,
Themselves high treason would employ
  If 'twould fulfill their needs.

Americans! resolve, proclaim
  That in our own dear land
Never, while the people reign,
  Shall treason's statue stand!
And he who dares erect it next
  On fair Columbia's breast.
With furtive or with false pretext
  Shall dangle from its crest!

5. Hendrix's real name was James McCormack. *New York Times*, Mar. 27, 1884, 8; Mar. 5, 1882, 5.

6. *National Police Gazette*, Mar. 18, 1882, 5, 7.

7. *New York Times*, Mar. 11, 1882, 5.

8. Ibid., Feb. 27, 1882, 8; Mar. 5, 1882, 5.

9. *Liberty* 1, no. 19, Apr. 15, 1882, 1.

10. *Chicago Tribune*, Aug. 22, 1886, 1.

11. Hendrix was arrested early on the morning of Monday, March 24, 1884, on the Fulton ferry by Roundsman McCarty for apparent public drunkenness. Hendrix had come from an anarchist meeting at the Germania Assembly Rooms earlier that night and had taken a few glasses of *weiss* beer. His fiancée accompanied him to the police station and demanded that a doctor be called for, but the night sergeant refused until Hendrix passed fully into unconsciousness, whereupon he was taken to Brooklyn Hospital. Hendrix died Tuesday evening, and a postmortem examination discovered a fracture at the base of the skull and "compression of the brain." The Central Labor Union issued a protest to Brooklyn mayor Seth Low demanding that he investigate the suspicious circumstances of Hendrix's death, though they did not imply that police caused his death, only that their "brutal neglect" had resulted in his death. Hendrix's fiancée complained of the police's disregard of her pleas to send for a doctor, not of any physical abuse to him. *New York Times*, Mar. 26, 1884, 5; Mar. 27, 1884, 8; Apr. 7, 1884, 8; Apr. 28, 1884, 8.

12. *New York Times*, Nov. 10, 1885, 1. The monument was reported to still lay

on its side in 1893 but was upright by 1899. *Albany Law Journal*, Mar. 18, 1893, 219; *New York Observer and Chronicle*, Sept. 7, 1899, 312.

13. *Alarm* (Chicago), Dec. 26, 1885, 3.

14. *Scientific American* 46, no. 16 (Apr. 22, 1882): 245.

15. Michael Davitt, *The Times' Parnell Commission: Speech in Defence of the Land League* (London: Kegan Paul, Trench, Trübner, and Co., 1890), 147.

16. *Progressive Age*, June 17, 1882, 1.

17. James Paul Rodechko, "Patrick Ford and His Search for America: A Case Study of Irish-American Journalism, 1870–1913" (PhD diss., University of Connecticut, 1967), 66, 74–75. Circulation figures are found on pp. 48–49.

18. *Irish World and Industrial Liberator*, Nov. 27, 1880, 3; Oct. 28, 1882, 3.

19. Ibid., Apr. 21, 1883, 8.

20. Jeremiah O'Donovan Rossa, *Rossa's Recollections, 1838 to 1898* (Mariner's Harbor, N.Y., 1898); Alyson Brown, *Irish Society and Prison: Time, Culture, and Politics in the Development of the Modern Prison, 1850–1920* (Suffolk, U.K.: Boydell Press, 2003), 165–66; Seán McConville, *Irish Political Prisoners, 1848–1922* (London: Psychology Press, 2003), 157, 175; Peter Berresford Ellis, *History of the Irish Working Class* (London: Pluto Press, 1985), 144.

21. David Montgomery, *Beyond Equality: Labor and the Radical Republicans, 1862–1872* (Urbana: University of Illinois Press, 1967), 376; Bruce Hoffman, *Inside Terrorism* (New York: Columbia University Press, 2006), 8; Lindsay Clutterbuck, "The Progenitors of Terrorism: Russian Revolutionaries or Extreme Irish Republicans?" *Terrorism and Political Violence* 16, no. 1 (2004): 154–81.

22. *New York Times*, Apr. 27, 1883, 3; Niall Whelehan, "Skirmishing, *The Irish World*, and Empire, 1876–86," *Éire-Ireland* 42, no. 1 (2007): 180–200.

23. *United Irishman* (New York), September 30, 1882, 4.

24. Paul Avrich, "Conrad's Anarchist Professor: An Undiscovered Source," *Labor History* 18 (Summer 1977), 307–402; *New York Times*, Apr. 7, 1884, 5, reports his Dr. Hodges alias. On the Rogers identity, see *Brooklyn Eagle*, Feb. 3, 1885, 4, Feb. 2, 1885, 4; on Scottish birth, see *Brooklyn Eagle*, Nov. 7, 1886, 13; *Truth* (San Francisco), May 26, 1883, 1. Joseph Conrad, *The Secret Agent: A Simple Tale* (1907; repr. New York: Modern Library, 2004).

25. William Edwin Adams, *Memoirs of a Social Atom* (London: Hutchinson and Co., 1903), 2:564. Adams's story checks out with contemporary source the *New York Times*, which reported that Mezzeroff gave a public speech extolling the use of dynamite to free Ireland for the Joe Brady Emergency Club in Kessel's Hall (*New York Times*, Apr. 7, 1884, 5).

26. *Truth* (San Francisco), Jan. 10, 1883, 3.

27. K. R. M. Short, *The Dynamite War: Irish Bombers in Victorian Britain* (Atlantic Highlands, N.J.: Humanities Press, 1979), 219.

28. *Brooklyn Eagle*, Apr. 14, 1883, 6; *New York Times*, Sept. 16, 1896, 1; *Independent* (New York), Feb. 5, 1885, 15.

29. *Brooklyn Eagle*, Feb. 2, 1885, 4.

30. *New York Times,* July 24, 1885, 12; Aug. 16, 1885, 2.

31. Ibid., Aug. 5, 1887, 5; Aug. 6, 1887, 5. John T. McEnnis, *The Clan-Na-Gael and the Murder of Dr. Cronin* (San Francisco: G. P. Woodward, 1889), 57.

32. *New York Times,* Apr. 22, 1883, 7. When asked if she was involved with the Irish rebels, Jeannie Byrnes denied the story, saying customs inspectors treated her horribly, believing the same.

33. *Irish World and Industrial Liberator,* July 21, 1883, 8.

34. *Citizen* (Chicago), Feb. 7, 1885, 3.

35. *Liberty* (Boston), Aug. 6, 1881, 2.

36. *Report of the Special Commission [of Parliament], 1888* (London: Eyre and Spottiswoode, 1890), 105.

37. Henri Le Caron, *Twenty-five Years in the Secret Service: The Recollections of a Spy* (London: William Heinemann, 1893), 188; *Brooklyn Eagle,* Feb. 9, 1885, 4; Jonathan W. Gantt, "Irish-American Terrorism and Anglo-American Relations, 1881–1885," *Journal of the Gilded Age and Progressive Era* 5, no. 4 (Oct. 2006), 325–57.

38. *Irish World and Industrial Liberator,* July 21, 1883, 8.

39. Report of Jan. 12, 1882, Report of June 14, 1882, in Reinhard Höhn, *Die Vaterlandslosen Gesellen: Der Sozialismus im Licht der Geheimberichte der Preußischen Polizei, 1878–1914,* Band I (1878–1890) (Köln: Westdeutscher Verlag, 1964), 117–18, 138–39.

40. Craig Phelan, *Grand Master Workman: Terence Powderly and the Knights of Labor* (Westport, Conn.: Greenwood Publishing Group, 2000), 88–89; Schneirov, *Labor and Urban Politics,* 125–26; Clarence Walworth Alvord, ed., *The Centennial History of Illinois* (Chicago: Illinois Centennial Commission), 4:456–57. After the events of May 1886, McPadden left the labor movement and operated a store in Chicago and later obtained a government job with the Internal Revenue Service, which he kept until his death. *The Samuel Gompers Papers: The Making of a Union Leader, 1850–86,* ed. Stuart Bruce Kaufman (Urbana: University of Illinois Press, 1986), 496.

41. *Irish World,* Sept. 23, 1882, 1.

42. *Iron Molder's Journal,* Mar. 31, 1886, 2. Timothy Messer-Kruse, "Strike or Anarchist Plot?: The McCormick Riot of 1886 Reconsidered," *Labor History* 52, no. 4 (Nov. 2011): 483–510.

43. HADC, Vol. L, 361–77. After the Haymarket trial, Gleason led the United Labor Party but after one election conspired with the Democrats to ruin the ULP by forming an offshoot, the Reformed United Labor Party (dubbed the "Free Lunch Party" by reporters), which endorsed Democratic candidates. Mittelman, "Chicago Labor in Politics," 407–27 (see ch. 3, n. 61). Carolyn Ashbaugh, *Lucy Parsons: American Revolutionary* (Chicago: Charles H. Kerr, 1976), 120.

44. Le Caron, *Twenty-five Years,* 243; *Vorbote,* Oct. 14, 1885, 2.

45. *Alarm,* Mar. 7, 1885, 1.

46. *Arbeiter-Zeitung,* Apr. 11, 1884.

47. James Chester, "Dynamite, and the Art of War," *United Service: A Quarterly Review of Military and Naval Affairs*, Apr. 1884.

48. *Truth*, June 30, 1883, 1.

49. *Truth* (San Francisco), June 30, 1883, 1.

50. *New York World*, Dec. 17, 1885, 1; *New York Times*, Dec. 17, 1885, 1. Dr. C. C. O'Donnell served one term as coroner of San Francisco. Ira B. Cross, *A History of Labor in California*, 97, 321. Saxton, *Indispensable Enemy: Labor and the Anti-Chinese Movement in California* (Berkeley: University of California Press, 1975), 195–97. Sylvia Sun Minnick, *Samfow: The San Joaquin Chinese Legacy* (Fresno: Panorama West Publishing, 1988), 149. A search of WorldCat reveals no extant issues of the *Dynamite*.

51. *New York Times*, Jan. 3, 1885, 1; Jan. 15, 1885, 1; Jan. 25, 1885, 1.

52. *Alarm* (Chicago), Feb. 7, 1885, 2.

53. Sartorius, *Der Moderne*, 176 (see ch. 2, n. 74).

54. *New York World*, Sept. 25, 1887, 1.

55. Bers, *Wilhelm Hasselmann*, 56–58 (see ch. 2, n. 62).

56. *Interocean*, Jan. 4, 1887, 8.

57. *New York Times*, Oct. 21, 1886, 8.

58. *Daily Evening Bulletin* (Maysville, Ky.), *Daily Northwestern* (Oshkosh, Wisc.), Dec. 30, 1886, 1. Newspapers in the West paid for news from wire services in New York, though at the time they did not include the name of the service in the byline.

59. *Olean (New York) Democrat*, Feb. 4, 1886, 4.

60. *Brooklyn Daily Eagle*, Sept. 30, 1886, 4; Oct. 6, 1886, 6; *New York Times*, Oct. 1, 1886, 8. A "Charles Zadeck" is listed in the Coroner's Inquest Index in the Westchester County Archives (Charles Zadek, October 19, 1886, Coroner's Inquest Index, Vol. 1: 1886–1909, Series 74, Westchester County Archives, Elmsford, New York). There is no evidence that Zadek was involved in the Dittmar explosion. Dynamite factories frequently blew up of their own accord. It was only a few months before another of the wooden sheds where dynamite was mixed detonated, blowing out all the lights along the nearby New York and New Haven Railroad and leaving only a rib bone and a piece of scalp of the worker who had been mixing nitroglycerin and clay. Dittmar's Baychester factory was blown up a second time in 1893 and again in 1895, severely wounding three workers and killing a fourteen-year-old girl. Dittmar's other plant, in Lakewood, New Jersey, was flattened by a nitroglycerin blast in 1902. *New York Times*, Mar. 7, 1887, 3; Mar. 8, 1887, 2; *Brooklyn Daily Eagle*, Mar. 7, 1886, 1; Nov. 7, 1893, 1; Sept. 15, 1895, 24; Dec. 11, 1902, 3.

61. Nettlau, *Anarchisten und Sozialrevolutionäe*, 382–84 (see ch. 1, n. 36). August Spies acknowledged receiving this letter on the witness stand (Testimony of August Spies, HADC, Vol. N, 94; Testimony of E.F.L Gauss, HADC, Vol. N, 106).

62. Testimony of M. D. Malkoff, HADC, Vol. M, 1–36.

63. *New York Times*, Jan. 26, 1885, 1.

64. *Chicago Tribune*, June 18, 1886, 5.

65. HADC, Vol. J, 240–42.

66. *Chicago Tribune*, Apr. 29, 1885, 2.

67. HADC, Vol. J, 242–45.

68. Ibid., 245–47. Treharn names "Lizzie Moore" but certainly meant Lizzie Holmes.

69. *Arbeiter-Zeitung*, Apr. 29, 1885, translated and transcribed as a trial exhibit, HADC, Vol. K, 721–32; Avrich, *Haymarket Tragedy,* 192. HADC, Vol. I, 97–98, 101–102.

70. *New York Times*, Jan. 2, 1886, 1.

71. *Chicago Tribune*, Dec. 27, 1885, 9; Dec. 29, 1885, 8.

72. HADC, Vol. J., 143–45. James Green implies that what Spies braggingly flourished was not a bomb at all but merely a common item that could have been made into one: "In January 1886, talk of bombs took a more dramatic turn when August Spies showed a newspaper reporter a piece of tube he said could be used as a casing for a dynamite bomb" (*Death in the Haymarket*, 141). In fact, what Spies flourished and even gave to the reporter was a specially cast round "czar bomb" of precisely the type thrown at police four months later.

73. *Chicago Daily News*, Jan. 14, 1886, 1; *Decatur (Illinois) Daily Republican*, Jan. 16, 1886, 1; *New York Times*, Jan. 15, 1886, 1. Testimony of Joseph Gruenhut, HADC, Vol. K, 71–72. Testimony of Harry Wilkinson, HADC, Vol. J., 152–56. Testimony of August Spies, HADC, Vol. N, 56–63.

74. *Chicago Tribune*, Jan. 17, 1886, 4; *New York Times*, Jan. 16, 1886, 4.

75. *Chicago Tribune*, Mar. 24, 1886, 1. Johann Most, *Revolutionaere Kriegswissenschaft* (Millwood, NY: Kraus Reprint, 1983).

76. *Autonomy* (Chicago), Apr. 1, 1886, 3.

77. *New York Times*, Mar. 10, 1886, 2. Though he carried fewer weapons than his compatriot, Willmund was sentenced to three and a half years in Sing Sing while Schlieman was given a two-month stint in the Tombs. Judge Smyth of the New York Court of General Sessions did not hide the fact that Willmund had drawn the harsher sentence because of this letter proving his dedication to the anarchist propaganda of the deed: "I understand that a night or two ago a meeting was held by men of your class who resolved to arm themselves and resist lawful authority. I give those people warning through you that if they are ever brought into this court and properly convicted they will receive no mercy or consideration at my hands. I am bound . . . to do what I can to stop this sort of thing, and to let men of your class know that the criminal laws of this country cannot be ignored" (*New York Times*, Apr. 27, 1886, 8).

78. *Brooklyn Eagle*, May 15, 1886, 4.

79. *Vorbote*, Oct. 14, 1885, 2.

80. The text of Smith's letter to Parsons is reprinted in Schaack, *Anarchy and Anarchists*, 227. Confirmation that it actually existed can be found in a report published in the *Illinois Staats-Zeitung* on May 16, 1886, 2, that mentions the discovery of the letter from Fred Smith to Parsons dated April 29, in which Smith requested explosives. The *Illinois Staats-Zeitung* confirmed many of the details later published in Schaack's account, including Smith's name, the date, and Smith's return address

on Woodland Avenue in Cleveland (though the newspaper reported that Smith's house number was 224 while Schaack reported it to be 193).

81. Schaack, *Anarchy and Anarchists*, 227. Spies admitted ordering dynamite from the Aetna Powder Company in his own defense testimony (Testimony of August Spies, HADC, Vol. N., 83).

82. *Alarm*, May 2, 1885, 4. Note that this meeting was not one of the American group's public "agitation" meetings, and although its proceedings were published in the *Alarm*, it seems that its resolutions were not primarily intended for their publicity value.

83. *Alarm*, May 30, 1885, 1.

84. Ibid., June 27, 1885, 1.

85. *Proceedings of the Joint Committee of the Legislature of the State of Kansas . . . To Investigate the Explosion Which Occurred at Coffeyville, Kansas, Oct. 18, 1888* (Topeka: Kansas Publishing House, 1891), 179, 191. Parsons's account can be found in L. Parsons, *Life of Albert Parsons*, 30 (see ch. 2, n. 3). C. A. Henrie, who was implicated in the Coffeyville bombing and evaded many of the committee's questions when asked if he was present at the gathering with Parsons at Whitley's house, testified, "I do not know whether I was or not" (*Proceedings of the Joint Committee*, 174).

86. Many thanks to Dr. Jeffrey Dunn, Professor Emeritus of the University of Toledo Chemistry Department for sharing with me his insight into this process.

87. *Alarm*, Apr. 4, 1885, 1; *Freiheit*, Jan. 31, Feb. 7, 14, 21, Mar. 10, 14, 21, 28, Apr. 4, June 27, July 25, 1885. Trautmann, *Voice of Terror*, 100–101.

88. Letter from M. Bachman in *Vorbote* (Chicago), Nov. 19, 1881, 4.

89. Richard T. Ely, *Christian Union*, May 1, 1884, 414; *Brooklyn Eagle*, Mar. 27, 1885, 4; Mar. 28, 1885, 4.

90. *Brooklyn Eagle*, Mar. 27, 1885, 4; Mar. 28, 1885, 4; Report of Mar. 4, 1884, Joun. NR. 1389, P.J.I.; Höhn, *Die Vaterlandslosen Gesellen*, 215–16.

91. Carlson, *Anarchism in Germany*, 259–67 (see ch. 2, n. 20).

92. *New York Tribune*, April 2, 1884, 1. J. Langhard, *Die Anarchistische Bewegung in der Schweiz* (Bern: Stampfli, 1909), 270.

93. *New York Times*, Feb. 11, 1884, 2; *Die Freiheit*, Feb. 16, 1884, 1 (translation from Richard T. Ely, *Labor Movement in America* [1886; New York: Macmillan, 1905], 262–63); *New York Times*, Aug. 9, 1884, 1; Goyens, *Beer and Revolution*, 41 (see ch. 2, n. 62).

94. *New York Times*, Mar. 23, 1884, 9; Mar. 25, 1884, 1.

95. Sartorius, *Der Moderne Socialismus*, 176.

96. Candace Falk, Barry Pateman, Jessica Moran, eds., *Emma Goldman: A Documentary History of the American Years* (Berkeley: University of California Press, 2005), 2:266–67. Carl Nold to Agnes Inglis, Sept. 28, 1933; Nold to Inglis, Jan. 8, 1931, Carl Nold Papers, Inglis Collection Box 14, Labadie Library, University of Michigan.

97. *Liberty* (Boston), Mar. 27, 1886, 1. Henry David does not mention Tucker's

arson allegations. Paul Avrich writes that Tucker "alleged that a number of Most's followers in New York . . . had collected large sums of money by insuring their dwellings, removing the contents, setting fire to the premises," but he fails to mention that Tucker also charged Most with turning a blind eye to the arson frauds. Avrich muddies the waters further by depicting the recriminations between Most and Tucker as mostly personal, not revolving around Tucker's charges that Most was knowledgeable and protective of the arsonists. Avrich then writes, "No evidence was ever brought forth to connect Most directly with the arsonists or with any other instances of violence" (*Haymarket Tragedy*, 174). Of course the "evidence" of Most's connection to the arsonists was the membership of a number of convicted arsonists in his group, his refusal to denounce them, and Justus Schwab's abrupt break with Most, his newspaper, and his anarchist organization.

98. *Liberty* (Boston), Apr. 17, 1886, 1.

99. Ibid., May 1, 1886, 8.

100. Ibid., 5.

101. Kohout and Kylian are described as anarchists in the *Brooklyn Daily Eagle*, Aug. 29, 1886, 16, Aug. 30, 1886, 4; *New York Times*, Nov. 30, 1885, 5. On Kylian's earlier attempted arson, see *New York Times*, Aug. 29, 1886, 5.

102. *New York Times*, Nov. 24, 1885, 1; Jan. 23, 1886, 8; Jan. 27, 1886, 3; Jan. 28, 1886, 8; Jan. 29, 1886, 8; Jan. 30, 1886, 8; Feb. 3, 1886, 8; Feb. 4, 1886, 8; Aug. 29, 1886, 5; Aug. 30, 1886, 8; Aug. 31, 1886, 8; Oct. 13, 1886, 6; Oct. 27, 1891, 9; *New York World*, Nov. 25, 1885, 1; Dec. 1, 1885, 8; *New York Tribune*, Nov. 24, 1885, 2; Jan. 23, 1886, 8; Jan. 26, 1886, 8; Jan. 27, 1886, 8; Feb. 4, 1888, 8; *New York Sun*, Aug. 29, 1886, 10.

103. *New York World*, Nov. 30, 1885, 1.

104. Ibid., Dec. 1, 1885, 8. Trautmann, *Voice of Terror*, 211.

105. *Liberty* (Boston), Mar. 27, 1886, 1; May 1, 1886, 5; emphasis in original.

106. On Nicolai and the *Freiheit*, see Goyens, *Beer and Revolution*, 117; on Wabnitz, see Goyens, *Beer and Revolution*, 73; on Kubisch (listed in the *Sun* as "Kubitsch"), see Goyens, *Beer and Revolution*, 27, 106. On Kaiser, see *New York Times*, June 4, 1890, 3. *New York Times*, June 3, 1885, 5.

107. *New York Tribune*, Oct. 20, 1887, 3; *New York Sun*, Nov. 11, 1887, 2; Nov. 12, 1887, 1.

108. *New York Tribune*, Oct. 21, 1894, 1.

CHAPTER 5. ANARCHISTS, TRADE UNIONS, AND THE EIGHT-HOUR WORKDAY

1. *Chicago Tribune*, July 9, 1885, 2.

2. Flinn and Wilkie, *History of the Chicago Police*, 237–39 (see ch. 2, n. 2).

3. *Chicago Tribune*, July 4, 1885, 1. It was reported that when he heard that many of his men were accepting free lunches on the tab of the streetcar company

at a downtown restaurant, Bonfield paid the proprietor for all the meals (*Chicago Tribune*, Oct. 23, 1885, 8).

4. *Chicago Tribune*, July 7, 1885, 1.

5. Ibid., July 8, 1885, 4.

6. Ibid., July 7, 1885, 1. See letter of Harrison to President Jones, *Chicago Tribune*, July 5, 1885, 1.

7. *Chicago Tribune*, July 6, 1885, 1.

8. *Alarm*, July 11, 1885, 2.

9. *Liberty*, Aug. 20, 1881, 4.

10. *Chicago Tribune*, Oct. 23, 1881, 11; Oct. 24, 1881, 6. As at least thirteen of the twenty-one delegates to the congress were from Chicago, and the wording of the trade union plank divided Spies and Parsons, the idea that support for trade unions was the unique and defining quality of the Chicago anarchist movement, as labor historians have long argued, seems rather leaky. Rather, the "Chicago Idea" was first articulated in San Francisco and was more an element of Burnette Haskell's attempt to bring international anarchism to the workers of the West than it was of Chicago's anarchist movement. Haskell consciously blended some of the doctrines of force with traditions of labor reform. The bylaws of Haskell's International Workmen's Association, Pacific Coast Division declared it "the duty of every member . . . to assist and aid the organization of the Knights of Labor, the various Trade Unions, Farmers Alliances and all other forms of organization in which the producers have organized . . . themselves." This duty rested uneasily alongside the "objects" of the association that included "to eradicate the false impression of the people that redress can be obtained by the ballot," and "to prepare the way for the direction of the coming social revolution by an enlightened and intelligent public thought" (*Truth*, May 19, 1883, 1).

The "Chicago Idea" entered into the labor history canon through the pen of Selig Perlman, who wrote part 6, "Upheaval and Reorganization (Since 1876)," of John R. Common's foundational *History of Labour in the United States*. There Perlman traces what he perceived to be a major schism between the "pure" East Coast anarchism of Johann Most and the Midwestern variant led by Chicago's labor-oriented radicals. According to Perlman, Most's "opposition to trade union action cost him the adherence of the revolutionary groups centering in Chicago." Such a split was evident, Perlman claims, because "a resolution proposed by Spies was passed, which referred to trade unions fighting for the abolition of the wage system as the foundation of the future society." Perlman then conceded that the "manifesto which the congress issued . . . was framed entirely in the spirit of Most's philosophy and contained no mention of trade union action" (Commons et al., *History of Labour*, 2:294–95).

By portraying the Pittsburgh Congress as being split between Most's more militant East Coast faction and the trade-union-oriented Chicago delegation, Perlman carves out a distinct identity for the Chicago anarchists that becomes the basis for subsequent historians to place them in a separate category and laid the groundwork for discounting their violent rhetoric in the run up to the Haymarket bombing. Perlman then quotes a passage from the *Alarm* to establish that Spies and Parsons had "a distinctly 'syndicalistic' . . . theory of the importance of trade unions": "The International recognizes in the trade union the embryonic group of the future 'free society.' Every Trade Union is, *nolens volens*, an autonomous commune in process of incubation" (Commons et al., *History of Labour*, 2:297). However, Perlman does not put this quote in its proper context. It was a response to criticism lodged in the Michigan labor weekly the *Labor Enquirer* that the *Alarm* has "decided upon a vigorous warfare against Trades unions as an important branch of their tactics." The *Alarm* does not deny these charges; in fact, it admits "[we] have on occasion found it necessary to criticize adversely the tactics, propaganda and aims of some Trades unions." The author (presumably Parsons) then quotes from the Pittsburgh Manifesto to show to what extent and to what capacity the International supports trade unions, which boils down to their being merely a vessel for revolutionary action and little else.

Thus is an article that is a justification for the *Alarm*'s hostile criticism of trade unions conscripted for the work of establishing the imagined uniqueness of the Chicago anarchists' stubborn support for unions (*Alarm*, Apr. 4, 1885, 3). Immediately following this justification for its criticism of trade unions, the *Alarm* devoted more column inches to reprint the recent resolutions of the New York group on "revolutionary action," which made no mention of trade unions but urged "every person to procure arms, rifles, pistols, etc. and drill and exercise with the same." The lead article on page 1 of this issue was an English translation of Johann Most's pamphlet "Explosives: A Practical Lesson in Chemistry: The Manufacture of Dynamite Made Easy." Though Perlman finds this issue of the *Alarm* supporting his contention that Chicago's anarchists were estranged from Most because of their deep support for trade unions, every statement in it points to the opposite conclusion. (Perlman's theory of a unique "Chicago Idea" is supported by only three citations: the *Alarm* of Oct. 4, 1884, which merely contains the Pittsburgh Manifesto; that of Nov. 22, 1884, which does not even mention trade unions; and that of April 4, 1885, discussed above.)

Paul Avrich also describes the Pittsburgh Congress as having "two distinct elements . . . elements divided by their attitude towards trade unions." Arrayed on one side were the "delegates from New York . . . led by Most, [who] declared their opposition to unions and to the struggle for immediate economic gains." On the other were the "delegates from Chicago . . . led by Parsons and Spies [who] . . . remained devoted to the cause of trade unionism." Of course, Chicagoans were not interested in "reformist unionism" but instead urged a "militant, revolutionary unionism" (*Haymarket Tragedy*, 72; see ch. 1, n. 11).

11. *Progressive Age* (Chicago), May 6, 1882, 1.

12. Philip S. Foner, ed., *The Autobiographies of the Haymarket Martyrs* (New York: Humanities Press, 1969), 128, 167, 177.

13. *Progressive Age* (Chicago), July 15, 1882, 1.

14. David, *History of the Haymarket Affair*, 93, 95–66 (see ch. 1, n. 11).

15. *Arbeiter-Zeitung*, Aug. 20, 1883. The general meeting then elected Parsons, Spies, George Meng, and Balthasar Rau as their delegates.

16. Alexander Saxton, *The Indispensible Enemy: Labor and the Anti-Chinese Movement in California* (Berkeley: University of California Press, 1971), 197–200; Chester McArthur Destler, *American Radicalism, 1865–1901* (1946; repr. Chicago: Quadrangle Books, 1966), 78–85.

17. *Vorbote*, Oct. 27, 1883, 1.

18. L. Parsons, *Life of Albert Parsons*, 125 (see ch. 2, n. 3). See Robert E. Weir, *Knights Unhorsed: Internal Conflict in a Gilded Age Social Movement* (Detroit: Wayne State University Press, 2000), passim.

19. Trautmann, *Voice of Terror*, 253–57 (see ch. 2, n. 61).

20. *Die Fackel*, June 22, 1884; *Arbeiter-Zeitung*, June 9, 1884.

21. Commons et al., *History of Labour*, 399–400; *Chicago Tribune*, Nov. 24, 1883, 7; Nov. 26, 1883, 8; Dec. 4, 1883, 2.

22. *Chicago Tribune*, Feb. 18, 1884, 8.

23. Ibid., June 8, 1884, 16; Nelson, *Beyond the Martrys*, 36–40 (see intro., n. 1); Richard Schneirov and Thomas J. Suhrbur, *Union Brotherhood, Union Town: The History of the Carpenter's Union of Chicago, 1863–1987* (Carbondale: Southern Illinois University Press, 1988), 23–27.

24. Ernest Ludlow Bogart and Charles Manfred Thompson, *The Centennial History of Illinois*, Vol. 4, *The Industrial State, 1870–1893* (Chicago: A. C. McClurg and Co., 1922), 463–64.

25. Nelson, *Beyond the Martyrs*, 44.

26. *Chicago Tribune*, Oct. 19, 1885, 8.

27. *Anarchist*, Jan. 1, 1886, 4.

28. *Labor Enquirer*, Apr. 25, 1885, 2.

29. *Alarm*, Oct. 18, 1884, 2. See also Oct. 25, 1884, 1.

30. Ibid., Nov. 8, 1884, 3.

31. Ibid., Apr. 18, 1885, 1.

32. *Chicago Tribune*, Aug. 21, 1886, 2.

33. *Labor Enquirer*, May 23, 1885, 3.

34. Ibid., Mar. 21, 1885, 2.

35. Most historians have assumed that the Haymarket rally was just a part of a larger mobilization of anarchists in support of the nationwide strike for the eight-hour workday. This assumption follows naturally from the coincident occurrences of these events. But creating this impression was also part of the defense strategy of distancing the Haymarket defendants from any sort of a conspiracy meant to radicalize the eight-hour protests into all-out revolution. Dyer Lum, whose *Concise History* well summarizes the still-prevalent view of the case, argues that the Chicago anarchists were motivated entirely by their interest in the eight-hour workday and had no ulterior aspirations. While admitting that initially the anarchists "held themselves aloof" from the eight-hour movement "because the movement did not

strike at the root of the evil," Lum claims that Spies, Parsons, and the other anarchist "leading spirits" threw themselves wholeheartedly into active support for the eight-hour workday once it became clear this was not just a theoretical debate but the ardent desire of most workers. "Whatever their individual views and expectations were regarding the 'eight-hour reform,'—the Internationalists are not narrow-minded theorists, and hence, instead of opposing the movement, they gave it their full support" (*Concise History*, 16, 19). Henry David, in the first academic study of the Haymarket affair, echoes Lum's characterization, finding that the anarchists at first "turned a deaf ear" to the eight-hour workday movement, because it represented "a compromise with the wage-system which they were struggling to abolish." But in early 1886 the anarchist leadership decided it was a true class struggle, and "the Chicago social-revolutionaries finally ended by entering whole-heartedly into the eight-hour movement" (*History of the Haymarket Affair,* 167–70). Paul Avrich followed David and Lum so closely in his own chronicle of the events leading up to the Haymarket bombing as to repeat both of their metaphors, writing that the "IWPA at first turned a deaf ear to the eight-hour campaign" and "held themselves aloof from the eight-hour struggle" (*Haymarket Tragedy,* 181–82). Likewise, David R. Roediger and Philip S. Foner go a bit further and disagree that the anarchists were ever critical of the eight-hour idea. Though relying mostly on Avrich and David for support—both of whom find that the anarchists were latecomers—Roediger and Foner state in their book on the eight-hour workday that it is just a "persistent myth . . . that they [anarchists] entered the eight-hour movement late and as opportunists." David R. Roediger and Philip S. Foner, *Our Own Time: A History of the American Working Day* (Westport, Conn.: Greenwood Press, 1989), 137.

36. Nelson, *Beyond the Martyrs,* 183.

37. *Alarm,* Oct. 11, 1884, 1.

38. *Socialist* (Chicago), July 26, 1879, 5.

39. Ibid., May 24, 1879, 1.

40. *Alarm,* Aug. 8, 1885, 1. David incorrectly cites this quote as coming from the *Alarm,* Aug. 5, 1885 (*History of the Haymarket Affair,* 180n40). In fact, the issue in which Parsons's editorial appears is dated Aug. 8, 1885. Roediger and Foner, who evidently borrowed from David without crosschecking his sources, also incorrectly cite Aug. 5, 1885 (*Our Own Time,* 324n62). See also Avrich, *Haymarket Tragedy,* 181–82.

41. Though he decries the fact that the eight-hour-workday reform leaves the structures of exploitation in place, Parsons still understands the eight-hour demand in Stewardian terms as part of the escalating historical logic of class struggle: "we can get no relief without striking at the root of the evil; namely, cutting off man's right to convert anything into private property. All short of this is useless patch-work, and every patch will cost more time, pain and bloodshed than will be necessary to destroy the whole right of private property, and settle the matter at once . . . The Alarm does not antagonize the eight hour movement; viewing it from the standpoint that it is an economic struggle, it simply points out that it is a lost battle, and further

proves that though the eight hour system should be established, the wage-workers would gain nothing. They would remain slaves to their capitalistic masters" (*Alarm*, Sept. 5, 1885, 4).

Using Ira Steward's economics but inverting his conclusions, Parsons pointed out that shortening hours placed additional competitive burdens on marginal producers leading to a concentration of ownership and a commensurate increase in the scale of production. It also induced employers to innovate and incorporate more machinery as a means of compensating for lost work hours. Where Steward emphasized the consumer benefits of such changes, Parsons stressed the burdens for the workers still bound to their factories. In the end, Parsons noted, shorter hours actually accelerated the exploitation of the worker by speeding up production and intensifying work.

In this way, Parsons seems to have discovered the moral gap in Steward's cold economic logic. One way of reading Steward is to see the eight-hour-workday movement as just a prelude to the seven-hour-workday battle, then a six-hour-workday fight, ad infinitum, each with its own sacrifices and toll in lives. Though this process could eventually usurp the usurpers, it seems to condemn the future to both continued exploitation and to the struggles of the past. On a purely utilitarian basis, it was better to have one revolution than many. The ethical scales tip back toward incrementalism only if a single revolution were either far more costly or doomed to defeat. From his vantage point in America's fastest-growing city, with its largest and newest immigrant working class, its hyper-exploitation, and its naked class struggle, Parsons had no reason to doubt the possibility of the appearance of a revolutionary moment, and this possibility is all that was needed to give him moral assurance of the rightness of his approach.

42. *Alarm*, Sept. 5, 1885, 4.

43. Ibid., Sept. 19, 1885, 1.

44. Bruce Nelson wrongly writes, "Although it hosted the federation's convention, Chicago's Trades Assembly neither endorsed the eight-hour demand nor established an eight-hour committee until October 1885" (*Beyond the Martyrs*, 179). Nelson pushes the movement back a little further than Eric L. Hirsch, who says, "Chicago unions began active agitation for the demand on November 11, 1885, when the Brickmakers and Stonemasons Union resolved that they would work only eight hours a day after May 1, 1886." Eric L. Hirsch, *Urban Revolt: Ethnic Politics in the Nineteenth Century Chicago Labor Movement* (Berkeley: University of California Press, 1990), 63.

45. *Chicago Tribune*, Sept. 8, 1885, 3. Report of the *Arbeiter Union* being a non-union shop is in *Chicago Tribune*, Oct. 5, 1885, 8.

46. Ibid., Sept. 8, 1885, 3; bracketed text in original.

47. *Alarm,* Sept. 19, 1885, 2.

48. Ibid., Oct. 17, 1885, 1.

49. Ibid.

50. Ibid. Paul Avrich notes Spies's resolution but misrepresents it as endorsing the eight-hour-workday movement, claiming, "While campaigning for shorter hour[s] . . .

the anarchists continued to urge the workers to arm themselves . . . A similar position was taken by the Central Labor Union, which endorsed the eight-hour cause." In fact, the resolution specifically denounces claims made by eight-hour-workday advocates and endorses violent action not so as to win the eight-hour workday but to attack the capitalists (*Haymarket Tragedy*, 184). While Avrich simply misrepresents the meaning of the CLU resolution, Roediger and Foner, in their book on the history of the eight-hour workday, overlook it altogether. Clearly aware of its existence because they denounce Henry David for "over simplification" and for perpetuating "a persistent myth . . . [that the anarchists] entered the eight-hour movement late and as opportunists," they then exclude it from their discussion of the position of the CLU in the fall of 1885 (*Our Own Time*, 137). Roediger and Foner specifically cite the page in David (*History of the Haymarket Affair*, 169) in which the CLU resolution is paraphrased as being of especial importance in spreading this myth (see 324n59). At one point in their analysis of the CLU's views of the eight-hour workday, they indicate that such views are documented in "two articles that appeared in the . . . *Alarm* in 1885." These articles are the issues of August 5 and September 5, 1885. Conveniently, they exclude the most important statement of the CLU's position, Spies's resolution, which was reported in the *Alarm* of Oct. 17, 1885. By excluding this most important evidence, Roediger and Foner are then able to conclude that the anarchist position was a belief that "eight hours meant nothing if capital still ruled," a position "arrived at with Parsons traveling away from Chicago, [which] was speedily overturned." It is true that Parsons was on tour when the CLU approved Spies's resolution. That week he was in South Bend, Indiana, extorting a crowd: "Voting, strikes, arbitration, etc. was of no use. Those who deprived the workers of the wealth they created, and held them by laws and the bayonet in subjection, would never heed the logic of anything but force—physical force. A winchester rifle and a dynamite bomb was the only argument that tyrants ever could or would listen to" (*Alarm*, Oct. 3, 1885, 4). However, there is no evidence that Parsons disagreed with the CLU resolution.

Likewise, Bruce Nelson, in his often cited *Beyond the Martyrs*, waters down the anarchist/CLU opposition to their not being "initially enthusiastic about shorter hours." Nelson finds this lack of enthusiasm was because of the anarchists' refusal to compromise, but they broke down as it became increasingly clear to many in the anarchist movement that the agitation over the eight-hour workday provided a good "opportunity to spread revolutionary ideas." Again, Nelson makes no mention of the important and revealing CLU resolution that clearly shows opposition to the eight-hour workday as principled, deep, and bridged only by the possibility of the eight-hour-workday movement turning violent and leading to revolutionary class conflict (*Beyond the Martyrs*, 180).

51. *Alarm*, Oct. 17, 1885; *Chicago Tribune*, Oct. 12, 1885, 8. On Magie, see *Chicago Tribune*, Aug. 10, 1881, 8; Feb. 12, 1882, 16; Feb. 21, 1882, 12.

52. A few historians have argued that the anarchists were opportunists using the eight-hour-workday movement for their own ends. See Chester McArthur Destler,

American Radicalism, 1865–1901 (Chicago: Quadrangle Books, 1966), 82. Originally published as "Shall Red and Black Unite? An American Revolutionary Document of 1883," *Pacific Historical Review* 14 (December 1945): 434–51. Likewise the authoritative labor history textbook by Foster Rhea Dulles and Melvin Dubofsky implies that the anarchists had an opportunistic agenda: "When in 1886 a movement spread across the country for general strikes in favor of the eight-hour day, the Chicago anarchists were ready to take advantage of every opportunity to preach their own doctrines of revolution." Foster Rhea Dulles and Melvin Dubofsky, *Labor in America* (Arlington Heights, Ill.: Harlan Davidson, 4th ed., 1984), 117. Though he does not pursue its implications, Paul Avrich does raise the possibility that the anarchists supported the eight-hour movement because they hoped it would lead to a revolutionary conflict: "In changing their position, the anarchists were prompted not only by loyalty to labor in a fight with the class enemy. They had come to view the eight-hour movement as an opportunity . . . it might grow in size and militancy and become an entering wedge for the social revolution" (*Haymarket Tragedy*,183). But most popular treatments of the Haymarket bombing have depicted the anarchists as sincere supporters of the eight-hour-workday campaign.

53. *Alarm*, Oct. 31, 1885, 2.

54. David, *History of the Haymarket Affair,* 168–69; Nelson, *Beyond the Martyrs*,180; Avrich, *Haymarket Tragedy*, 41–43, 181–82.

55. *Illinois vs. August Spies et al.* trial evidence book, People's Exhibit 32: *Anarchist* (Newspaper) article, "Call! Workingmen and Fellows!!" Jan. 1, 1886; *Autonomy* (Chicago), Apr. 1, 1886, 3, 4.

56. HADC, People's Exhibit 81: *Arbeiter-Zeitung* (Newspaper) article, untitled, Dec. 29, 1885.

57. HADC, People's Exhibit 83: *Arbeiter-Zeitung* (Newspaper) article, untitled, Dec. 31, 1885.

58. *Illinois vs. August Spies et al.* trial evidence book, People's Exhibit 96: *Arbeiter-Zeitung* (Newspaper) article, "The Eight Hour Movement," Mar. 19, 1886.

59. Testimony of Joseph Gruenhut, HADC, Vol. K, 84–85.

CHAPTER 6. FROM EIGHT HOURS TO REVOLUTION

1. *Chicago Tribune*, Jan. 4, 1886, 11; *Jonathon Swinton's Paper*, Jan. 10, 1886, 1.

2. *Jonathon Swinton's Paper*, Jan. 24, 1886, 1, 4; Feb. 14, 1886, 1; *Chicago Tribune*, Jan. 17, 1886, 6; Jan. 23, 1886, 5.

3. *Chicago Tribune*, Apr. 5, 1886, 1; HADC, People's Exhibit 83: *Arbeiter-Zeitung*, Dec. 31, 1885, 4; *Chicago Tribune*, Dec. 28, 1885, 8.

4. *Chicago Tribune*, Dec. 28, 1885, 8; HADC, People's Exhibit No. 81: *Arbeiter-Zeitung*, Dec. 29, 1885, 4. Harry Barnard, "*Eagle Forgotten*": The Life of John Peter Altgeld (Indianapolis: Bobbs-Merrill Co., 1938), 92.

5. *Alarm*, Feb. 6, 1886, 2; *Chicago Tribune*, Feb. 1, 1886, 8.

6. *Chicago Tribune*, Feb. 15, 1886, 8. Simpson's membership in the TLA is mentioned in *Chicago Tribune*, Apr. 6, 1886, 1.

7. *Chicago Tribune*, Mar. 1, 1886, 3; Milton F. Small, "The Biography of Robert Schilling," (unpublished master's thesis, University of Wisconsin, 1953); Destler, *American Radicalism*, 15 (see ch. 5, n. 16).

8. *Chicago Tribune*, Mar. 1, 1886, 3; Mar. 7, 1886, 15.

9. Ibid., Mar. 16, 1886, 1. Schilling's quotation is a paraphrasing of his remarks by a *Tribune* reporter.

10. Ibid., Mar. 20, 1886, 1; Mar. 29, 1886, 1. George Schilling's remarks are a reporter's paraphrasing. Mar. 30, 1886, 1; on Baptist ministers: Apr. 4, 1886, 12; Mar. 27, 1886, 3. The Chicago city council also passed an ordinance requiring all city printing contracts to be given only to firms that were unionized. It had been mentioned at a meeting of the TLA in November 885 that such a rule would cut out the anarchist *Arbeiter-Zeitung* from city printing contracts because its typographers did not belong to the recognized typographers union (*Chicago Tribune*, Nov. 16, 1885, 8).

11. *Chicago Tribune*, Mar. 29, 1886, 1.

12. Unions affiliated with the CLU were listed in the *Alarm*, Apr. 24, 1886, 4; those who marched with the CLU were identified in the *Chicago Times*, Apr. 26, 1886, 1. Numbers of newly chartered unions and members are extracted from a table in the *Illinois Bureau of Labor Statistics, 1886*, 172–78, 187.

13. Testimony of Luther V. Moulton, HADC, Vol. I, 275–83.

14. *Arbeiter-Zeitung*, Apr. 22, 1886, qtd. in HADC, People's Exhibit 91.

15. *Chicago Tribune*, Apr. 4, 1886, 12; *Chicago Tribune*, Apr. 9, 1886, 3; *New York Times*, Apr. 10, 1886, 9.

16. *Alarm*, Apr. 24, 1886, 3.

17. *Chicago Tribune*, Apr. 12, 1886, 6.

18. *Chicago Times*, Apr. 26, 1886, 4; *Arbeiter-Zeitung*, Apr. 26, 1886, qtd. in HADC, People's Exhibit 92.

19. Schaack, *Anarchy and Anarchists*, 122 (see ch. 1, n. 3). Schaack reproduces a number of documents he claims were taken as evidence during the investigation into the Haymarket trial but were not introduced during the subsequent trial. There is no particular reason to believe that these are not genuine.

20. *Arbeiter-Zeitung*, Apr. 30, 1886, qtd. in HADC, People's Exhibit 93; May 1, 1886, qtd. in People's Exhibit 94.

21. *Chicago Times*, Apr. 30, 1886, 2–3; May 1, 1886, 2–3; May 2, 1886, 5–6; Apr. 29, 1886, 8.

22. *Chicago Mail*, Apr. 28, 1886, 1; the actions of the furniture workers was denounced at a Knights of Labor Eight-Hour meeting the following night (*Chicago Times*, Apr. 29, 1886, 8).

23. *Chicago Times*, Apr. 30, 1886, 2. Richard Schneirov, in his *Labor and Urban Politics* (see ch. 2, n. 33), notes the differences between the Eight-Hour League and the anarchists, but implies that the idea that anarchists pushed workers toward

more irreconcilable demands was manufactured by the press. "After the Eight Hour Association condemned the furniture workers' demands, the press blamed 'foreign communists' for the shift in strategy and began identifying the eight hour movement with anarchism and the CLU" (198). Schneirov argues against his own evidence—the reports he cites merely report on anarchist encouragement of workers' more maximum demands. There is no evidence, at least none that Schneirov cites, that any of these reports were exaggerated. Indeed, in the very next paragraph, Schneirov observes that "it was the anarchists who championed eight for ten" (198).

24. *Chicago Times*, Apr. 30, 1886, 3; *Chicago News*, Apr. 29, 1886, 1.

25. Excerpt from the *Eight Hour Day*, qtd. in *Chicago Mail*, May 1, 1886, 3.

26. *Knights of Labor* (Chicago), May 15, 1886, 8.

27. *Chicago Mail*, May 1, 1886, 4. Avrich embellishes his quotation of the *Chicago Mail*'s editorial by adding an exclamation point to the final line, "make an example of them if trouble does occur," where one is not present in the original version (*Haymarket Tragedy*, 187; see ch. 1, n. 11).

28. *Chicago Tribune*, May 3, 1886, 2.

29. *Chicago Times*, Apr. 29, 1886, 8.

30. Ibid., May 1, 1886, 2–3; May 2, 1886, 5–6; *Chicago Journal*, May 3, 1886, 1.

31. *Chicago Times*, May 2, 1886, 5–6; *Chicago Journal*, May 1, 1886, 6; *Chicago Mail*, May 1, 1886, 1.

32. *Chicago Times*, May 2, 1886, 5–6.

33. Ibid., May 1, 1886, 2–3.

34. *Arbeiter-Zeitung*, May 1, 1886, qtd. in HADC, People's Exhibit 63A.

35. *Chicago Interocean*, May 3, 1886, 2.

36. *Chicago Tribune*, May 3, 1886, 2.

37. *Chicago Times*, May 2, 1886, 5–6.

38. Ibid., May 3, 1886, 2–3.

39. Ibid., Apr. 29, 1886, 8.

40. Ibid., May 4, 1886, 2–3.

41. Ibid.; *Chicago Journal*, May 3, 1886, 1.

42. *Chicago News*, Apr. 29, 1886, 2.

43. *Chicago Herald*, May 2, 1886, 1.

44. Ibid.

45. *Chicago Times*, May 3, 1886, 2–3; *Chicago Mail*, May 3, 1886, Extra edition, 1; *Die Fackel*, May 2, 1886, qtd. in HADC, People's Exhibit 72.

46. August Spies testified that the *Arbeiter-Zeitung* appeared each day at 2:00 in the afternoon (Testimony of August Spies, HADC, Vol. N, 30–31).

47. *Chicago Times*, May 4, 1886, 2–3.

48. Ibid. Lucy Parsons led an organizing meeting of the sewing girls the day before (*Chicago Interocean*, May 3, 1886, 2).

49. *Chicago Mail*, May 3, 1886, Extra edition, 1.

50. *Chicago Times*, May 2, 1886, 5–6.

51. Testimony of Henry Witt, HADC, Vol. M, 220. The organizing meeting was

held in a "Mr. Letker's saloon" located on the corner of Blue Island Avenue and Twentieth Street (five blocks from where the lumber rally of May 3 took place and the same distance in the opposite direction from where Witt lived). Frederick Breest, the recording secretary of this union, also testified that it had only existed since April 4 (HADC, Vol. M, 218, 224, 232).

52. *Die Fackel*, Mar. 7, 1886, 8; *Chicago Tribune*, Mar. 16, 1886, 1; Clipping dated Mar. 1, 1886, McCormick Harvesting Machine Co. Papers, Series IX Letterbooks, State Historical Society of Wisconsin. *Illinois Staats-Zeitung*, Mar. 2, 1886, 4.

53. *Illinois Staats-Zeitung*, May 2, 1886, 3; May 3, 1886, 3. Testimony of Frank Haraster, HADC, Vol. I, 412. *Chicago Daily News*, May 3, 1886, 5:00 ed., 1. HADC, Vol. I, 407. The lumber worker's employers did not take the union's petition seriously, "the peculiar orthography of which was regarded as a capital joke by those receiving it" (*Chicago Times*, May 1, 1886, 2-3).

54. Testimony of E. T. Baker, HADC, Vol. I, 401; Testimony of James Fraser, HADC, Vol. I, 395. Paul Avrich constructs an account of Spies's actions in these crucial moments that had no basis in Spies's own recollections. Avrich writes: "Spies addressed the meeting. He called on his listeners to stand firmly together and they would carry the day. He did not mention the McCormick lockout, nor did he counsel violence. As he was finishing up a bell rang at McCormick's, signaling the end of the workday. At this, some two hundred men detached themselves from Spies's audience and rushed towards the plant to join the pickets in heckling the scabs. Spies pleaded with them not leave, but his words fell on deaf ears" (*Haymarket Tragedy*, 189). Likewise James Green followed suit and wrote, "Spies continued to speak, urging the lumber shovers not to join the rush on the plant" (*Death in the Haymarket*, 169-70; see ch. 1, n. 11). It is true that several defense witnesses claimed that Spies urged the crowd to remain, but Spies himself, either in his report of the riot written that same day, or in his testimony from the witness chair, or in his *Autobiography*, made no such claim. Rather, Spies admitted he did nothing to restrain the crowd, claiming he did not understand why the mob was running off toward the factory and simply continued his speech. Testimony of August Spies, HADC, Vol. N, 23-23; Testimony of Henry Witt, HADC, Vol. M, 222; Testimony of Frederick Breest, HADC, Vol. M, 231; Testimony of Albert Schlavin, HADC, Vol. M, 234.

55. *Chicago Herald*, May 4, 1886, 1; *Arbeiter-Zeitung*, May 4, 1886, translation given as approved by defense counsel, People's Exhibit No. 63, Haymarket Trial Transcript; Chicago Historical Society, *Robinson's Atlas of the City of Chicago, 1886* (E. Robinson, 1886). HADC, People's Exhibit No. 63, 4-6.

56. *Chicago Tribune*, Sept. 13, 1886, 6.

57. *Illinois Staats-Zeitung*, May 15, 1886, 4; *Chicago Tribune*, Sep. 24, 1886, 8; Dec. 18, 1886, 8. One of the men prosecuted, Joseph Breda, was arrested five days after the riot, and police told the judge at his trial that Breda admitted being "a socialist" and drilling armed men in the southwestern district. The state's attorney was about to enter into evidence dynamite, fuses, anarchist publications, and bomb molds found in Breda's house, but Judge Joseph Gary would not allow it and the next day dropped

the charges against Breda (*Chicago Tribune*, Sep. 25, 1886, 7). William Casey was dismissed from the police force on July 7, 1887, after it was discovered that he had promised to marry a young widow but failed to tell her he already had a wife and family (*Chicago Tribune*, July 8, 1887, 5). See also Joseph Chada, *The Czechs in the United States* (Washington, D.C.: SVU [Czechoslovak Society of Arts and Sciences] Press, 1981), 162. Both Dejnek and Mikolanda later provided affidavits to Governor Altgeld alleging they were beaten and offered bribes to testify in the Haymarket trial. However, they failed to mention to the governor or his assistants that they had actually been convicted of crimes that took place the day before the Haymarket bombing. Both Paul Avrich and Henry David mention Dejnek and Mikolanda's later affidavits to Governor Altgeld but are silent on the attempted lynching of Officer Casey (Avrich, *Haymarket Tragedy*, 222; David, *History of the Haymarket Affair*, 224).

58. Testimony of Franz Hein, HADC, Vol. J, 184.

59. Facsimiles of the two broadsides can be found in Avrich, *Haymarket Tragedy*, Illustrations 11 and 12 (unpaginated; located between pages 278 and 279).

60. *Chicago Mail*, May 4, 1886, 5:00 edition, 1.

Epilogue

1. "Joseph Dietzgen: A Sketch of His Life by Eugene Dietzgen," in Joseph Dietzgen, *Philosophical Essays on Socialism and Science, Religion, Ethics; Critique-Of-Reason and the World-At-Large* (Chicago: Charles Kerr, 1906), 16–29.

2. Dietzgen to Sorge, May 17, 1886, in *Briefe und Auszüge aus Briefen von Joh. Phil. Becker, Jos. Dietzgen, Friedrich Engels, Karl Marx u.A. an F.A. Sorge und Andere* (Stuttgart: Verlag von J.H.W. Dietz, 1921) 221–22; Dietzgen, *Philosophical Essays*, 28. See also, David, *History of the Haymarket Affair*, 532–33 (see ch. 1, n. 11).

3. Frank H. Brooks, "Ideology, Strategy, and Organization: Dyer Lum and the American Anarchist Movement," *Labor History* 34, no. 1 (1993): 57–83.

4. Dyer D. Lum, *The Great Trial of the Chicago Anarchists* [originally published as *A Concise History of the Great Trial of the Chicago Anarchists in 1886: Condensed from the Original Record* (1887; Chicago: Socialistic Publishing Company; repr. New York: Arno Press, 1969).

5. In quoting from an article penned by Albert Parsons on the eight-hour workday, such alterations are serious. Compare, for example, Lum's version and the actual text of a passage that begins, "Will the manufacturing kings grant the modest request under such circumstances? No, sir. The small ones cannot, and the big ones will not."

> Lum: "They will fill your place by drawing from the army of the unemployed . . . You will interfere . . . Then comes the police and militia!"
>
> Alarm: "They will then draw from the army of the unemployed; the strikers will attempt to stop them. Then comes the police and militia . . . Say, workingmen, are you prepared to meet the latter; are you armed?—A"

6. Clara Kirk, "William Dean Howells, George William Curtis, and the 'Haymarket Affair,'" *American Literature* 40, no. 4 (1969), 487–98.

7. L. Parsons, *Life of Albert Parsons*, 256–57 (see ch. 2, n. 3).

8. J. Seymour Currey, *Chicago: Its History And Its Builders, A Century of Marvelous Growth*, (Chicago: S. J. Clarke Publishing Company, 1912), 1:391.

9. Joseph Kirkland, "Some Notable Trials," in *History of Chicago, Illinois*, ed. Joseph Moses and Joseph Kirkland (Chicago: Munsell and Co., 1895), 208.

10. James Green, *Taking History to Heart: The Power of the Past in Building Social Movements* (Amherst: University of Massachusetts Press, 2000), 137. Gregory Kealey, "Herbert G. Gutman, 1928–1985," *Monthly Review* (May 1986): 23–26; Joseph S. Murphy and Joan Wallach Scott, "Herbert G. Gutman, 1928–1985," *Radical History Review* (1986): 107–12.

11. David, *History of the Haymarket Affair*, 75, 105.

12. Destler, *American Radicalism, 1865–1901*, 434–51 (see ch. 5, n. 16).

13. Foner, *Autobiographies of the Haymarket Martyrs* (see ch. 5, n. 12); Lara Kelland, "Putting Haymarket to Rest?" *Labor: Studies in Working-Class History of the Americas* 2, no. 2 (2005): 33–34. Aside from the occasional reprinting of Henry David's 1936 PhD thesis on the event, *History of the Haymarket Affair*, and the publication of a college reader of sources on the event in 1959, *Autobiographies of the Haymarket Martyrs* was the first popular account of the Haymarket Riot to come out since International Publishers, another Communist Party front, issued Alan Calmer, *Labor Agitator: The Story of Albert R. Parsons* (New York: International Publishers, 1937). Robbins may also have run across Bernard R. Kogan's *The Chicago Haymarket Riot: Anarchy on Trial: Selected Materials for College Research Papers* (Boston: D. C. Heath, 1959) while studying at Kent State University. Lum, *Great Trial*.

14. Among the many works published in this period was an avalanche of theses. Billie Stevenson's dissertation focused on the ideas and rhetoric of Chicago's anarchists in "The Ideology of American Anarchism," at the University of Iowa in 1972. Kenneth Kann earned his PhD at the University of California, Berkeley, in 1977 with "Working-Class Culture and the Labor Movement in Nineteenth-Century Chicago." Eric Hirsch took advantage of the abundance of materials close at hand at the University of Chicago and finished his dissertation, "Revolution or Reform: An Analytical History of an Urban Labor Movement," in 1981. Richard Schneirov's "The Knights of Labor in the Chicago Labor Movement and in Municipal Politics, 1877–1887," of 1984 was the second dissertation produced on this topic at Northern Illinois University since 1969, following Ralph Scharnau's "Thomas J. Morgan and the Chicago Socialist Movement, 1876–1901," and soon followed by a third, Bruce C. Nelson's "Culture and Conspiracy: A Social History of Chicago Anarchism, 1870–1900," in the centennial year of 1986.

15. Avrich, *Haymarket Tragedy*, 67, 74 (see ch. 1, n. 11).

16. Ibid., 163.

17. Ibid., 175.

18. Green, *Death in the Haymarket*, 96 (see ch. 1, n. 11). Green repeats his thesis again on 129, again with no documentary evidence to sustain it: "Johann Most, the world's leading anarchist in 1885, exerted a strong hold on Parsons, Spies and the Chicago Internationals, but they did not fully embrace his view that individual acts of violence would provoke a revolution; indeed, they faithfully adhered to the lesson they had learned from Karl Marx: that socialism could be achieved only through the collective power of workers organized into aggressive trade unions."

19. Ibid., 141.

20. Ibid., 360–61n52.

21. *Chicago Tribune*, May 1, 1998, 1.

INDEX

Ackerman, Fred, 61–62
Adams, William Edwin, 108
Adelman, William, 184
Aetna Powder Company, 124
Alarm, The (Chicago), 78, 104, 116,
 125–27, 135, 148, 150, 153, 160, 163;
 post-Haymarket, 180–81
Alexander II, Czar, 69–71, 75, 121
Allegemeiner Deutscher Arbeiterverein
 (ADAV), 43–44, 45, 47, 62
Altgeld, Gov. Peter, 4
American Federation of Labor, 149
anarchism: German, 53–58; historiography
 of, 4–5, 8, 195n34, 196n37, 218–19n35,
 220–21n50, 221–22n52, 226n5; nihilism,
 30–31, 69–78; revolutionary, 30–31;
 terminology of, 7, 190n7. *See also*
 boring-from-within; dynamite; International Working People's Association;
 Propaganda by the Deed
Anarchist, Der (Chicago), 14, 123, 148, 156
anarchists, Chicago: Autonome Gruppen,
 123, 148; beliefs, 5–7, 95–96, 178; Board
 of Trade protest (1885), 119–20; Chicago
 Conference (IWPA), 86–91; dynamite,
 114, 119–25; eight-hour movement,
 147–48, 149–57, 159–60, 162–64,
 166–72; immediate revolution doctrine,
 58–59; Johann Most, 91–92; North Side
 Group, 156, 159, 173; Northwest Side
 Group, 10–11, 12–13, 114, 120; Paul
 Grottkau, 62–68; Pittsburgh Congress
 (IWPA), 94–98; political disillusionment

theory, 52, 65–68; revolutionary preparations, 163–65, 177–78; Streetcar Strike
 of, 1885 139–40; views of trade unions,
 140–49
anarchists, Milwaukee, 160
anarchists, New York City: André monument bombing, 103–4; arrival of German
 socialist refugees, 58; arson, 131–36;
 criminal activities, 127–31; Social Revolutionary Club, 61
*An-Archist: Socialistic Revolutionary Re-
 view* (Boston), 80–81, 204nn23–24
Ancient Order of Hibernians, 108
André, Major John, 100–101
André Monument, 100–105, 208n4,
 209n12
Andrews, Stephen Pearl, 89
Anti-Coolie League, 124
Anti-Monopoly Party, 155
Anti-Socialist Law (Germany), 55–56, 66
Arbeiter-Zeitung (Berne, Switzerland),
 39–40, 44
Arbeiter-Zeitung (Chicago), 1–2, 9, 12–13,
 19, 22, 25, 52, 119–20, 135, 165, 173;
 banned by Bismarck, 64; dynamite,
 124–25; SLP factionalism, 62–64, 67, 99
Arnold, Benedict, 100
Artley, Sylvester, 51, 66
Avrich, Paul, 185–86

Bachmann, Moritz A., 61, 132
Bakunin, Mikhail, 7, 32–33, 42–43, 72,
 115; Propaganda by the Deed, 37; revo-

THE WORKING CLASS IN AMERICAN HISTORY